THE ADDAMS FAMILY
AND THE MUNSTERS
PROGRAMME GUIDE

THE
ADDAMS FAMILY
AND
THE MUNSTERS
PROGRAMME GUIDE

John Peel

First published in 1994 by
Virgin Books
an imprint of Virgin Publishing Ltd
332 Ladbroke Grove
London W10 5AH

Text copyright © John Peel 1994

Typeset by Robin Davies, London

Printed and bound in Great Britain by
Cox & Wyman Ltd, Reading, Berks

ISBN 0 86369 837 9

CONTENTS

This one is for Honnie Gladden, Blondie Kissme and Nela Pen – the three strangest girls I almost know.

With special thanks to Andrew Pixley.

Note: American spellings have often been used in programme titles. This is not an error, so please don't blame the poor typesetters or proofreaders!

Origins

As American television entered its third decade with the start of the sixties, it seemed that the airwaves were dominated by Westerns and sitcoms – *Gunsmoke* and *Bonanza* were heading the former, and *The Andy Griffith Show* and *The Danny Thomas Show* ruled the latter. The push was on to find new formats that might draw audiences in and to expand the horizons of the shows. In 1960, for example, *The Flintstones* became the first animated series to be shown in primetime, and it was highly successful.

Most of the sitcoms then airing were very simple formats based about 'average' American families. Father worked – and we were often not told even what his job was! – Mother kept house – Donna Reed even wore pearls to do the vacuuming! – and the basically good-natured kids got into scrapes rather than trouble with the law. The title of Robert Young's long-running (1954–63) series summed it up: *Father Knows Best*.

The Danny Thomas Show (known as *Make Room For Daddy* at the start of its run) was on the air from 1953–65 and highly rated during its entire run. Thomas played Danny Williams, an entertainer, with two children, Rusty and Terry. Each story centred around his being a trifle bombastic, the kids being a trifle bratty and everything being warmly resolved by the end. Another well watched show was *Leave It To Beaver* (1957–63), in which Theodore 'Beaver' Cleaver and his older brother, Wally, eternally got into scrapes out of which their parents (Ward and June) had to help them. Even *Dennis The Menace* (1959–63) was more mischievous than menacing. Suburbia, it seemed – at least from TV – was populated only by nice folks with loveable, if sometimes rascally, kids. Problems were minor and crises were generally minor things, too, that were blown out of proportion by over-reacting adults. *I Love Lucy* (1951–61) and *The Lucy Show* (1962–74) gave us the prototype over-reacting adult, Lucille Ball.

Naturally, this complacency couldn't go on unchallenged. *The Beverly Hillbillies* (1962–71) broke the mould slightly with the Clampett family moving from the mountains to Beverly (Hills, that is). The classic fish-out-of-water syndrome took place, but with the rustic Clampetts almost always the winners. In the battle against complacency, the Clampetts fired the first shots. It was possible to send up conventional values and get ratings, too. (Incidentally, many of these shows have been revived as movies in the past few years. Is it just for the sake of nostalgia, or is it because the same grounds still need to be covered today?)

At the same time, there were other odd entries. Police shows were always popular TV fare – *The Naked City* (1958–63), with its catch-phrase: 'There are eight million stories in the Naked City . . .' and *Dragnet* (1952–59 and 1967–70) with its 'Just the facts'. Naturally, there had to be a spoof, and this was *Car 54, Where Are You?* (1961–63), created by Nat Hiken, who had earlier created *You'll Never Get Rich*, sometimes known as *The Phil Silvers Show* (1955–59), with Phil Silvers as the money-hungry Sergeant Bilko. *Car 54* was a modest success for its two seasons (unlike the recent movie revival), but was noted most for its characters. Gunther Toody (Joe E. Ross) was an excitable type, partnered with the hulking, quiet Muldoon – played by Fred Gwynne. Another regular on the show was the grouchy Officer Schnauser, played by Al Lewis. Gwynne and Lewis worked marvellously well together, and when the show was cancelled both received a number of offers for new series.

I'm Dickens – He's Fenster (1962–63) was a slapstick series about the misadventures of two construction workers

8

who were always getting into trouble, Fenster (Marty Ingels) and Dickens (John Astin). Astin was particularly noted for his comedic skills, but the show didn't do well enough to warrant renewal, and he, too, went looking for a new show.

Then came the new 1963 season. One of the highly loved (even if not ratings-popular) series was *The Twilight Zone* (1959–65), hosted by Rod Serling, and dealing with the unexpected. It was bound to occur to someone eventually that here was fertile ground for satire, and so it happened. Ray Walston – most noted then for his role as the Devil in *Damn Yankees* – wafted down out of the skies and onto TV sets as *My Favorite Martian* (1963–66). He was promptly adopted as his 'Uncle Martin' by reporter Tim O'Hara (Bill Bixby). Tim discovered that Martin had almost magical powers by virtue of his strange birth, and these powers opened new vistas for stories. *My Favorite Martian* became a ratings winner for CBS and the hunt was on to add more out-of-this world comedies.

ABC responded with *Bewitched* (1964–72), the story of a young wife who happens to also be a witch, Samantha (Elizabeth Montgomery, daughter of Robert Montgomery, on whose show she got her acting start). Her husband, Darrin (Dick York, replaced by look-alike Dick Sargent) wants her to give up the witchery and just be normal. Her mother, Endora (Agnes Morehead) despises normal, and constantly causes trouble. (The show was terribly similar, in fact, to the 1958 movie of the play *Bell, Book And Candle*. That starred Kim Novak as witch Gillian Holroyd who gives up her craft to marry a human, played by Jimmy Stewart.) Also airing the same year on ABC was an oddity called *The Addams Family*.

Meanwhile, CBS had learned from their own success. Along with *My Favorite Martian*, they commissioned two further way-out sitcoms. First was *My Living Doll* (1964–65), which had Dr Robert McDonald (Bob

Cummings) looking after the 'perfect woman' – Rhoda (Julie Newmar, later Catwoman to TV's *Batman*). She was, in fact, an android, and Dr McDonald had to keep this a secret. The second series was *The Munsters*.

The third network, NBC, arrived late into the fantasy sitcom market, airing their own entries a year later. *My Mother The Car* (1965–66) was about Dave Crabtree (Jerry Van Dyke, then hoping to rival his brother Dick's success) discovering that his mother has been reincarnated as a car . . . It is widely – and probably accurately – considered the worst TV series ever made. The other show was a deliberate copy of *Bewitched* called *I Dream Of Jeannie* (1965–70). Jeannie (Barbara Eden) is a genie discovered by Major Nelson (Larry Hagman) and who falls in love with him. Magic and bizarre happenings abound, as in *Bewitched*.

The Addams Family and *The Munsters* both arrived at the same time and, on first glance, seem quite alike: a weird family living in a haunted house. In fact, the shows were terribly dissimilar in important respects, and in many ways their appearance at the same time is no more than coincidental.

The Addams Family

The Addams Family was developed from the outrageous and popular cartoons created by Charles Addams. Addams was born in Westfield, New Jersey, in 1912. His father was a naval architect, and Addams inherited his father's drawing abilities. One of his earliest jobs was as an illustrator for *True Detective* magazines – he had to draw diagrams showing where bodies were found in the tales.

In private life, he was an avid collector. He had a collection of medieval arms and armour, and another of vintage cars (including a 1928 Bugatti and a 1932 Aston Martin) which he drove around on Long Island. He married three times, the last time in 1980. The ceremony was held in a pet cemetery, both bride and groom dressed in black.

His best-known characters first appeared in a *New Yorker* cartoon in 1938. Over the years, the members of the family grew and evolved, but they were never named until the TV show. The characters were partially based on people he knew. 'I've always thought of myself as Uncle Fester', he admitted. 'We share certain attitudes and even look a little alike.'

He died in 1988. The originals of many of his cartoons were donated to the New York Public Library, which holds showings of the works on a regular basis.

Turning the cartoons, which were simply one-panel jokes, into a show was a challenge. For one thing, the characters weren't really named, and there hadn't been much about them established. The concept came from Executive Producer David Levy, and he had firm ideas in mind, wanting to tone down some of the gruesomeness but to retain the strangeness of the cartoons. Levy was well-experienced in TV, having produced *Face The Music* (1948–49), an early variety series and *You Asked For It* (1950–59), in which viewers requested what they'd like to see. He became an executive for NBC before returning to production with *The Addams Family*. He later went on to produce *The Pruitts Of Southampton* (1966–67), also with John Astin in the cast, and the police series *Sarge* (1971–72) (which had Harold 'Oddjob' Sakata in the cast).

Levy set about writing up the premise for the show, and developed many items, such as Thing. (So many, in fact, that when the first movie came out in 1991, Levy sued the producers, claiming that he had been the creator of the Family and demanding payment.) He had able help in Nat Perrin, who served as producer for the show. Perrin had worked with TV superstar Red Skelton, and had produced shows for two rising newcomers – *The Johnny Carson*

Show (1955–56) for Carson (who would later dominate American late-night TV for over two decades) and *How To Marry A Millionaire* (1957–59), which starred a young actress named Barbara Eden. When the time came to write the pilot script, Perrin brought in two people who'd worked with him on both series, Seaman Jacobs and Ed James.

Jacobs was a veteran scripter, having worked extensively with both Bob Hope and George Burns. Ed James had also written for *Leave It To Beaver* and *The Many Loves Of Dobie Gillis*. Together, the two writers and two producers hammered out the pilot story, in which the Addams clan would be introduced.

Casting the series had a few problems. John Astin had been Levy's only choice to play Gomez, and he was involved from the very beginning, even on discussions. It was inspired casting, and Astin has never been better than playing the part of Gomez. Mortitia was another matter, and several auditions were held before Carolyn Jones was chosen. For her role, she was required to wear a long, jet-black wig and a very tight dress to accentuate her figure (which is why she's often seen sitting down – it was so much easier than standing in that dress!).

Uncle Fester was a real problem. Jackie Coogan was only one of several actors who were auditioned for the role, but the network was wary of casting him. He'd been involved in an arrest for possession of drugs (Coogan claimed in court that he had no idea how the marijuana found in his house during a small party had come to be there and was let off) and twice for drunkenness, but he was certainly the best candidate for the role. A young executive named Harve Bennett finally determined his cast. Bennett has since gone on to become producer of the highly successful *Star Trek* motion pictures. Coogan went on the wagon, and proved to be both a great hit in the part and also absolutely reliable. Rounding out the cast were Blossom Rock as Granny and

Ted Cassidy as Lurch. The children were played by young-sters Ken Weatherwax and Lisa Loring.

The guiding concept for the show is simply that the Addams Family marches to the beat of a very different drummer. They see themselves as perfectly normal, and find the odd behaviour of visitors rather perplexing. Though some of the Family members are on the odd side (Cousin Itt, obviously, as well as Lurch), most *look* normal, even if they don't act it. The series' wit is mostly satirical, con-trasting the Family's values with those of the rest of the world. The Family might seem odd, but that they love one another deeply is never questioned. Gomez, for example, doesn't want to send his children to school because he dislikes the idea of getting rid of them.

One very unusual element in the show is that Gomez and Mortitia are very sexual. Most sitcoms at this time showed married couples as polite or even loving, but it was hard to imagine them actually getting passionate. Gomez and Mortitia, by contrast, are more than happily married – they're deliriously in love and constantly making plans to consummate it. It's all done with surprisingly good taste, but the sexual heat between them is very real.

Interestingly, the Addams Family shows absolutely no interest in television (unlike the Munsters). There isn't one in their house, though there are plenty of books. Nor do they go to the cinema. They prefer to amuse themselves, albeit in rather off-beat ways.

The Munsters

Unlike *The Addams Family*, which was a show born out of the conviction of one man, David Levy, *The Munsters* was much more of a group decision. At this time, Universal Studios had a very healthy TV production company, with many popular series to their credit. *Alfred Hitchcock Presents* (later *The Alfred Hitchcock Hour*) (1955–65), for example, and the highly-popular *Wagon Train* (1957–65). Universal had (and still has) their own city aimed at the production of their TV shows. Though producers would be assigned to projects, the technical crews – photographers, art directors, musicians and so forth – would be alternated between productions. A director of photography might work on *Wagon Train* one week, *The Munsters* the following week and *Alfred Hitchcock* a week later. By contrast, the same team worked together constantly on *The Addams Family*.

When Universal was looking around for sitcom ideas, an intriguing suggestion came forward. In the forties and fifties, Universal's staple productions that had brought in lots of money had been their series of monster movies. They had copyrighted their designs for the Frankenstein monster (played by Boris Karloff) and Dracula (Bela Lugosi), and had created their own creatures, such as the gill-man in *The Creature From The Black Lagoon*. These films had been recycled over and over again, and were tremendously popular with youngsters, who seemed intrigued with monsters. Since Universal owned the copyright on them all, why not create a sitcom spoof of the genre, and utilize their products?

Irving Paley was Production Executive for the new series. He'd previously produced *Blondie* (1957), an unsuccessful spin-off from the daily comic strip, and the rather better received *Ichabod And Me* (1961–62) about a small-town newspaper. He would later produce *Pistols'n'Petticoats* (1966–67), a spoof Western. Paley's producers and writers for the new show were men he'd worked with on these shows, Joe Connolly and Bob Mosher. Connolly and Mosher were prolific writers (together they wrote over 1500 scripts in their careers), and they were highly regarded since they had created and produced *Leave It To Beaver*. They were a very hands-on team whose influence suffused *The Munsters*.

14

The original format for the show was written by Allan Burns and Chris Hayward. Burns went on to help create the much loved *Lou Grant* (1977–82) and *Rhoda* (1974–78), both spun off from *The Mary Tyler Moore Show* . Hayward worked on *Barney Miller* (1975–82) and *The Bullwinkle Show* (1961–62). After their original outline for *The Munsters* was in, however, the team immediately moved on to create . . . *My Mother The Car*. Not a great career move, but they overcame it.

The original outline was enough to show to the network, and they went for the show. Fred Gwynne and Al Lewis were the only people in mind for the roles of Herman and Grandpa. The script had been one of three that Gwynne was offered. 'I sort of smelled something that I liked', he told *TV Guide* (July 10th, 1965). 'There was some sort of fascination when I read the script and knew that I would be different, even physically. I like the point of view, a little bit of the satire of the old movie monsters.' He and Lewis agreed to play the roles. The final major role was offered to Yvonne de Carlo. She had returned to work on almost anything that came her way at this time, as her stuntman husband had been badly injured in a stunt that went wrong. She had a family to support and immense medical bills. The security of a series was the main lure for her.

Filling out the cast was young actor Butch Patrick as wolfman-like son Eddie and a minor actress named Beverly Owen who played Marilyn, the beautiful blonde niece (named, naturally, for Marilyn Monroe). She was simply one of many pretty girls that Universal would sign on and hope would prove to be an asset. In fact, she turned out to be woefully unsuited to the part, and was unceremoniously replaced by a look-alike, Pat Priest, after 13 episodes. The replacement was managed quite seamlessly; when I mentioned this to actor Al Lewis, he didn't even realize that two girls had played the role!

The original pilot shot was a 15-minute segment that was incorporated later into the second episode, but it showed that there were a number of rough edges to smooth out. Norm Liebmann and Ed Haas were brought in to rework the concepts. Leibmann later worked on *Kolchak – The Night Stalker* (1974–75), with real monsters, though he was not credited on-screen for his work, *Good Times* (1974–79) and *Baretta* (1975–78). Haas stuck mainly with comedy, on *The Jerry Lewis Show* (1967–69) and *The John Byner Comedy Hour* (1972).

The Munsters was quite different to *The Addams Family*. For one thing, it was a spoof of the old monster films rather than a satire of modern attitudes. Herman and his family simply thought of themselves as perfectly average people, despite every indication about them that they were not. And, though they were a close family, they were not overly loving. In 'Love Locked Out,' for example, Lily refuses to allow Herman into their bedroom. Can you imagine Mortitia denying Gomez her bed? Unthinkable! And Grandpa is very much the irascible and often downright nasty old man. Herman – being gentle here – is not overly bright, but he does mean well. He's a big fan of TV (often quoting *Leave It To Beaver*, a nice in-joke reference to the show's producers) and very, very gullible. Many of the episodes centred about Herman goofing up and the rest of the family having to solve the problem. In *The Addams Family*, there was none of that sort of thing. Gomez and Mortitia were far too bright to need setting straight. So, despite their superficial similarities and the odd coincidence in both shows airing at the same time – and being cancelled together – they are in fact quite different in format.

The Munsters name was arrived at by combining 'fun' and 'monsters'. Herman is quite obviously Frankenstein's monster. In fact, the latest Frankenstein turns up ('Johan'), as do other versions of Herman – prototypes, if you like – in 'Knock Wood, Here Comes Charlie' and 'Johan'. Fred Gwynne had to undergo two hours of makeup at the start of each day at the hands of makeup man Karl Silvera.

A latex mask applied over his skull provided the flattened pate. Grey makeup, overlaid by yellow, added to the cadaverous appearance. Bolts and washers (rubber) were applied to his neck, and mascara and eyeliner made his eyes look sunken. A wig (real human hair) was fastened over the appliance and sprayed. Black nail polish coloured his fingernails. (In the first episode, he was considered too horrific and not funny enough, so the makeup was altered for subsequent stories to make him more amusing.) The scars and stitches were actually nothing more than lines drawn on him with felt-tip markers!

To increase his already huge six foot five inch frame, Gwynne wore heavy leather boots (ten pounds each) with five inch lifts. 'For the first three weeks', he told *TV Guide*, 'my back, everything hurt. My body was not used to the costume and the high-heeled boots stretched my tendons.' The outfit was also incredibly hot, and he lost ten pounds in the first weeks of filming. Lemonade and salt tablets had to be kept available on the set for him to make up for all the sweating he did. He even hired a masseur to help him to recover at the end of each day.

Al Lewis and Yvonne de Carlo had a better time of it, since they only needed wigs and a white makeup applied. This still took them two hours at the start of the day, however. Butch Patrick's makeup was mostly a wig and pointed ears, while Pat Priest got off very lightly indeed!

Though Grandpa and Lily were supposed to be vampires, their taste for fresh blood was quite subdued. Much more was made of Grandpa's skills as a mad scientist, and he was constantly inventing things, many of which either failed to work or had unexpected effects. To provide the special effects for his lab, Ken Strickfaden, then 70 years old, was lured out of supposed retirement. Strickfaden had actually worked on many of the same horror films that *The Munsters* was sending up, including *Frankenstein*.

Another allocation for the show was money to create special vehicles. Merchandising was strong at the time, and Universal knew that a successful show could net considerable sums in model kit sales, for example. A special car for the family was thus called for (the Addams, even though theoretically richer, had to settle for a normal roadster). The Munster Koach was born, at the then high cost of $20,000. It was constructed mainly from fibreglass by joining the body of a 1927 Model T to that of a touring roadster. (It had a 133" frame when it was finished.) Curtains and trims gave the car its very distinctive look.

The sales of the merchandising rights proved so phenomenal that the producers were asked to add a second car later in the series. As a result, the Dragula was born: a 350 horsepower hot-rod car, its form taken from that of a coffin. This cost a 'mere' $10,800!

The Addams Family

Background

It's not surprising that visitors to the Addams Family house tend to get a little . . . nervous. At first glimpse, Gomez, head of the household, appears normal enough: wearing a huge grin beneath his moustache, and often smoking an impressive (and expensive) cigar, Gomez wears an impeccable pin-striped business suit. He *looks* like any decent, hard-working father of a family. When you scratch the surface, however, his looks are about the only normal part of him.

Mortitia, his loving wife, puts you on alert from the start. She's the drop-dead gorgeous (accent on the *dead*), with a taste for black. Not only does she wear it, she decorates with it. Her favourite dress has long flowing tendrils, she pets a brass dragon that smokes, and she keeps carnivorous plants as pets.

The children . . . Wednesday is demurely dressed – almost retro in her fashion tastes – and carries a headless doll. Pugsley is a rolly-poly, jolly character with a taste for explosions. Then there's Uncle Fester: bald, startling and with a high pitched nasal voice that could shatter glass. Grandma is the very epitome of a witch, down to her cauldron and chants. Frequent visitors include a mobile hairball called Cousin Itt and a blonde bombshell sister of Mortitia's called Ophelia, whose favourite moves are judo tosses. Men *really* fall for her.

And it isn't just the direct relatives who are strange. The butler, Lurch, looks as if he's a not-too-well preserved corpse, with a gravelly voice and immense strength. Then there's Thing. He (and he's definitely male) appears to be no more than a hand who lives in boxes. There are boxes all about the house, and at any time Thing might pop up from one. He seems to be the brains of the Family, even if there's no sign of where he keeps his brain. He loves to help out, but somehow visitors find him rather alarming.

If you're paying a call at the house as a visitor, you'll discover that the Family home is definitely one that reflects the tastes of this strange brood.

The Family mansion has been chosen 'Spookiest House of the Year' by *Strife* magazine. Outside on the gate (which opens by itself) is a sign: 'Beware of the Thing'. Their address is 001 Cemetary Lane (or North Cemetary Drive) in the Greenbriar/Woodlawn area of town, and their phone number is Cemetary 13. The door pull tugs back when pulled on. There are numerous tunnels under the house, and vampire bats brood under the eaves. The main room has a polar bear skin on the floor that growls when stepped upon. One wall sports a swordfish's head that has cousin Farouk's foot protruding from its mouth. There is a large stuffed bear (which Fester burns down from time to time), a moosehead with floppy antlers, a stuffed two-headed turtle and a suit of samurai armour along with a normal suit of armour (in which Fester can often be found resting). There's a painting on one wall of a giraffe in a business suit, who Wednesday says 'used to be a friend of my Daddy's'.

Thing has been Gomez's friend and companion since childhood. He communicates with the Family by tapping out Morse code messages. He travels in the glove compartment of the Family car. When the mail arrives, it's announced by a foghorn, and Thing always collects it and brings it into the Family room. For the dance sessions, Thing plays either castanets or the tambourine. He sometimes turns the pages for Lurch at the harpsichord. Thing is engaged to Lady Fingers, hand (!) maid to Princess Millicent.

Gomez is a lawyer by profession, known as 'Loophole' Addams. As a young man, he was something of a hypochondriac until Mortitia inflamed his blood and cured him. He's fond of cigars (striking matches on Lurch's hand) and his favourite lunch is eye of newt. He's independently wealthy and, among other things, owns a game reserve in Nairobi, a mango plantation, a crocodile farm, Mount Everest Tapioca Mines and an insurance company. To relax, he crashes model trains on elaborate sets. He once bought a real railroad, the Big Swamp And Southern, just to play with that, too. He also practises Zen yoga, standing on his head (and smoking a cigar). He belongs to the Zen Yoga Society, headed by Drashi Dumo. He's originally from Castille, part of the Spanish branch of the Addams clan. He loves flamenco dancing, and is appalled to discover he has no Gypsy blood in him. Nothing turns him on as much as his wife speaking French. 'Tish, that's French!' he cries, and starts kissing her beginning at her fingertips. They relax by fencing with one another. They've been married just over 13 years. Their honeymoon was spent in a cave in Death Valley.

Mortitia is the younger daughter of Granny Frump. The family came from Swamptown High. Before she met Gomez, she was engaged to Rupert Styx, and Gomez is still a little jealous of Styx's good looks (long fingernails and a sneer when he smiled). Mortitia feeds meatballs to her carnivorous plant, Cleopatra. She clips the heads off roses and throws them away, keeping only the stems. Her favourite chair is a large rattan throne. She practises hypnotism, at which she excels, and is constantly knitting. As a child, she had two pet vultures, Hubert and Henry. She has an older sister, Ophelia.

Uncle Fester is from the Frump side of the family. He is DC current (110 volts), and lights bulbs by placing them in his mouth. He waxes his head to keep it shiny. His blunderbuss is named Genevieve. One of his old girlfriends is Queenie, who was a bearded lady in a circus. His favourite way to relax is to explode dynamite caps. His normal body temperature is minus 3 degrees, and he eats mercury to perk himself up. He has a habit of falling in love with his pen pals. He keeps pet hawks to drive away robins and other depressingly cheerful birds. He has a tree house in the back garden, and is often found simply perched in trees.

Lurch, the butler, crushes hats when he takes them at the door. He plays the harpsichord, generally a piece called 'The Anxiety Tango'. He never drinks. His mother is very over-protective.

Wednesday is eight (six in the pilot), and her middle name is Friday. She has a pet tarantula named Homer and breeds pedigree spiders. She dated the invisible man's invisible son for a while, but isn't not seeing him any more. She carries about her favourite doll, named Marie Antoinette. Wednesday chopped its head off with her toy guillotine.

Pugsley is ten (eight in the pilot), very inventive and a big fan of science. He likes to build gadgets – disintegrators, ham radios, computers, missiles, ray-guns. His favourite clock has a wolf's head and howls on the hour. He has a pet lizard on a leash, and has baby vultures painted on his bedroom door. His room is decorated with signs from blasting sites.

Cousin Itt is an Addams, and spends a great deal of time with the Family. Itt appears to be nothing much but a bowler hat on a huge pile of hair. He speaks in a high-pitched, fast voice that, oddly, people somehow understand. His IQ is 320. When his high-speed voice is slowed down to a normal pace it comes out as a deep, rich baritone. He spent 15 years at the West Africa Institute of Music, supplying hair for violin bows. He also practises magic, tells jokes and is something of a ladies' man.

Ophelia is Mortitia's older sister and the white sheep of the family. She's blonde, dresses in white and strews petals wherever she walks. Daisies grow out of her head, the roots apparently extending throughout her body. She plays the violin with such ferocity that she saws it in half. Her voice is odd, and she can sing either as a chorus or as an alto and bass at the same time. She's very dreamy and out of touch with any kind of reality, even that of the Addamses.

Not all of the Addams Family are as eccentric as this branch. Aunt Abigail, who lives in Boston, is socially prominent and not overly fond of Gomez. She evens tries to remove him as head of the Family finances.

The Family enjoys moonbathing, which is much nicer than sunbathing, though Fester has a tendency to moonburn. The house has a fully-equipped torture chamber, where the Family likes to relax.

The Family pets: Aristotle the Octopus; Kitty, a full-grown lion (who belonged to Mortitia before she married Gomez); Fang, the jaguar. They also have a tank with two piranhas, Tristan and Isolde.

Relatives

In the course of the series, numerous relatives of the Family are mentioned. These include:

Cousin Imar (three-armed); Cousin Clott (who was electrocuted); Cousin Blink; Cousin Farouk (it's his foot in the swordfish's mouth); Cousin Gripe; Cousin Melancholia (engaged to Fred); Cousin Creep; Cousin Blob; Cousin Slimy (who has two heads); Cousin Plato (who also has two heads); Cousin Manuel (who's a pyromaniac); Cousin Nanook; Cousin Cringe; Cousin Crimp; Cousin Grope; Cousin Trivia; Cousin Droop; Cousin Bleep; Cousin Fungus (who lives in the tunnels under the house); Cousin Vague; Cousin Cackle; Cousin Turncoat; Cousin Slump; Cousin Blah and Cousin Goop.

Grandpa Slurp; Grandpa Squint; Grandfather Malaprop; Grandpa Droop.

Grandma Squint; Grandmother Frump (Mortitia and Ophelia's mother).

Aunt Blemish; Aunt Trivia; Aunt Millicent (who prefers being known as Princess Millicent); Aunt Drip.

Great Uncle Grizzly. Uncle Blight; Uncle Crimp; Uncle Droop.

Great-Great-Great-Grandmother Slice, 'the belle of the French Revolution'.

Great-Grandfather Pegleg, an old sailor who was made to walk the plank; Great-Grandfather Blob.

General Credits

Produced by	Nat Perrin
Developed for Television by Executive Producer	David Levy
Based on Characters created by	Charles Addams
Associate Producer	Herbert W. Browar
Director of Photography	Arch R. Dalzell
Art Director	Edward L. Ilou
Film Editor	Gerald S. Shepard, Joe Harrison, ACE, Douglas Hines, Jim Faris, James D. Ballas, ACE
Assistant Director	Jack Voglin
Editorial Co-ordinator	Robert Freedman
Production Co-ordinator	Richard Greer
Music	Vic Mizzy
Set Decorator	Ruby Levitt, except: Claude Carpenter (episodes 1, 2, 6)
Music Co-ordinator	Dave Kahn
Script Supervisor	Stanley Olsen, except: Stanley K. Scheuer (episode 52)

Properties	Joe Thompson
Sound Editor	George Eppich
Casting	Kerwin Coughlin
Costume Supervisor	Myrtle Logan
Makeup	Norman Pringle, SMA
Hair Stylist	Myrl Stoltz
Chief Electrician	Harry Hopkins
Key Grip	Roy L. Kight
Special Effects	Larry Chapman (alone episodes 1, 2) and Bob Overbeck (Season One) Joseph A. Zomar and Bob Cole (Season Two)
Sound Mixer	Earl E. Spicer
Sound Recorder	Don Bassman (Season One); Ray Regula (Season Two)
Boom Man	Al Boyle (Season Two)
Sound Recorded by	Todd-AO
Automobiles furnished by Filmways	Ford Motor Company

Cast

Mortitia	Carolyn Jones
Gomez	John Astin
Uncle Fester	Jackie Coogan
Lurch	Ted Cassidy
Grandmama	Blossom Rock
Wednesday	Lisa Loring
Pugsley	Ken Weatherwax
The Thing	'Itself'*

*Actually, it was generally Ted Cassidy, unless there were scenes where Thing and Lurch had to interact, such as in the opening story.

25

| Cousin Itt | Felix Silla (episodes 20, 27, 32, 34–36, 39, 40, 45, 47, 54, 59, 62–64); Roger Arroyo (episodes 47, 53) |

Season One

1) The Addams Family Goes To School
18 September 1964

| **Written by** | Seaman Jacobs and Ed James |
| **Directed by** | Arthur Hiller |

Cast

Mr Hilliard	Allyn Joslyn
Miss Comstock	Madge Blake
Miss Morrison	Nydia Westman
Postman	Rolfe Sedan

Sam Hilliard is the truant officer for the Sherwood School, and he arrives at the Addams Family house to complain about the fact that Wednesday and Pugsley have never been to school. Mortitia is busy feeding the man-eating plants, and Gomez is crashing trains. Gomez claims that Wednesday is well educated, and show the shocked Hilliard a box containing spiders. 'Pedigree!' he exclaims happily. 'Ever known a child who could raise thoroughbred spiders?' When Fester's knife-throwing almost kills him, Hilliard flees in terror. When the school authorities insist that the children attend, Gomez is appalled as he is opposed to regimented schooling, but he has to give in. The principal, Miss Comstock, is happy with their decision, but Gomez and Mortitia aren't when Wednesday comes home and throws a tantrum. She hates the fairy stories they've been read, as all the ogres and monsters get killed. Appalled again, Gomez has Lurch fetch Hilliard. He's very nervous when dragged in, so Gomez offers him the use of the rack to calm him down. He then demands Grimm's fairy stories be removed from the curriculum before he'll allow his children to return to school. Hilliard agrees to anything to escape the madhouse.

For the opening scene in this story, featuring Hilliard and the terrified postman, a real house was filmed on location. For the rest of this show (and the series), a painting was used to establish the scene. Wednesday's age is given as six and Pugsley's as eight. By the next episode, however, they've somehow aged two years each to match the ages of the children playing the roles.

Sam Hilliard (Allyn Joslyn) would appear in two further episodes (4 and 59) to suffer at the hands of the Family. By the final episode, he is a school principal, but still a nervous wreck. Madge Blake (Miss Comstock) is best known for her role as Aunt Harriet on TV's *Batman* series, and from movies like *Singin' In The Rain* (1951).

2) Mortitia And The Psychiatrist
25 September 1964

Written by   Hannibal Coons and
                             Harry Winkler
Directed by   Jean Yarbrough

Cast
Dr Black   George Petrie

The Family is appalled when Pugsley gets a Boy Scout uniform, and can't believe they'd failed him. Fester thinks Gomez spoils the boy. Gomez has seen Pugsley playing

27

with a bat – not a live one, but a *baseball* bat. Then he gets a poodle puppy, and Mortitia is aghast: 'Where did we fail?' She calls Dr Black, child psychologist, and he informs them that it's a common phase, a cry for more attention, and suggests they let it play out. They shudder at being called 'Dad' and 'Mom', but bear up. Pugsley even starts helping old ladies across the street and won't blow up trains any more. Mortitia thinks it's time for serious remedies and insists Black make a house call. There are wholesome things which Pugsley has placed all over the house, but Black naturally assumes that it's the normal Addams Family furnishings they are complaining about. He has a long talk with Pugsley to release his 'antagonisms'. By the end of it, the Family is thrilled to have Pugsley back to normal and throw out all the wholesome junk. Black quits practising to go back to school.

3) Fester's Punctured Romance
2 October 1964

Written by   Jameson Brewer
Directed by   Sidney Lanfield

Cast
Miss Carver   Merry Anders

Fester is feeling lonely and unwanted and has been stealing the paper to read the lonely hearts' column. Gomez takes his photo and sends it in. A cosmetics salesgirl, Miss Carver, arrives, and they think she's a mail order bride. Fester doesn't think she's his type, especially when she offers him a free sample or will deal for cash. Eventually the poor girl can take no more and bolts. Fester thinks he's had a narrow escape from marrying a lunatic and vows off marriage.

Merry Anders was a regular on *How To Marry A Millionaire* (1957–59), along with Barbara Eden.

4) Gomez The Politician
9 October 1964

Written by   Hannibal Coons and
                                    Harry Winkler
Directed by   Jerry Hopper

Cast
Mr Hilliard   Allyn Joslyn
George Bass   Eddie Quillan
TV Announcer   Bill Baldwin
Reporter's Voice   Bob le Mond

The Addams Family has a history of happily backing the losers in elections. George Bass, a campaigner for Sam Hilliard, calls on them. He accidentally convinces Gomez that Hilliard is a loser, and the Family wants to help run the campaign – putting Lurch on TV to appeal to the female voters, for example, and having Fester write the campaign song. Hilliard refuses their help (and Kitty as a mascot), but Gomez works for him anyway. As a result, Hilliard loses disastrously and quits politics forever.

5) The Addams Family Tree
16 October 1964

Written by   Hannibal Coons and
                                    Harry Winkler and
                                    Lou Huston
Directed by   Jerry Hopper

Cast

Mr Pomeroy	Frank Nelson
Harold Pomeroy	Kim Tyler
Professor Simms	Jonathan Hole

Wednesday and Pugsley are less than a hit at Harold Pomeroy's birthday party when they turn up with a tarantula as a gift. After a fight, they return home. Gomez wants to challenge Pomeroy to a duel, but Fester thinks he has a better idea – shoot him in the back. Pomeroy arrives and Gomez instead apologizes. He's disturbed when Pomeroy rants on about his family tree, so Gomez decides to trace his own ancestors. Pomeroy meanwhile discovers that the Addams own land he wants and tries to be friendly. Gomez has ferreted out the man's *real* ancestors – pirates and crooks – making Pomeroy panic and bolt. Actually, Gomez liked him better for those relatives!

6) Mortitia Joins The Ladies League
23 October 1964

Written by	Phil Leslie and Keith Fowler
Directed by	Jean Yarbrough

Cast

Oscar Webber	Peter Leeds
Mrs Magruder	Dorothy Neumann
Mrs Page	Pearl Shear
Gorgo	George Barrows

Gomez visits his old friend Oscar Webber at his circus, which has gone downhill. Pugsley plays with Gorgo 'The Killer Gorilla' and the two become friends. Meanwhile,

Mortitia has invited the Ladies League to tea. They're on a membership drive and agree to come. Gorgo breaks out of the circus to visit his pal Pugsley, to Lurch's disapproval. Gomez isn't worried: 'Any boy who loves cobras, toads and apes can't be all bad.' Lurch feels even worse when Gorgo does a better job of the laundry than he's ever done. 'Lurch', Gomez tells him, 'there's some things you can do and some things an ape can do.' It doesn't cheer Lurch up. The Ladies League arrives for tea, but they aren't prepared to see a gorilla serve it, and bolt. Webber arrives looking for Gorgo and is appalled to find him doing the laundry. But Gomez has a winning idea: Webber bills Gorgo as 'The World's Most Domesticated Gorilla' and exhibits him doing housework in an apron – and makes a fortune.

George Barrows (Gorgo) appeared in many gorilla roles (it was his own costume), including the camp classic *Robot Monster* (1953) and the worst ever episode of *The Man From UNCLE*, 'The My Friend The Gorilla Affair'. He appeared in the following episode of the show minus his costume.

7) Halloween With The Addams Family
30 October 1964

Written by	Keith Fowler and Phil Leslie
Directed by	Sidney Lanfield

Cast

Claude	Don Rickles
Marty	Skip Homeier
Policeman	George Barrows

Gomez gets a new knife in the mail, which Wednesday admires. 'Nice knife', she comments. 'Can I play autopsy with it?' Gomez wants it for carving an image of Fester – into a pumpkin, as the Family prepares for their favourite holiday, Halloween. Mortitia makes the punch, with help from Thing. 'It's so nice to have a Thing around the house', she observes. Meanwhile, two bank robbers, Claude and Marty, are on the run. Their car runs out of fuel outside the Addams house, where they hide. Wednesday and Pugsley (dressed – ugh! – as normal children) go trick or treating while Gomez invites the crooks in to celebrate. He offers them treats, but sees that their bag is full of money. He apologizes for being cheap and gives them several hundred dollars. Marty and Claude get greedy for the rest they've spotted. Mortitia tells Gomez, 'When we're together, darling, every night is Halloween.' Thing, more astute, takes Marty's gun and substitutes a banana. Gomez reads their guests a poem, then gets them to bob for (live!) crabs, unaware that the guests are merely hiding from the police. When offered another game, Marty exclaims, 'Try it again? I'd rather wrestle a lion!' Mortitia, ever obliging, calls Kitty. Marty, thinking fast, suggests hide and seek. The Family think this is tame, but oblige their weird guests. Marty and Claude run off with all the cash they can find, but are picked up by the police. Gomez reads in the paper that they've been sent up the river. Mortitia approves, 'They needed a vacation.'

8) Green-Eyed Gomez
6 November 1964

Written by	Keith Fowler and Phil Leslie
Directed by	Jerry Hopper

Cast

Lionel Barker	Del Moore

| Mildred | Pattee Chapman |
| Charlie | Jimmy Ames |

Lionel Barker, an old friend of Mortitia's, arrives at the
house. Gomez is jealous of him, but he's actually a con
man, working with his partner, Charlie, to fleece the family. Gomez tries to drive him out by making him comfortable, and when that doesn't work he decides that jealousy
can work both ways. He hires a maid, Mildred, in an effort
to make Mortitia jealous, but the maid just drives Gomez
crazy. When Gomez tries to make her more assertive,
Mortitia does become jealous. Gomez decides he wants to
make Mortitia happy, by killing himself to free her to marry
Lionel. All his efforts fail, however. Lurch gets Gomez and
Mortitia back together by playing their favourite dance, and
everything is resolved – especially since Mildred and Lionel
have eloped together.

9) The New Neighbors Meet
The Addams Family
13 November 1964

Written by   Hannibal Coons and
                    Henry Winkler
Directed by   Jean Yarbrough

Cast
Amanda Peterson	Cynthia Pepper
Hubert Peterson	Peter Brooks
Mr Wentworth	Eddie Marr

Hubert and Amanda Peterson are newlyweds, and they
have leased the house next door. Their bliss starts to erode
immediately when they see the Family washing their pet
octopus and Fester testing dynamite caps. Hubert tries to

get out of the lease, but Gomez turns out to be the landlord and won't hear of it. Mortitia, thinking the couple need to relax, has Lurch bring them over for a game of bridge. The couple are far from relaxed when they finally escape. The Family thinks that it's their appalling taste in decorating affecting the neighbours, so they redecorate the house for them in Addams style. Hubert has an inspiration, claiming his company is transferring him to Hong Kong. Gomez promptly buys the company to prevent the move – he's dead set on helping the couple, and can't understand why Amanda faints.

10) Wednesday Leaves Home
20 November 1964

Written by   Hannibal Coons and
                          Harry Winkler
Directed by   Sidney Lanfield

Cast
Sergeant Haley   Jesse White
Officer Johnson   Ray Kellogg

Wednesday has been playing with Fester's dynamite caps without permission, so Mortitia punishes her by not allowing her to play with her spider. Wednesday decides to run away from home, but hides out in Pugsley's room. The police are called in, in the form of Sergeant Haley, but when he arrives, Fester has found Wednesday. Mortitia decides to use reverse psychology on Wednesday, who promptly runs away for real. She shows up at Haley's desk at the police station. He calls the Family, who insist Wednesday isn't really missing. Haley is being driven crazy by the Family. Fester collects Wednesday, and the next missing

34

person reported is Haley – he's run away, unable to take any more!

11) The Addams Family Meets The V.I.P.s
27 November 1964

Written by   Keith Fowler and
                           Phil Leslie
Directed by   Sidney Lanfield

Cast
Ila Klarpe   Stanley Adams
Miri Haan   Vito Scotti
Sam Harris   Frank Wilcox

Two foreign visitors to the US want to see a typical American family. They pick a name from the phone book, and their host, Sam Harris, almost dies: it's the Addams Family. He can't refuse them, as they accuse him of censorship. When they reach the house, they think Cleopatra (Mortitia's man eating plant) is a secret weapon. Seeing Thing, they believe he's a radio-controlled robot. Then they see Fester being recharged, and Lurch in action. Staggered, they almost walk into Pugsley's science project – a disintegrator ray. Convinced that the Americans are years ahead in research, the V.I.P.s vow that their Government will have much better relationships with them from now on.

12) Mortitia The Matchmaker
4 December 1964

Teleplay by   Hannibal Coons and
                           Harry Winkler
Story by   Maury Geraghty
Directed by   Jerry Hopper

Cast

Charles P. Harvey	Lee Goodman
Melancholia	Hazel Shermet
James Ferguson	Barry Kelley
Fred	Hal Baylor
Cab Driver	Lennie Bremen

Cousin Melancholia's intended, Fred, has joined the Foreign Legion, so Mortitia determines to find her a new man, and phones up Hasty Marriage. Gomez, meanwhile, calls his lawyer, Harvey, for business matters. Harvey hates to go over, but his firm needs Gomez's business. When he arrives, Mortitia thinks he's Melancholia's new beau and hits him with love dust. Then Fred arrives – he joined the American Legion, not the Foreign Legion. Thinking Harvey is flirting with his girl, he punches out his lights and takes his girl back. When Harvey recovers, Mortitia promises to find him another cousin to marry. Gomez likes him, too, which prompts the poor lawyer to flee and join the Foreign Legion.

13) Lurch Learns To Dance
11 December 1964

Teleplay by	Jay Dratler, Jerry Seelen and Charles Marion
Story by	Jay Dratler
Directed by	Sidney Lanfield
Choreography by	Jack Baker

Cast

Sally O'Rourke	Penny Parker
Fred Walters	Jimmy Cross

Lurch is about to turn down his annual invitation to the Butlers Ball as usual. He admits he doesn't go because he can't dance. Gomez insists on rectifying this and calls the Fred Walters Dance School. One of his teachers, Sally, has been mouthing off to the clients, so he sends her to the Addams as punishment. When she first sees her client, she faints. When she finally manages to teach Lurch some steps, *he* faints. Sally then runs away. Wednesday tries to teach him next, but she only knows ballet. Mortitia attempts to teach Lurch the Twist, but it puts his back out. Gomez cures him by putting him on the rack: 'Another triumph for medical science!' Gomez then takes over the teaching, and throws out his back, but Lurch gets the idea. At the Ball, no one asks him to dance – until Mortitia arrives. She and Lurch dance the tango, knocking them all dead. They return home with a trophy.

4) Art And The Addams Family
18 December 1964

Written by   Harry Winkler and
                             Hannibal Coons
Directed by   Sidney Lanfield

Cast
Sam Picasso   Vito Scotti
Bosley Swain   Hugh Sanders

Mortitia has taken up painting (she throws the paint at the canvas) and Gomez has art critic Bosley Swain evaluate her work. Swain tactfully suggests a teacher, and Grandma calls Spain for Picasso, getting oddball Sam Picasso instead. He tries hard, but Bosley thinks the man is a crook. Gomez likes Sam, and decides (against Sam's wishes) to restore Sam's good name. Wednesday tries coaching him, but Sam keeps trying to escape his dungeon workshop. Swain sees Wednesday's paintings, thinking they're Sam's, and raves. Sam manages to return to Spain to take up the safer occupation of bullfighting, while the whole Addams Family takes up brushes.

15) The Addams Family Meets A Beatnik
1 January 1965

Teleplay by	Henry Sharp and
	Sloan Nibley
Story by	Jack Raymond
Directed by	Sidney Lanfield

Cast

Rockland Cartwright III	Tom Lowell
Rockland Cartwright II	Barry Kelly
Mr Benson	Barry Brooks

Rocky Cartwright, a beatnik, crashes his motorbike into the house. He's amazed by the Family, and they're enamoured of him. He's hurt his leg and has to stay overnight. He admits he's run away from home. His father is a rich tycoon, out looking for his lost son. Rocky wants to hide, so Wednesday and Pugsley deflect the searchers. The Addams decide to cheer Rocky up by throwing him a surprise party – and invite his father. Rocky's presents are hidden and he has to hunt for them. The last one is his father, who realizes he can't interfere in his son's life. If the Addams can accept Rocky as he is, then so can his own father. Reconciled, they leave together, and Rocky gives Fester his motorbike.

16) The Addams Family Meet The Undercover Man
8 January 1965

Written by   Harry Winkler and
                              Hannibal Coons

Directed by   Arthur Lubin

Cast

Mr Hollister	George Neise
Mr Briggs	Rolfe Sedan
Mr Conkey	Norman Leavitt

Hollister is an undercover operative who's been picking up odd radio signals from the Addams house. Convinced they're spies, he recruits the postman, Briggs, to help. Briggs panics when he gets in the house, though, and flees. Hollister then tries the plumber, Conkey, who's been called in to fix Kitty's water fountain. When Conkey acts suspiciously, Gomez thinks Conkey is a spy and calls the authorities – ending up with Hollister. Mortitia is convinced that Hollister is a spy, so they capture him and toss him in the dungeon. Then he realizes that the source of the odd signals is Pugsley's new ham radio. Washington vouches for Hollister, so the Family allow him to go.

17) Mother Lurch Visits The Addams Family
15 January 1965

Written by   Jameson Brewer

Directed by   Sidney Lanfield

Cast

Mother Lurch	Ellen Corby

Lurch's mother is coming to visit, and he confesses that she doesn't know he's just the servant. Mortitia sees no problem: he can pretend the house is his, and she'll be maid and Gomez the butler, while the others move out to the cottage. Gomez tries to coach Lurch to be the gentleman, but it's hard going. He even reads the papers backwards: 'I like the funnies.' Mother Lurch arrives, a tiny old lady who wears out Gomez and Mortitia with her demands. She doesn't like Gomez and aims to stay as long as it takes to get him into shape. Matters get worse, and she eventually has Lurch fire Gomez and Mortitia. Fester and Grandma aim to straighten out Mother Lurch, but she thinks they're the replacements and hires them. Happy now, she goes home. The only problem left is that Lurch won't let Gomez or Mortitia back in the house since they've been fired.

Best known for her role as the Grandmother on *The Waltons*, Ellen Corby's small frame and large personality made a nice contrast to Ted Cassidy's Lurch. This was the first episode to introduce one of the show's catch phrases: 'Tish, that's French!'

18) Uncle Fester's Illness
22 January 1965

Written by	Bill Lutz
Directed by	Sidney Lanfield

Cast

Dr Milford	Lauren Gilbert
Hunter	Loyal 'Doc' Lucas

Fester's feeling ill, losing his voltage. Mortitia suggests a good moonbathing, but he only gets moonburn. The family doctor, Mbongo, has given up making house calls and returned to Africa. Reluctantly, Fester agrees to see a normal doctor, but doesn't care for Dr Milford. He won't take his coat off to be examined, and then eats the thermometer. The mercury picks Fester up, and Gomez thinks the doctor is a genius. He wants him to check Thing next, but Milford flees.

19) The Addams Family Splurges
29 January 1965

Teleplay by	George Haight and Lou Huston
Story by	George Haight
Directed by	Sidney Lanfield

Cast

Ralph J. Hulen	Roland Winters
Harwood Widdy	Olan Soule
Announcer	Bill Baldwin

Gomez and Pugsley build a new computer, Wizzo, because the family wants somewhere new and interesting to visit. Wizzo suggests the Moon, and the family love the idea. Their financial advisor, Hulen, tries to talk them out of it because they'd need billions. Fester suggests betting on horses, using Wizzo to predict the results. They would have won billions – except that Hulen hated the idea and never placed the bets. He schemes to make certain they 'lose' their money on a rank outsider – which then wins at 100-to-1. He faints. The horse is disqualified, so the Family is glad he didn't place the bets after all. They agree to give up on going to the moon, and will take up fishing instead. They now want him to buy them a nuclear submarine . . .

41

20) Cousin Itt Visits The Addams Family
5 February 1965

Teleplay by	Henry Sharp
Story by	Tony Wilson
Directed by	Sidney Lanfield

Cast

Park Commissioner Fiske	Alan Reed
Announcer	Bill Baldwin

Fiske is the new Zoo commissioner, and plans expansion. Fester complains about all the robins in the parks as they're too cheery. Gomez agrees to support the new fund drive and donates $150,000 (and 20 cents to cover the cost of gas to visit them). Meanwhile, Cousin Itt arrives for a visit and settles into the attic. He's good at magic tricks, but restless. Mortitia thinks they should get him a job to keep him longer, but what – 'Too short for an actor, too tall for a producer,' she sighs. Gomez ponders the idea that Itt could join the Beatles. Then they discover he has a way with animals and think he'd be perfect for a curator's job at the zoo. Fiske is thrilled, thinking Itt is an exhibit and puts him in a cage. Later, on the radio, there's news of an escaped beast. Gomez and Mortitia arm themselves to defend the house, prompting Gomez to recall their safari: 'No one could skin a hippopotamus like you could.' Tish disagrees, 'Darling, any housewife can do that.' The escaped animal is Itt, of course. Fiske arrives and the Family sorts out what happened. They're outraged about the treatment Itt received, but Itt enjoyed it and only came back for his brushes. Fiske, horrified, says he'll reserve separate cages for the whole Family at the zoo. Mortitia is appalled – it's a family cage or nothing!

Along with his usual 'Anxiety Tango', Lurch plays a

little Hungarian dance music and Spanish style for Gomez and Mortitia.

21) The Addams Family In Court
12 February 1965

Written by   Harry Winkler and
                                               Hannibal Coons

Directed by   Nat Perrin

Cast

Judge Harvey Saunders	Hal Smith
Lt Poston	James Flavin
Mrs Harvey Saunders	Lela Bliss
Police Woman	Gail Bonney
Bailiff	Ray Walker

Grandma's been telling fortunes as Madame Bovary, helped by Thing. She's even set up a tent in the living room. Mortitia is appalled and wants her to stop. It's too late, though, as the police arrest her. Gomez decides to be her lawyer, as 'Loophole' Addams. He refuses to let Grandma be sworn in, as telling the whole truth would cramp her style. The Judge orders Gomez off the case, and Mortitia takes over. She accuses the police of harassment, and the Judge finds the whole family in contempt. The Judge's wife arrives, and turns out to be one of Grandma's best clients. She insists that her husband dismiss the case.

Hal Smith was best known for his role as the town drunk on *The Andy Griffith Show*.

22) Amnesia In The Addams Family
19 February 1965

Written by   Phil Leslie and
                                               Keith Fowler

Directed by   Sidney Lanfield

Regulars only

Gomez is playing with his clubs and hits himself on the
head. When he recovers, his personality has drastically
altered – he's normal. He's just insured his life for $1
million, and thinks the family is trying to kill him and
collect. He wants Mortitia to wear some cheerier clothes.
She thinks another blow on the head might cure him, but
hasn't the heart to do it. Fester does, however, and Gomez
is restored. Unfortunately, Lurch has the same idea and hits
Gomez again . . . Then Grandma 'cures' him, only for
Pugsley to reverse it . . . Mortitia is going crazy with the
flip-flopping personalities. Gomez panics, certain they're
trying to kill him, and runs into a suit of armour. The blow
cures him – but Fester's hit *his* head and everything starts
again.

23) Thing Is Missing
5 March 1965

Teleplay by   Bill Lutz
Story by   Lorraine Edwards
Directed by   Sidney Lanfield

Cast
Sam Diamond   Tommy Farrell
Mr Boswell   Charles Wagenheim
Detective   Ray Kellogg

After Fester accidentally insults Thing, Thing disappears.
Gomez plays Sherlock Holmes to deduce who did it, decid-
ing it must be Lurch because the butler always does it.
Gomez offers a reward, and gets lots of things, but no

Thing. Then a ransom note arrives, and Gomez realizes: 'He's been Thingnapped!' They call in a detective, Sam Diamond, since the ransom is to be paid in diamonds (the best they have, which are all cursed). Diamond has to drop the diamonds at the cemetery at midnight. He returns, shaken, to report that a hand grabbed the loot. He can't understand why they're so happy, but the Family realizes that it was all a hoax by Thing, who's been feeling neglected. He wanted to see if they cared enough to ransom him.

24) Crisis In The Addams Family
12 March 1965

Teleplay by	Sloan Nibley and Preston Wood
Story by	Preston Wood
Directed by	Sidney Lanfield

Cast

Arthur J. Henson	Parley Baer
Horace Beesley	Eddie Quillan
Secretary	Bebe Kelly

Fester's in trouble for breaking the water mains for the fourth time in a row. Their insurance policy pays up, but is cancelled. Fester decides he'd better get a job to raise money himself, so he becomes an insurance salesman. Unfortunately, it's for their old company, and the only policy he sells is to the Family. Henson, the manager, wants Gomez to cancel, but Gomez refuses, saying it would break Fester's heart. Henson then calls the company's owner to report a swindle, but it turns out that Gomez *is* the owner. Gomez promotes Henson's underling to be Henson's new boss. Fester then breaks the water mains again, but at least their insurance covers it . . .

This was the first of six episodes featuring Arthur Henson (Parley Baer), the Family's unfortunate insurance salesman. He returns in episodes 29, 30, 39 (as mayor), 55 and 62. Parley Baer's credits stretch back to the days of radio (he was Chester in *Gunsmoke*) and up to modern days with guest roles on *Quantum Leap* and *The Flash*.

25) Lurch And His Harpsichord
19 March 1965

Written by	Harry Winkler and
	Hannibal Coons
Directed by	Sidney Lanfield

Cast

Mr Belmont	Byron Foulger
Workmen	Lennie Bremen,
	Ray Galvin

Lurch's harpsichord turns out to be a rare survivor of an extinct make, so Gomez is persuaded to donate it to the local museum. Lurch is left inconsolable, so the Family attempts to get him interested in other pursuits, to no avail. Finally, Gomez and Fester make the ultimate sacrifice – they build Lurch a replacement.

26) Mortitia, The Breadwinner
26 March 1965

Written by	Phil Leslie
Directed by	Sidney Lanfield

Cast

Mr Blooker	Milton Frome
Man	John 'Red' Fox
Woman	Maxine Semon
Woman	Ceil Cabot

The stockmarket has collapsed, and thousands of people are going broke. Fester and Mortitia think that the Family has lost all its money, while Gomez has bought a railroad to play with. Mortitia rallies the Family to make money without telling Gomez, as it would upset him. Fester and Lurch start an escort service, Mortitia teaches fencing and the kids start a henbane stand. Thing sells pencils. None of these are successes. Gomez is planning a vacation and the Family think he's lost his mind out of shock. Mortitia decides to sell her jewels, so Fester blows open the safe. Inside is a railroad stock. Having heard about some mystery man buying railway stock, Mortitia has Blooker the broker sell it – to Gomez. He's puzzled by the whole thing as all their money is safe, except for that in the railroad, which sank into a swamp.

27) The Addams Family And The Spacemen
2 April 1965

Written by	Harry Winkler and
	Hannibal Coons
Directed by	Sidney Lanfield

Cast

Professor Altshuler	Vito Scotti
Mr Hinckley	Tim Herbert
Mr Gilbert	Jimmy Cross
Announcer's Voice	Bob le Mond

There have been sightings of UFOs, and when Hinckley investigates, he comes across the Family on a midnight picnic. He takes Lurch and Itt for aliens, while they believe the same of him and his assistant. The two 'aliens' seem shocked, so Gomez and Mortitia lock them up for their own good. They then call Professor Altshuler for advice. He thinks Martians have invaded and rushes over to see what the Addams Family has found. It turns out that Hinckley is his assistant, and the UFOs were Pugsley's home made missiles.

28) My Son, The Chimp
9 April 1965

Teleplay by   Henry Sharp
Story by   Don Quinn
Directed by   Sidney Lanfield

Cast
Boy's Voice   Robert Nunn

Fester's working on a new experiment that goes (inevitably) wrong. An organ grinder's chimp wanders into the house when Fester's experiment blows up. Pugsley was watching, and was knocked through a wall. When the smoke clears, Fester sees the chimp and thinks he's transformed Pugsley. Mortitia thinks the chimp is nice, but wants her son back. Fester tries contacting the spirit world for advice. Pugsley, in the other room, hears and replies. Thing finds Pugsley and tries to explain to Fester that he's behind a secret door. He's eventually freed and the chimp returned to his owner. Wednesday turns up with a new boyfriend – the invisible man's invisible son.

29) Mortitia's Favorite Charity
16 April 1965

Teleplay by	Elroy Schwartz and
	Jameson Brewer
Story by	Elroy Schwartz
Directed by	Sidney Lanfield

Cast

Mr Henson	Parley Baer
Mrs Atherton	Maida Severn
Mr Clayton	Donald Foster
Jason	John Lawrence

There's a local charity auction being run by Mr Henson, and the Addams Family hear about it. He doesn't want their items, but they insist. Mortitia offers a baby strangler plant, a whipping table and a moose's rear clock (the tail swishes on the hour). Eventually, though, Henson takes some items. Pugsley is depressed and hides in the chimney because one of the items was his wolf's head clock. Mortitia decides she'll have to get it back. At the auction, Henson almost likes a suit of armour the Family gave – until he discovers Fester is still inside it. At the auction, however, Clayton buys the clock. Mortitia wonders how to cheer up Pugsley when Lurch turns up with the clock. It howls on the hour, and so unnerved Clayton that he paid Lurch to get rid of it!

30) Progress And The Addams Family
23 April 1965

Teleplay by	Bill Freedman and
	Ben Gershman
Story by	Cecil Beard and Clark Haas
Directed by	Sidney Lanfield

Cast

Mr Henson	Parley Baer
Phoebe Henson	Natalie Masters
Scotty	John Hart
Mike	Dick Reeves

Henson has now been made city Commissioner, and he condemns the Addams Family house to evict them and build a freeway in its place. When the explosives expert arrives to set the charges to destroy the house, Gomez has him thrown out. Henson comes over, giving them 24 hours to vacate. Gomez decides that he'll fight them legally – but sneakily. He calls the Hensons over and announces he's bought a new plot of land, where he aims to relocate the Addams family house. It's the plot next to the Henson house . . . The next day, they begin to move the house (as their current neighbours cheer), but Henson hastily revokes the freeway plan and buys the plot from Gomez. The Addams Family home now is returned to its old site.

31) Uncle Fester's Toupee
30 April 1965

Written by	Harry Winkler and Hannibal Coons
Directed by	Sidney Lanfield

Cast

Madelyn Smith	Elisabeth Fraser
Max	Frederic Downs

Fester's pen-pal from Paris, Madelyn, is coming to visit him. He's told her he has a lot of hair and is very athletic. Gomez calls in Max, a toupee salesman. Max is terrified and leaves the house at a gallop, forgetting his samples.

Fester can't decide which to keep. Madelyn arrives, and is attracted to Fester, and when she speaks French, he's hooked. Then she starts to realize that Fester's not what he appears to be and finally storms out. Fester's not too bothered. He uses the spare wigs for target practice.

32) Cousin Itt And The Vocational
7 May 1965

Written by   Hannibal Coons and
                             Henry Winkler
Directed by   Sidney Lanfield

Cast
Mortimer Phelps   Richard Deacon

Itt is trying to decide on a career. Mortitia suggests he become a marriage counsellor, and she and Gomez pretend to have problems for Itt to solve. 'You just think of me as a plaything', she accuses Gomez. Itt manages only to make matters worse, and Gomez and Mortitia spend the night apart. Both make up in the morning, but realize Itt isn't cut out to be a marriage counsellor. They call in Phelps, a vocational guidance expert. Phelps thinks Itt is impossible, but stays when Gomez offers him big money. Itt takes a Rorschach test, and gets them all right. And when Itt takes word association, he again passes – though Phelps isn't sure how he understood Itt! Phelps becomes enthusiastic, and decides that the best possible career for Itt is . . . as a marriage counsellor. Gomez calls: 'Lurch, show this quack the door!' Itt finally gets a job in Pango Pango, an island in the South Seas, as a tourist guide.

33) Lurch, The Teenage Idol
14 May 1965

Teleplay by	Phil Leslie
Story by	Carol Henning, Ed Ring and Mitch Persons
Directed by	Sidney Lanfield

Cast

Mizzy Bickle	Herkie Styles
Gladys	Laurie Mitchell
Susie	Noanna Dix
Claire	Pam McMyler
Joan	Jacque Palmer
Tommy	Patrick Moore

Mortitia has a wonderful thought – Lurch is such a marvellous musician, would he not make a great pop star? Mizzy Bickle, record promoter, agrees once he hears Lurch, but Lurch is reluctant. Gomez insists, and when the recording is played on the radio, Lurch becomes a huge star. Kids storm the house, and Lurch likes it. Lurch starts to neglect his butlering duties, and fan mail starts arriving by the truck-load. Bickle wants Lurch to do a world tour, which Lurch agrees to. He gives the Family a signed photo of himself. Gomez likes it, 'Best picture you ever took, Lurch. Doesn't look a bit like you.' Outside the house, Lurch encounters the down side of fame when his fans mob him. He decides he prefers the safe life with the Family and gives up showbiz.

34) The Winning Of Mortitia Addams
21 May 1965

Teleplay by	Jameson Brewer and Charles Marion

| Story by | Charles Marion |
| Directed by | Sidney Lanfield |

Cast

| Dr Francis Chalon | Lee Bergere |
| Drashi Dumo | Jan Arvan |

Fester reads an article that claims that apparently happy marriages are dangerous, because there is sickness hidden within. Since Gomez and Mortitia are so happy, Fester thinks he'd better help out and make them have a few fights for their own good. He has Gomez thrown out of his yoga society in Mortitia's name, but it backfires because Gomez enjoys being with Mortitia all that time he would have spent on yoga. Fester then calls the article's author, Dr Chalon, who comes to offer advice. He's very attracted to Mortitia, and Fester stirs this up to cause trouble. Chalon is the best swordsman in France, and Gomez challenges him to a duel. Fester's getting worried, but Gomez would rather be dead than lose Mortitia. Chalon calls off the fight, declaring that their marriage is perfect just the way it is.

Season Two

35) My Fair Cousin Itt
17 September 1965

| Written by | Phil Leslie |
| Directed by | Sidney Lanfield |

Cast

Eric von Bissell	Sig Ruman
Bennie	Jimmy Cross
Sam Derrick	Douglas Evans

Gomez has written a play for the Family to celebrate Wednesday's birthday. Cousin Itt wants to be in it, and is brilliant as the hero, Claude, to Fester's disgust – he wanted the role. Now all they need is a director, so Gomez decides to hire a professional. Erich von Bissell wants to rekindle his faded career, and thinks the play beneath him until Gomez offers $50,000. Meanwhile, Fester locks Itt in a chest so he can play the hero, but is in turn locked in the iron maiden by Lurch, who also wants the role. When Itt is freed, von Bissell refuses to work with him, especially when he hears Itt's voice. Offended, Itt hides up the chimney. Mortitia coaxes him down and works on improving his voice. Itt slows his speech down to reveal a deep baritone, which von Bissell adores. Itt now gets airs and won't do a silly amateur play. Mortitia is appalled and tries in vain to get the old Itt back. Gomez brings over producer Sam Derrick, who wants Itt to be the star of his next picture – a monster movie. Itt is so incensed that his voice returns to normal.

36/37) Mortitia's Romance
24 September, 1 October 1965

Written by   Harry Winkler and
                                  Hannibal Coons
Directed by   Sidney Lanfield

Cast
Granny Frump   Margaret Hamilton
Minister   Edward Schaaf
                               (part 2 only)

It's Mortitia and Gomez's 13th anniversary, a cause for celebration. Mortitia tells the children how they met. Gomez was supposed to marry her sister, Ophelia (also played by

Carolyn Jones). Gomez was 22, and a hypochondriac. Mama invited Ophelia and her mother, Mrs Frump, over. Ophelia is a blonde, sweetly good-natured and with a habit of strewing petals everywhere. Gomez is unimpressed, but when her sister Mortitia arrives, it's love at first sight. She has Kitty and Cleo with her. Mrs Frump insists that Ophelia, the older sister, marry first, but Gomez hates her. She's not only too bright and cheery, but also a judo expert with a habit of making men literally fall for her. Using judo, Ophelia forces Gomez to propose to her. Mortitia tries to congratulate him, and they blow up trains together. Mortitia is obviously the one for him, especially when she speaks French and inflames his blood. But what are they to do about Ophelia? Mortitia calls her Uncle Fester, but he's no help. Gomez tries his Cousin Itt, who's better. He suggests Gomez shoot himself. Mortitia thinks it's a good idea, and aims to join him. Thing, however, stops them.

In part two, the plans for the wedding continue. When Fester arrives, he's astonished to find that anyone wants to marry Ophelia, but then learns the truth. He decides that the perfect solution is to have Cousin Itt marry Ophelia, so Gomez can have Mortitia. Ophelia is a mystery fan, and nobody is more mysterious than Itt! She's quite entranced with Itt. Meanwhile Gomez tries to hide in the tunnels under the house. Mortitia finds him and forces him to talk to Ophelia. Gomez explains that he can't marry her, and to his surprise Ophelia doesn't care – she's smitten with Itt. Gomez then proposes to Mortitia, who accepts. The wedding continues, with a different bride than planned. Ophelia, though, throws over Itt – he's too much of a playboy for her liking.

Guest star Margaret Hamilton had a long career, but is still best known for her role as the Wicked Witch in *The Wizard Of Oz* (1939).

38) Mortitia Meets Royalty
8 October 1965

Written by   Leo Rifkin
Directed by   Sidney Lanfield

Cast
Princess Millicent   Elvia Allman

Princess Millicent (who is actually Aunt Millie from Iowa) arrives for a visit in a sedan chair. She's a snob, even though her husband squandered all her money but oil stocks. She has a literal handmaiden, Lady Fingers, a hand that Thing falls desperately in love with. Millicent insists that they spruce up the place, and dress accordingly. Fester the Jester is not amused. They finally can take no more, and take her to a hotel. Oil is discovered on her property and she's rich again. Mortitia is relieved that she's gone, and will give no more orders: 'The Addams Family is a democracy again.' 'Exactly!' Gomez agrees. 'From now on, I give the orders around here. But – nobody has to obey them!' Thing is depressed, missing Lady Fingers, and Gomez agrees to allow Millicent back. 'See – even the pages have turned over a new leaf!' But Millicent has fired Lady Fingers and hired a new maid, Esmeralda, another disembodied hand. Thing goes missing, and Millicent discovers one of her bracelets has been stolen. She thinks Thing is guilty, but Gomez proves Esmeralda is the thief: 'And an old hand at it!' Thing returns with Lady Fingers. The two are engaged. Millicent hires her back, and Thing promises to wait for Lady Fingers.

39) Gomez, The People's Choice
15 October 1965

Teleplay by	Henry Sharp
Story by	Joseph Vogel and
	Marvin Kaplan
Directed by	Sidney Lanfield

Cast

Mayor Arthur Hensen	Parley Baer
Reporter	Jack Barry
Clyde Arbogast	Eddie Quillan
1st Workman	Lennie Bremen
2nd Workman	Bart 'Buzz' Greene

Gomez is insulted by his latest tax bill, which is only $84, and complains to the mayor. Hensen misunderstands and offers him a rebate, convincing Gomez and Mortitia that he's incompetent. Mortitia convinces Gomez to run for office, so Fester gets out Wizzo (their computer) to help with political questions. Unlike Hensen, Gomez won't lie and cheat, and the reporter who interviews him discovers Gomez has odd views, such as aiming to preserve picturesque slums. The Mayor challenges Gomez to a TV debate, which Gomez wants to weasel out of, but then gets utterly preoccupied with. Mortitia is distraught and tries to get him to quit. When that doesn't work, she tries to convince people not to vote for Gomez, but her efforts all backfire. Gomez is about to be elected, but is disqualified on a technicality, which makes everyone happy again, especially the Mayor.

57

40) Cousin Itt's Problem
22 October 1965

Written by   Carol Henning, Ed Ring
                                            and Mitch Persons

Directed by   Sidney Lanfield

Cast

Myrtle Mae Dragwater	Meg Wyllie
Delivery Boy	Frankie Darro

Cousin Itt is shedding hair, and the Family is worried that he'll lose his great good looks along with his hair. Fester gets out his chemistry set to produce a batch of hair restorer and prevent a disaster.

41) Halloween – Addams Style
29 October 1965

Written by   Hannibal Coons and
                                            Harry Winkler

Directed by   Sidney Lanfield

Cast

Penelope Sandhurst	Yvonne Peattie
Henry Sandhurst	Bob Jellison
Cousin Cackle	Don McArt

Mrs Sandhurst, one of the neighbours, shocks Wednesday by telling her that there are no such things as witches. Wednesday returns home in tears, and the Family has to rally around to prove that Mrs Sandhurst is wrong and to restore Wednesday's faith in her favourite holiday.

42) Mortitia, The Writer
5 November 1965

Written by   Hannibal Coons and
                          Harry Winkler
Directed by   Sidney Lanfield

Cast
Boswell   Peter Bonerz

Mortitia disapproves of the books the children are assigned
from school, since they portray giants, goblins and ghouls
as the bad guys. She sets up an office in a cave and starts
writing better stories such as 'The Good Giant Slays Sir
Lancelot' and 'Cinderella, The Teenage Delinquent'. Gomez
is worried because she seems so obsessed and is afraid he'll
lose her to her work. She asks him to send her story to
Demon Press (she likes the name), and Gomez agrees to
Fester's suggestion to change it and make it unprintable.
When he does, though, Boswell, the publisher, arrives –
thinking Mortitia is a genius. He asks for $5,000 to publish
the book, convincing Gomez he's a con artist. Gomez gives
him $10,000 to get rid of him. Mortitia returns to work, on
Goldilocks next: 'Trust a blonde to bring on trouble.' Gomez
discovers that Boswell was for real, and Mortitia's book is
selling like crazy becoming the standard work for schools.
When she reads it, though, she's appalled: the witches are
bad and all her other innovations are changed. Gomez confesses what he did, and Mortitia thinks he was very wise –
he's proved to her that publishers have no idea what good
literature is!

43) Mortitia The Sculptress
12 November 1965

Written by   Harry Winkler and
                                       Hannibal Coons
Directed by   Sidney Lanfield

Cast

Sam Picasso	Vito Scotti
Bosley Swain	Hugh Sanders

Mortitia wants to do something to add to life artistically, so she decides to take up sculpting. Lurch carries in a huge rock for her and she sets to work. Three months later, Fester still isn't impressed, so Gomez calls in art critic Swain for an informed opinion. He suggests blowing the sculpture up, and Gomez has to hide this opinion from Mortitia. He decides that the best way out of this is to get someone to buy it, and hires Sam Picasso (last seen in episode 14) to do the deed. Picasso and Mortitia instead decide to sponsor starving artists. Gomez is driven to distraction (and near-bankruptcy) by this, as Mortitia neglects everything to concentrate on her work. Then she finds the children making fudge and is horrified. She decides she's been neglecting them and gives up sculpture. Gomez is more than happy, because he's been feeling neglected also, and Tish promises to make it up to him.

44) Gomez, The Reluctant Lover
19 November 1965

Teleplay by   Charles Marion and
                                       Leo Rifkin
Story by   Charles Marion
Directed by   Sidney Lanfield

Cast

Isobel Dunbar	Jill Andre
Mr Jennings	Tom Brown Henry

Pugsley is all melancholic because he's in love. Gomez tries to cheer him by buying him a pneumatic drill, but Pugsley already has one. Pugsley tries to write a love letter, but he can't get it right, so he copies one of his father's old ones to his mother. He then sends the love letter to his teacher, Miss Dunbar. She's horrified and goes to visit Pugsley's father. Naturally, Gomez knows the letter by heart and she thinks he sent it. She's charmed and attracted to Gomez and attacks him, because she's shy and mousey. Gomez tries to put her off, without success. Fester sees him 'romancing' Miss Dunbar and tells him: 'I don't know about you, but I come from a long line of stool-pigeons.' He tells Mortitia, who confronts Gomez. Gomez explains that he's only wooing Miss Dunbar to show her she is an attractive woman and can get a man of her own. He's afraid to reject her because it might damage her self-esteem. Mortitia doesn't buy it, and is about to leave him. Then the principal, Jennings, arrives to look for Miss Dunbar and when he sees the new version falls for her. She then rejects a relieved Gomez and everyone is happy again.

45) Feud In The Addams Family
26 November 1965

Teleplay by	Rick Richards and Jerry Gottler
Story by	Rick Richards
Directed by	Sidney Lanfield

Cast

Mr Courtney	Fred Clark

| Mrs Courtney | Virginia Gregg |
| Robespierre | Kevin Tate |

Abigail Addams wants to have Gomez removed as the head of the Family fortune, and is in town on a visit. Meanwhile Mrs Courtney wants to get to know her, and she annoys her husband by encouraging their young son, Robespierre, to get along better with Wednesday, who's in love with Robespierre. Mrs Courtney thinks Wednesday's family is Abigail's and agrees to visit for tea. Meanwhile, Wednesday is getting advice from her relatives on how to catch men – along with a rope, a gun and love dust. The Courtneys are taken aback when they arrive and meet Itt and Fester. Fester thinks they're spies when they mention Abigail's name, and gets obsessed. He breaks their pens, thinking they're bugged. Gomez helps Courtney to invest and he promptly loses all his money. It finally dawns on Courtney that his wife was completely wrong, and they leave, laughing hysterically. Abigail finally drops her plans to sue Gomez.

When Fester is ranting on about spies, he suspects that the Courtneys are working for THRUSH – the villains from *The Man From UNCLE*, which was then at the height of its popularity.

46) Gomez, The Cat Burglar
3 December 1965

| **Written by** | Phil Leslie |
| **Directed by** | Sidney Lanfield |

Cast

| Sergeant Rogers | Ken Mayer |
| Officer Hix | Bill White |

After a large meal, Gomez gets sleepy. That night, he sleep-walks, and when he returns doesn't get up till four in the afternoon. The news is filled with the story of a cat burglar on the loose. He sleep-walks again that night, and the cat burglar strikes again. Fester stands guard, but falls asleep, and the Family is worried. Fester and Mortitia find the stolen loot in their basement, and are afraid Gomez is the cat burglar sought by the police. They have to keep him from going out. Mama realizes that her yak stew is what's making him sleep-walk, and Mortitia hypnotizes Gomez to find out why he's stealing. He's been reading about Robin Hood, and has been influenced to imitate him. Mortitia wants to use hypnosis to cure him, but speaks French and he awakens. They lock him in the basement, but he escapes, returning at three a.m. with more loot. The others waken him and he realizes what he's been doing and is aghast. This time, though, the police have followed him. To prevent them from arresting Gomez, Mortitia hypnotizes them and gets them to return the loot.

47) Portrait Of Gomez
10 December 1965

Teleplay by	Leo Salkin, Bill Lutz and Henry Sharp
Story by	Leo Salkin and Bill Lutz
Directed by	Sidney Salkow

Cast
Examiner	Tom D'Andrea
Photographer	Ralph Montgomery

Strife magazine calls to tell Gomez that they're sending a photographer round. He thinks he's been chosen their Man of the Year. Mortitia wants to supply her own picture of

Gomez for the cover, but Cleopatra eats her favourite photo of Gomez. The photographer who took it is now out of business, so Fester volunteers to take a new one. When this doesn't come out properly Gomez retreats to the chandelier in despair. Mortitia tracks down the photographer, and discovers he's now taking photos for drivers' licences. All they need is for Gomez to apply for his licence – but he can't drive. Lurch has to teach him, but when Gomez takes his test he terrifies the examiner. He can't understand why Gomez even wants a licence. When Gomez explains, the examiner tells him that the photographer was fired anyway. Back to square one (and having given up driving) Gomez has Mortitia paint his portrait. The photographer from *Strife* arrives, but he wants to photograph the house – chosen Spookiest House of the Year. The Family is tremendously proud.

48) Mortitia's Dilemma
17 December 1965

Written by   Jerry Gottler and
                                   John Bradford
Directed by   Sidney Miller

Cast
Don Xavier Molinas   Anthony Caruso
Consuella   Yardena
Maria The Duenna   Bella Bruck
Señor Cardona   Carlos Rivas

There's a letter for Gomez from Camplona, Spain – an old family friend, Don Xavier Molinas is coming to visit. Don Xavier's daughter, Consuela, is getting married and has assumed it's to Gomez. They arrive with her Duenna, and Mortitia catches onto the problem. She thinks Gomez is two-timing her or building up a harem. She goes to Itt for advice and he suggests using psychology. Gomez hires flamenco dancer Señor Cardona to entertain his guests, and the dancer and Consuela fall for one another. Gomez is still oblivious of everything until Don Xavier announces that he is betrothed to Consuela. Gomez naturally refuses to marry her. Don Xavier is insulted and challenges Gomez to a duel. During the fight, Thing prevents Don Xavier from running Gomez through, and Gomez accidentally brings the chandelier down on Cardona. Consuela is upset and announces that she's going to marry the dancer. Everything is resolved and everyone is happy once more.

50) Uncle Fester, Tycoon
31 December 1965

Written by	Sloan Nibley and Preston Wood
Directed by	Sidney Salkow

Cast

Thaddeus Logan	Roy Roberts
Dr Brown	Harold Peary

Fester gets a letter from another of his pen-pals, Diana the bearded lady. Overcome with emotion, he proposes to her by mail. Mortitia is worried about him and poses as Diana's mother (complete with beard) to try and talk him out of it. She accuses him of being unable to support her 'daughter', so Fester decides he has to get a job. He enrols in a correspondence course in business and starts getting into it. He gets very aggressive and hones his bargaining ability. He impresses Logan with his skills and is offered a job. Meanwhile, worried, Gomez calls in a psychiatrist, Dr Brown, to help cure Fester. When Logan comes to see Fester, Gomez thinks he's the psychiatrist and that he's trying to take Fester off to an institution. Gomez manages to get rid of Logan, and Fester decides he's had enough of work and gives up on his plans to marry. When the real Brown arrives he thinks Fester's crazy, but the Family thinks he's cured.

51) Mortitia And Gomez vs Fester And Mama
7 January 1966

Teleplay by	Sloan Nibley and Preston Wood
Story by	Lila Garrett and Bernie Kahn
Directed by	Sidney Salkow

Cast

Inez Thudd	Irene Tedrow
Motel Proprietor	Loyal 'Doc' Lucas

Mortitia thinks Mama and Fester are spoiling the children. Fester arrives, hallucinating from too much sun, and with his dynamite. When they take it from him he's upset. When a hurricane hits the Gulf Coast, Gomez and Mortitia aim to go and enjoy it, employing Miss Thudd to look after the children. Fester and Mama are insulted and threaten to leave. Since they have no money, they decide to split the house instead – painting a line down their half (including half of Lurch!). Gomez and Mortitia check into the Last Chance Motel, which is dirty, wet and next to a smelly glue factory – absolutely perfect! Then they discover that Miss Thudd's bag has been accidentally brought along, and it contains treats for the children. 'She can't be all bad', argues Gomez. 'Really?' asks Mortitia. 'Reading Dr Spock?'

'Oh', apologizes Gomez. 'I thought it was Dr Spook.' They rush home, concerned for the children, only to discover that Mama and Fester have fired Miss Thudd and are looking after the children themselves. Gomez and Mortitia are vastly relieved and apologize. The hurricane now hits the house, so the whole Family is happy again.

52) Fester Goes On A Diet
14 January 1966

Written by   Hannibal Coons and
Harry Winkler
Directed by   Sidney Lanfield

Cast
Himself	Jack La Lanne
Dr Motley	William Keene
Yvette	Peggy Mondo
Mailman	Rolfe Sedan

Pugsley has been exercising, much to his parents' disapproval. Fester gets a letter from his French pen-pal, Yvette, who is coming to visit. He decides he has to get into shape, with the help of fitness guru Jack la Lanne. Gomez and Mortitia can't understand why he's doing this and think he's ill. They call in Dr Motley, who panics at some of the results when he tests Fester and flees. When Fester accidentally hypnotizes himself in an attempt to get fit, Mortitia uses the opportunity to question him. She comes to the conclusion he wants to become an astronaut. NASA isn't amused when she tries to talk them out of employing Fester, since they have no idea what's going on. Fester uses a mummy case as a steam bath to lose weight, and explains about Yvette. When she arrives, she's rather overweight and jilts Fester because he's too skinny!

53) The Great Treasure Hunt
21 January 1966

Written by   Hannibal Coons and
                                         Harry Winkler
Directed by   Sidney Lanfield

Cast

Captain Grimby	Nestor Paiva
Mr Brack	Dick Reeves

In the attic the Family discovers great-grandfather Pegleg's old sea chest. There's a treasure map in it. Gomez explains that Pegleg was buried at sea with 'full military honours – handcuffed, blindfolded, dropped off a plank'. Mortitia wants to search for the treasure, but half the map is missing, so the first search is for the rest of the map. When Gomez finds it they charter a boat from Captain Grimby and his mate, Brack. Grimby becomes infected with greed, especially when Gomez offers him $200,000 for the charter. The sailors try to steal the map, but Fester walks in on them. They torture him to make him open the safe, but he enjoys that. He only gives them the combination when they stop. The safe is booby-trapped, and they're scared off. Also in the safe is a code book for the map. When they check it, it turns out that the treasure is buried under the house, not at sea. They dig it up – chocolate gold pieces, so everyone is happy!

54) Ophelia Finds Romance
28 January 1966

Written by   Hannibal Coons and
                                         Harry Winkler
Directed by   Sidney Lanfield

Cast

Horatio Bartholomew	Robert Nichols

Ophelia needs help with her latest romance. She met Horatio at a Lonely Hearts' Club, and Grandma Frump objects to him. Gomez and Mortitia both think he's a phoney, and try to convince Itt to marry Ophelia instead. She won't listen to them, and prefers Mama's opinion because Mama likes him. Horatio claims to have studied at Heidelberg, so Gomez fences with him – and loses. He also loses at cards to him. Mortitia tries to prove he's a ladies' man by flirting with him, but he rejects her for Ophelia. Then Gomez discovers that Horatio is actually the second richest man in the world and not a phoney after all. He tries to make up for his suspicions by teaching Horatio Zen yoga, but Horatio hates it. Ophelia decides that this means he's unsuitable and breaks with him. Itt reappears, having decided he'd like to marry Ophelia, and she carries him off. Nobody is too surprised, however, when she breaks off that romance as well.

55) Pugsley's Allowance
4 February 1966

Written by	Harry Winkler and
	Hannibal Coons
Directed by	Sidney Lanfield

Cast

Dr Henson	Parley Baer
Mrs Henson	Natalie Masters
Dr Bird	Jack Collins
Mr Glenville	Robert S. Carson
Bennie	Tim Herbert

Pugsley wants some money and offers to work. This horrifies his parents – Addams don't work! – but they agree to let him work to teach him a lesson. Pugsley tries to get a job at the hospital, helping with operations, but is thrown out. Then he tries counting cash in a bank vault, which gets him thrown out again. Next Pugsley tries to join a funeral service, only to discover it's merely the front for a bookie named Bennie. Pugsley convinces Wednesday to join him and they offer to trim hedges, wash the car and clear the attic for the Hensons (who should know better by now). Henson cons them, offering fifty cents for all the work. But when he checks on their work, the hedge is cut as hideous creatures, the car was washed by filling it with water and the attic isn't merely cleared – it's gone. He threatens to sue Gomez, who threatens a counter-suit for exploiting the kids. Hensen apologizes quickly, and Gomez buys his ruined house. He then gives Pugsley the job of clearing another attic for a fair rate. Pugsley is happy, and this time he'll clear it using dynamite . . .

56) Happy Birthday, Grandma Frump
11 February 1966

Written by	Elroy Schwartz
Directed by	Sidney Lanfield

Cast

Granny Frump	Margaret Hamilton
Dr Jonley	George Petrie

Annoyed by not being asked to contribute to a charity drive, Gomez decides he'll build his own old folks' home. Meanwhile, Granny Frump's birthday is coming up and she's been invited over. Gomez and Mortitia plan to send her to a beauty clinic, but Pugsley thinks she's heading for the retirement home. Fester thinks that's a good idea, but reluctantly suggests that she should make herself too useful to be sent away. Granny tries hard, but she overdoes it and upsets Lurch by stealing his chores. Wednesday tries to cheer her up by suggesting she act young. Granny overdoes that, too, dressing and acting like a child. Gomez and Mortitia think she's cracked up, and call in Dr Jonley to examine her. Fester discovers the truth and explains to Granny – who then mistakes Jonley for the beautician and insists on being taken away. She enjoys the mental hospital for a while, but leaves when they won't give her a perm.

George Petrie played another psychiatrist in episode 2.

57) Mortitia The Decorator
18 February 1966

Written by	Gene Thompson
Directed by	Sidney Salkow

Cast

Eleanor Digby	Jeff Donnell
Joe Digby	Eddie Quillan

Mortitia is caught up in the National Beautification Programme and decides to become a decorator. Their new neighbours are the Digbys, and he's an insurance salesman. Gomez asks him to insure their art collection for a million dollars, and invites him to visit with his wife. They're taken aback by the Addams's house, and Mrs Digby explains that they have to decorate their home. Mortitia offers to help, and Mrs Digby faints. Once the insurance papers are signed, Mrs Digby claims she can't afford to use Mortitia, thinking that will end matters. The Family feels sorry for the neighbours and order Lurch to take over a few decorating items. Fester disapproves and tries to sabotage this by substituting

71

a genuine antique desk he loathes – a true classic. Mrs Digby thinks she's misjudged Mortitia and asks her to do the rest of the house. Mortitia complies, turning the garden into a desert, the house into a jungle and the basement into a swimming pool by flooding it. Mrs Digby faints again. Mortitia likes the house so much she's loathe to part with it, and buys it from the Digbys for a showroom. They offer their neighbours a new home and more decorating help. Surprisingly, the Digbys emigrate to Timbuktu.

58) Ophelia Visits Mortitia
25 February 1966

Written by   Art Weingarten
Directed by   Sidney Lanfield

Cast
Montrose   George Cisar

Ophelia is still having problems getting a man. As Gomez observes: 'In the school of romance, I'm afraid she's just a drop-out.' After her latest beau, Montrose, has jilted her (the sixth this year), he joined the Peace Corps. Fester decides to help her by joining the Corps also to enable him to look for Montrose. When he takes the exam, though, the Peace Corps returns him home – nowhere in the world is quite ready for him. The family daren't break this news to Fester, who's keen on his plan, so they have to try and convince him to stay. Gomez pretends he's lost all his money and needs help, so Fester stays. Mortitia claims to need inspiration from Fester for her paintings, so he dresses as an angel and suspends himself from the roof. Ophelia is still pining for Montrose, who has quit the Corps and returns to her.

72

59) Addams Cum Laude
4 March 1966

Written by   Sloan Nibley and Bill Lutz
Directed by   Sidney Lanfield

Cast

Sam Hilliard	Allyn Joslyn
Secretary	Carol Byron
Mrs Bennet	Pat Brown

The school principal threatens to expel the children after they've been playing with dynamite caps. Mortitia has heard that Sam Hilliard is now running a private school, Mockridge Hall, and wants to get the children in. He's strapped for cash and can't turn Gomez down when he offers $10,000. Still, when Pugsley and Wednesday bring their pets to school, he expels them. Gomez thinks he's cracked under the money problems and he buys the school to run it properly. He renames it Addams Hall. Hilliard resigns immediately, so Mortitia persuades Gomez to take over. The parents of the other pupils insist that Hilliard return or they'll take their children out. Mortitia is touched by their loyalty to Hilliard (actually, they're terrified of Gomez), and Gomez brings him back with a promise not to interfere. Wednesday and Pugsley decide they prefer their old school, and return there.

60) Cat Addams
11 March 1966

Written by   Paul Tuckahoe
Directed by   Sidney Z. Cherry

Cast

Dr Marvin P. Gunderson	Marty Ingels
Jungle Doctor	Loyal 'Doc' Lucas

Kitty Kat, the Family's lion, is off his food. Grandma is worried about him, so she insists on calling in the best medical advice that Gomez's money can buy – Dr Gunderson.

Marty Ingels had starred with John Astin in *I'm Dickens . . . He's Fenster*.

61) Lurch's Little Helper
18 March 1966

Written by	Phil Leslie
Directed by	Sidney Lanfield

Regulars only

Mortitia is afraid that they are overworking Lurch, so Gomez builds him a robot assistant. Lurch doesn't like 'Smiley' until he realizes he's now the Head Butler. He then has Smiley do all of the work in his stead. The problem is that Smiley is too strong, and this causes all kinds of complications – and he simply can't cook. Gomez begins wishing he'd never had this particular bright idea, since Lurch has stopped working. They decide to cure him by telling him he's no longer needed and he can take a long rest. Lurch is now worried, because he likes his job, and he's afraid he's been replaced. Thing suggests a spot of sabotage. When Gomez rings for Smiley, Lurch appears, with a wrench, to announce that Smiley has resigned . . .

Smiley was actually Robbie the Robot, from *Forbidden Planet* (1956) and *The Invisible Boy* (1957).

62) The Addams Policy
25 March 1966

Written by   Henry Winkler and
                                 Hannibal Coons

Directed by   Sidney Lanfield

Cast

Mr Henson	Parley Baer
Mr Digby	Eddie Quillan

Mortitia has a new flame thrower, which Fester tests, setting their polar bear on fire. They claim this on the insurance, infuriating Henson. His clerk, Digby, had forgotten to cancel the Family's coverage. Digby is in a quandry as Gomez wants the bear replaced, but he can't find one big enough. Henson, furious, has Fester re-enact the accident, and then fires Digby. Gomez feels sorry for the clerk and decides to help him by opening his own insurance company. The Family will be his staff, and they will specialize in covering people conventional insurance rejects. When their first client arrives, Fester gives him a medical exam that almost breaks his leg. Grandmama uses her crystal ball to work out his life expectancy and reveals him to be Henson in disguise. Gomez threatens to remove all his companies' insurance from Henson's firm, and Henson – faced with staggering income loss – has to back down and rehire Digby. Digby manages to replace the bear rug, but Fester promptly sets it on fire again.

Eddie Quillan had previously played insurance salesman Digby in episode 57, along with insurance salesman Horace Beesley (also working for Henson) in episode 24, and Clyde Arbogast (yet again working for Henson!) in episode 39. He was a regular on *Julia* (1968–71) and *Hell Town* (1985).

63) Lurch's Grand Romance
1 April 1965

Written by   Gene Thompson and
                             Art Weingarten
Directed by   Sidney Lanfield

Cast
Trivia   Diane Jergens

Mortitia's best friend Trivia arrives for a visit. She's into
show-biz and very theatrical. Lurch falls for her, but she
has no time for him. Wednesday tries to teach Lurch modern dance to help him snare Trivia, but that's a failure.
Fester offers Lurch advice about women, which merely
discourages Lurch, and he decides to kill himself. Gomez
tries to help out by writing a suicide note, but Lurch changes
his mind and decides to live. Mortitia suggests serenading
Trivia, another shambles, and Grandmama suggests a love
potion. That works all too well, and Trivia attacks Lurch –
and then Gomez. The potion just makes her insatiable for
all men. Fester tries to explain, but she goes for him next,
and then Itt. Finally, the potion wears off, and she returns to
normal. Lurch is glad to see her leave. Grandmama can't
understand what went wrong, but will test the potion on
herself next . . .

64) Ophelia's Career
8 April 1966

Written by   Harry Winkler and
                             Hannibal Coons
Directed by   Sidney Lanfield

Cast

Mr Rudolpho	Ben Wright
Signor Bellini	Ralph Rose

Ophelia arrives in tears as usual, as she's been jilted yet again. Mortitia thinks she should take up a career to distract her from her bad track record with men. Chemistry is a failure, so Cousin Itt offers to teach her singing. This doesn't work too well, and she sings like he talks. Gomez hires Signor Bellini to finish the job. He gets furious with her, and Ophelia manages to sing choral music – in a chorus of voices, which stuns him. Six months later, she's audition-ing for Rudolpho, the great impresario. Fester tries to calm her nerves by giving her a throat tonic – which ruins her voice. Mortitia tries to console her sister by writing a new opera for her, 'Afternoon In A Swamp'. Ophelia tries again to take up her career, and even cuts a record, which she sends the Family. She now has a two-tone voice . . . alto and bass.

Hallowe'en With The New Addams Family

The Addams Family survived so well in syndication that an attempt to revive it was perhaps inevitable. Comic-book humour was transferring to the TV screens by 1977. *Wonder Woman* was flexing her muscles and other body parts, and Charles Fries had already produced the pilot for the short-lived TV version of *Spiderman*, and *The Incredible Hulk* was about to burst on the scene. Quirky humour seemed to be coming back, and Fries opted to try an updated ver-sion of *The Addams Family* to see if the show could still work its old magic. If the ratings had allowed, the show would have returned to production once again. However, the ratings – and the critical reviews – sank the attempt.

Almost the entire cast of the original show returned for this new version, but instead of being studio-bound, it was videotaped on location in a real house. The special effects team rigged up a few extra touches, such as cauldrons and a graveyard instead of a backyard, but none of the old Addams' touches were really evident inside the house. The television movie was highly publicized, and first transmitted on 30 October 1977 – Halloween, naturally.

Written by	George Tibbles
Directed by	David Steinmetz
Music by	Vic Mizzy
'A Merry, Shh, Creepy Hallowe'en'	
Words by	David Levy
Music by	George Tibbles
Produced by	David Levy
Executive Producer	Charles Fries
Director of Photography	Jacques R. Marquette, ASC
Associate Producer	Paul Pieratt
Art Director	Bill Ross
Production Manager	William P. Owens
Assistant Director	Peter Barth
Technical Director	Jim Swick
Audio	Jack Tossman
Casting	Caro Jones
Videotape Editor	Ken Baker
Technical Operations Supervisor	Fred Donelson
Stage Managers	David Wader, Paul Pieratt, Jnr
Special Effects	Knott Limited
Costume Designer	Jim Kessler
Makeup	Carol L. Dary

Hair Stylist	Helen Grizuk
Costume Supervisor	Vou Lee Giokaris
Properties	Randall 'Ted' Berkeley
Set Decorator	Edward Parker
Production Controller	Linda Sohy
Assistant to Director	Lynn Tanke
Production Assistant	Joseph John Kontra
Location Video Facilities	Spectrum Video
Executive in Charge of Production	Malcolm Stuart

'The Addams Family' created for television by David Levy based upon the original cartoons by Charles Addams

Charles Fries Productions, Inc.
in association with Wilshire Productions, Inc.

Cast

Gomez	John Astin
Lurch	Ted Cassidy
Uncle Fester	Jackie Coogan
Mortitia	Carolyn Jones
Pancho	Henry Darrow
Granny	Jane Rose
Mother Frump	Elvia Allman
Mikey	Vitto Scotti
Boss Crook	Parley Baer
Little Bo Peep	Patrick Campbell
Fake Gomez	Dean Sothern
Cousin Itt	Felix Silla
Wednesday, Snr	Lisa Loring
Pugsley, Snr	Ken Weatherwax
Wednesday, Jnr	Jennifer Suprenant
Pugsley, Jnr	Ken Marquis
Fake Mortitia	Terry Miller

79

Hercules	David Johns
Atlas	Clinton Beyerle
First Cop	George Ranito Jordan
Countess Dracula	Suzanne Krazna
Thing	Itself

Gomez's brother, Pancho, is staying with the Family while Gomez goes to a lodge meeting in Tombstone, Arizona. Gomez is jealous of his brother, who once courted Mortitia. Halloween is nigh, and Pancho tells the legend of Cousin Shy, who distributes gifts and carves pumpkins. Actually, Gomez has been lured off by crooks, who've bugged the house in order to steal the Family fortune. Lafferty, the boss, sends Mikey to investigate. Wednesday Snr is home from music academy, where she studied the piccolo (she breaks glass with it). Pugsley Snr is home from Nairobi medical school, where he's a witch doctor. Mikey panics and flees after treading on Kitty Kat's tail. The crooks have a fake Gomez and Mortitia to help in their plans, along with two strong-arm goons, Hercules and Atlas. Gomez returns home for the Halloween party and trimming the scarecrow. Lafferty poses as Quincy Addams (from Boston) to get in. He has his men tie up Gomez and Mortitia and his doubles take their places, confusing Pancho, who's still got the hots for Mortitia. Lurch scares off the thugs and terrifies the assistant crook. Fester, trying to be nice, puts Lafferty on the rack. Lafferty tries to escape through the short cut and steps on Kitty Kat's tail. When the police arrive, they surrender. The Family is then free to celebrate Halloween happily.

Gomez has suddenly acquired a look-alike brother who was previously unknown. He's also a Mason. Most of the Family is reunited for this film, including the older children, though they also have two younger look-and-name-alike children. Lady Fingers returns as Mother Frump's aide. In the cemetery out back are graves for Uncle Faustus, Salem Addams, Uncle Morbid and Charles Freeze Addams. The person whose foot is in the swordfish's mouth has now become Cousin Ahab.

One joke in the movie, where the crooks decide to 'Let Mikey do it', is based on a then-popular breakfast cereal commercial.

This was an attempt to revive the old series using most of the original cast (minus Blossom Rock, who was too old and ill to return). It failed abysmally in the ratings, mostly because it isn't very funny. Oddly, the writer of this revival had never worked on the original *Addams Family* – but had worked extensively on *The Munsters*.

The Addams Family

Despite the first failed attempt to breath new life into *The Addams Family*, the series was too intriguing to be left alone for long. With the coming of age of the baby boomers who had grown up on this and other series, Hollywood was discovering that revived nostalgia could sell. The astonishing success of the grim *Batman* (1989) film proved that there was a market, and *Dick Tracy* (1990) – an abject failure – proved that it had to be done well.

The script for *The Addams Family* (1991) was considered to be a potential winner from the start. Ignoring a lot of the TV show setting, the script went back to the original Charles Addams' cartoons for most of their inspiration, including the most famous one of all: the Family pouring boiling oil on cheery Christmas carollers. The film thus had a much blacker humour than the show, which was essentially harmless fun. In America, there were complaints from several quarters that the second film, especially, was *too* nasty. It didn't hurt the box office, though.

Written by	Caroline Thompson and Larry Wilson
Based on the characters created by	Charles Addams
Directed by	Barry Sonnenfeld
Music by	Marc Shaiman
Conducted by	Hummie Mann
Dance music orchestrated by	Peter Golub
Produced by	Scott Rudin
Executive Producer	Graham Place
Director of Photography	Owen Roizman, ASC
Production Designer	Richard MacDonald
Film Editors	Dede Allen, ACE and Jim Miller
Costume Designer	Ruth Myers
Co-Producer/Unit Production Manager	Jack Cummins
Casting	David Rubin, CSA
1st Assistant Director	Joe Camp III
2nd Assistant Director	Ian Foster Woolf
Visual Effects Supervisor	Alan Munro
Additional Photography	Gale Tattersall
Choreography	Peter Anastos
Visual Effects Co-Supervisor	Chuck Comisky
Properties	Robin Miller
Stunt Co-ordinator	David Ellis
Supervising Sound Editor	Cecelia Hall, MPSE
Sound Mixer	Peter F. Kurland
Rerecording Mixers	Gregg Landaker, Gary Summers and Michael Minkler
Fencing Choreography	B.H. Barry
Makeup Design	Fern Buchner
Hair design	Anthony Cortino
Wigs	Paul Huntley

Casting Associate	Debra Zane
Extras Casting	Charlie Messenger
Art Director	Marjorie Stone McShirley
Associate Producers	Bonnie Arnold and Paul Rosenberg
Set Decorator	Cheryal Kearney
Assistant Art Directors	Erin Cummins and Paul Sonski
Special Effects Co-ordinator	Chuck Gaspar
Script Supervisor	Tom Johnston
Music Editor	George A. Martin
Orchestrations	Mark McKenzie, Steve Bartek, Ralph Burns, Dennis Dreith, Jack Eskew and Thom Sharp
Titles and Optical Effects	Cinema Research Corporation
Main Title Design	Pablo Ferro and Allen Ferro
Special Prosthetics and mechanical devices	Alterian Studios, Inc; Tony Gardner
'Thing' prosthetics and puppets	David Miller Studios
Puppeteers	J. Eustermann, Eric Friedler, Bruce Fuller, Jim McPherson, Dianna Smith, William Sturgeon, Tommy Williamson, Jnr, John Robles and David Penikas
Model train crash	Ron Thornton Effects
Matte Art Composites	Illusion Arts; Bill Taylor and Syd Dutton

'The Addams Groove', music by Hammer/Pilate; lyrics by Hammer; performed by Hammer

83

'The Addams Family Theme' by Vic Mizzy
'Mamushka', music by Marc Shaiman, lyrics by Betty
Comden and Adolph Green

Cast

Mortitia Addams	Anjelica Huston
Gomez Addams	Raul Julia
Uncle Fester	Christopher Lloyd
Abigail Craven	Elizabeth Wilson
Wednesday Addams	Christina Ricci
Granny	Judith Malina
Tully Alford	Dan Hedaya
Lurch	Carel Struycken
Judge Womack	Paul Benedict
Thing	Christopher Hart
Margaret Alford	Dana Ivey
Pugsley Addams	Jimmy Workman
Cousin Itt	John Franklin
Digit Addams	Tony Azito
Dexter Addams	Douglas Brian Martin
Donald Addams	Steven M. Martin
Cousin Ophelia Addams	Allegra Kent
Sloth Addams	Richard Korthaze
Lumpy Addams	Ryan Holihan
Flora Amor	Maureen Sue Levin
Fauna Amor	Darlene Levin
Employment Agent	Kate McGregor-Stewart
Susan Firkins	Lela Ivet
Little Tully	Whitby Hertford
Lois Addams	Patty Maloney
Swedish Blonde	Victoria Hall
Pre-Teen Gomez	Jimmy Ross
Pre-Teen Fester	Ryan Anderson
Teenage Gomez	Daniel Pikus

Teenage Fester	Michael Hittesdorf
Teenage Flora	Lauren Walker
Teenage Fauna	Valeri Walker
Girl Scout	Mercedes McNab
Long Arm Addams	Joe Zimmerman
Fingers Addams	Steve Welles
One-Armed Bass Player	Eugene Jackson
Snake Charmer	Richard Tanner
Conductor	Marc Shaiman
Jugglers	The Passing Zone; Jonathan Wee and Owen Morse
Stunts	Randy Kovitz, Keith Campbell, Mary Peters, Danny Rogers and David Welch
Special appearance by	Sally Jessy Raphael

'The producer and director wish to gratefully acknowledge the consulting services and assistance of The Lady Colyton in the making of this film.'

Gomez is unhappy, as the 25th anniversary of his brother Fester's disappearance is approaching. 'Don't torture your-self, Gomez', Mortitia advises him. 'That's my job.' Mean-while, the Family lawyer, flat-broke Tully Alford, arrives, with his wife, Margaret. His plans to fleece the Family fail. He owes money to Mrs Craven, who has her thuggish son, Gordon, threaten Tully. Tully notices that Gordon looks a lot like Fester, and a plan evolves for the three of them to get their hands on the Family's money. When the annual seance is held by the Addams Family, Fester arrives at the door, accompanied by Mrs Craven, posing as Dr Pinderschloss, a psychiatrist. She claims that Fester was fished out of the ocean after being stranded with amnesia in the Bermuda Triangle. Wednesday is very suspicious of this story, but Gomez accepts the newcomer.

Wednesday plays with Pugsley in the electric chair, a new game called 'Is there a God?' Gomez shows Fester the vault – below the house and down an underground river. The combination is '2-10-11: eyes, fingers, toes'. Gomez admits his own jealousy drove Fester away and asks for forgiveness. Fester agrees, but he's forgetting too much, and Gomez is growing suspicious of him. 'Dr Pinderschloss' cures Gomez's suspicions, and Fester starts to settle in. That night is the children's school play, and Fester helps them to make fall-apart limbs that spray the shocked audience with blood. Gomez throws a party to welcome Fester home, and they dance the traditional Mamoushka. Mrs Craven is furious with her son, and Wednesday overhears them plotting. Tully gets an idea and has the local judge (who loathes the Family) issue an order declaring that the Family treasures and property belong to the older brother – Fester. The Family is thrown out.

They have to take a room at a motel. Wednesday and Pugsley attempt to sell lemonade, while Mortitia gets a job telling stories to children (leaving them shocked and in tears). Thing delivers overnight letters, while Gomez becomes addicted to chat-shows and sitcoms. Mortitia returns to the mansion to try and talk sense to Fester. She's captured and tortured. Just as she's enjoying herself, Thing returns with Gomez to the rescue. Gordon, finally, has become fed up with his mother and Tully and switches sides to help the Addams's. He causes a hurricane that sends Tully and Mrs Craven spinning into graves. The children bury them. 'Are they dead?' asks Pugsley. 'Does it matter?' replies Wednesday. Gordon is hit by a lightning bolt which restores his memory. He really *is* Fester, and was lost in the Bermuda Triangle. The Family is together again. Margaret Alford falls in love with Cousin Itt, and the children all join happily in a game of 'wake the dead'. Bring your own shovel . . .

The major change for the film is that now Fester has become Gomez's older brother (born in 1947). After a fight over Flora and Fauna 25 years ago, Fester left home, and never returned. Lurch is, strangely, silent, save for a few groans. He also plays the organ now, instead of his old harpsichord. Gomez and Mortitia recall their first meeting, at a funeral, where they fell in love. At the end of the film, Mortitia announces she's expecting, and has knitted a baby suit with three legs. Thing is also finally freed of his boxes, thanks to a great deal of special effects work.

New members of the Family mentioned (along with those in the credits) are: Uncle Midnight, Aunt La Borgia, Cousin Fletch, Uncle Imar, Uncle Atlas, Great Aunt Lavinia, Great Aunt Calpurnia and Cousin Balthazar – all buried in the Family cemetery at the back of the house. Gomez and Fester's parents were killed by an angry mob. Fester's pet vulture, Muerto, is also buried in the cemetery.

The movie cost something along the lines of $30 million to make. The director, Barry Sonnenfeld, was a novice; before this movie he'd been director of photography on films like *Raising Arizona*, *Miller's Crossing* and *Misery*. He wasn't the first choice, either. Tim Burton was, but he and Terry Gilliam both passed when offered the film. Writer Larry Wilson had worked on *Beetlejuice*, and Caroline Thompson on *Edward Scissorhands*, so neither were new to the genre of comedy/horror. Despite this, their script suffered major overhauls at many stages, and was rewritten by (uncredited) Paul Rudnick, whose compensation was that he got to write the sequel alone.

The Addams's house was specifically constructed for this film at a cost of over $100,000. Shots of a model house were also used. For the sequel, only the model was used, as the full-sized house was demolished.

Raul Julia is best known for his stage work, and as a regular on the children's show *Sesame Street*. His films include *Kiss Of The Spider Woman* (1985), *Tequila Sunrise* (1988) and *Presumed Innocent* (1990). Anjelica Huston is the daughter of director John Huston, and won an Oscar for her work in his *Prizzi's Honor* (1985). Her other films include *The Witches* (1990) and *The Player* (1992). Christopher Lloyd rose to fame as the Reverend Jim on *Taxi* (1979–83), and cemented his appeal with the *Back To The Future* movies. Carel Struycken has appeared regularly on *Star Trek – The Next Generation* as Mr Homm.

Addams Family Values

1993

Written by	Paul Rudnick
Based on the characters created by	Charles Addams
Directed by	Barry Sonnenfeld
Music by	Marc Shaiman
Conducted by	Artie Kane
'Addams Family Theme' by	Vic Mizzy
Produced by	Scott Rudin
Executive Producer	David Nicksay
Director of Photography	Donald Peterman, ASC
Production Designer	Ken Adam
Film Editors	Arthur Schmidt and Jim Miller
Visual Effects Supervisor	Alan Munro
Costume Designer	Theoni V. Aldredge
Unit Production Manager	D. Scott Easton
1st Assistant Directors	Burt Harris and Mark McGann
2nd Assistant Director	Ian Woolf

Casting	David Rubin, CSA
Associate	Debra Zane
Associate Producer	Susan Ringo
Music Supervisor	Ralph Sall
Tango Choreography	Peter Anastos
Choreography Camp Chippewa	Adam Shankman
Art Director	William J. Durrell, Jnr
Set Decorator	Marvin March
Assistant Art Directors	Charles Breen, Lauren Cory and John Leimanis
Camera Operator	David E. Diano
Sound Mixer	Peter Kurland
Script Supervisor	Judy Townsend
Anjelica Huston's Makeup	Fern Buchner
Anjelica Huston's Hair Stylist	Toni-Ann Walker
Makeup Supervisor	Kevin C. Haney
Makeup Artists	Kathrine James, Fred C. Blau, Cheri Minns and Gerald Quist
Supervising Hair Stylist	Susan Germaine
Hair Stylists	Kim Santantonio and Susan Schuler-Page
Wigs	Bill Fletcher
Properties	Emily Ferry
Special Effects Supervisor	Albert Delgado
Sound Supervisor	Cecilia Hall
Music Editors	Scott Stambler and Nancy Fogarty
Rerecording Mixers	Robert J. Litt, Greg P. Russell, CAS, and Frank A. Montano
Orchestrations	Jeff Atmajian, Brad Dechter, Hummie Mann and Michael Starobin
Stunt Co-ordinator	Gary Hymes

89

Titles and Opticals	Cinema Research Corporation
Title Design	Pablo Ferro and Allen Ferro
Visual Effects Unit:	
Associate Supervisor	Brian Jochum
Director of Photography	Keith Peterman
Key Visual Effects Assistant	Fred Toye
Visual Effects Producer	Robin Griffin
Prosthetics Co-ordinator	Karen Murphy
Digital/Optical Visual Effects	VCE/Peter Kuran

'Thing' and 'Pubert' puppets and prosthetics created by David B. Miller Studio
Special prosthetics, mechanical devices and house miniatures by Alterion Studios, Inc.

Motion Control Photography	Image-G
Matte Paintings	Illusion Arts, Inc.
	Syd Dutton and Bill Taylor, ASC

'The producer and director wish to gratefully acknowledge the consulting services and assistance of The Lady Colyton in the making of this film.'

Cast

Mortitia Addams	Anjelica Huston
Gomez Addams	Raul Julia
Fester Addams	Christopher Lloyd
Debbie Jellinsky	Joan Cusack
Wednesday	Christina Ricci
Granny	Carol Kane
Pugsley	Jimmy Workman
Lurch	Carel Struycken
Joel Glicker	David Krumholtz
Thing	Christopher Hart

Margaret	Dana Ivey
Gary Granger	Peter MacNicol
Becky Granger	Christine Baranski
Pubert Addams	Kaitlyn and Kristen Hooper
Amanda Buckman	Mercedes McNab
Don Buckman	Sam McMurray
Ellen Buckman	Harriet Sansom Harris
Mrs Glicker	Julie Halston
Mr Glicker	Barry Sonnenfeld
Desk Sergeant	Nathan Lane
Cousin Itt	John Franklin
Cousin Aphasia	Charles Busch
Cousin Ophelia	Laura Esterman
Flora Amor	Maureen Sue Levin
Fauna Amor	Darlene Levin
Dementia	Carol Hankins
Donald	Steven M. Martin
Dexter	Douglas Brian Martin
Lumpy Addams	Ryan Holihan
Delivery Nurse	Lois de Banzie
Forceps Nurse	Vickilyn Reynolds
Heather	Cynthia Nixon
Mrs Montgomery	Edye Byrd
Delivery Room Doctor	David Hyde Pierce
Obnoxious Girl	Andreana Weiner
Host	Peter Graves
Lawyer	Rick Scarry
Flirting Woman	Monet Mazur
Flirting Man	Francis Coady
Driver	Ian Abercrombie
Moving Man	Chris Ellis
Concetta	Camille Saviola
Passport Clerk	Zack Phifer
Jorge	Tony Sharloub

91

Irwin	Jeffrey van Hoose
Mordecai	Micah Winkelspecht
Wheelchair Camper	Matthew Beebe
Consuela	Kristy Shirvani
Esther	Jamie Gordon
Yang	Michael Hata
Jamal	Joey Wilcots
Camper #1	Jason Fife
Camper #2	Karl David-Djerf
Young Debbie	Haley Peel
Pubert's Voice	Cheryl Chase

Mortitia is going to have a baby – *now*! 'It's an Addams!' announces Gomez, proudly, and they name it Pubert. Wednesday and Pugsley think it's to replace one of them, and decide they have to kill it first. Gomez and Mortitia decide they need a nanny to help out, and eventually they hire Debbie Jellinsky. She's almost as weird as they are, and Fester is smitten with her. Gomez advises him: 'I hope that someday you'll know the indescribable joy of having children – and of paying someone else to raise them.' Debbie is, in fact, a black widow who marries and then murders wealthy men for their money, and has set her sights on Fester. When she realizes that Wednesday is suspicious of her, Debbie cons the parents into sending the children to summer camp. When they arrive at Camp Chippewa, Pugsley asks what it means. 'It's an old Indian word', Gomez explains. Adds Wednesday: 'It means orphans.' It's a bright and perky camp for privileged children.

They don't fit in too well, but Wednesday excels when it comes to telling ghost stories. She makes friends with another misfit kid, Joel Glicker, and together they try to break out of the camp. Meanwhile, Debbie gets Fester to propose, and they're married in the graveyard at a Family gathering. Itt officiates, and Wednesday catches the bouquet. The honeymoon is in Hawaii, where Debbie tries again and again without success to murder Fester. She is forced to live with him, but insists on their own home and won't allow him to see the rest of the Family. Pubert becomes angelic, the rest of the Family troubled. Meanwhile, at camp, Wednesday is brainwashed into being good and manages to smile. She's to play Pocohontas in the end of camp play, but instead she leads an Indian raid, reducing the place to rubble. Debbie tries to kill Fester by blowing up the house, but he survives that, too. Thing comes to his rescue with a car, and Debbie, now utterly deranged, follows, vowing: 'I'll get you, and your little hand, too!' She trails them to the Addams house, where she puts the Family into electric chairs. She's about to fry them all when Pubert gets free and reverses the current, killing her instead.

Writer Paul Rudnick had performed uncredited rewrites on the first film. He's best known for his columns for *Premiere* magazine under the pseudonym of Libby Gelman-Waxner. There are some fun touches in this story, including Gomez arm-wrestling Thing. Itt and Margaret now have a baby, Whatt. And the wedding music is 'Sunrise, Sunset', from *Fiddler On The Roof*. Once again, though, the movie is stolen by Christine Ricci's magnificent performance as Wednesday. Rudnick wisely gives her the lion's share of this film.

Production Designer Ken Adam is best known for his work on numerous entries in the *James Bond* series.

Mercedes McNab (the perky girl scout in the first film) is a delight in this one as Wednesday's foil. Director Barry Sonnenfeld has a cameo as Joel's father. Carol Kane is best known from *Taxi* (1981–83) (with Christopher Lloyd) and movies such as *Scrooged*. She replaces Judith Malina (the only member of the first film's cast not to return) as Granny.

Joan Cusack was a regular on *Saturday Night Live* (1985–86).

Director Sonnenfeld explained to *Starburst* (January 1994) how he saw the appeal of the family: 'They are the perfect family unit in my estimation. The husband and wife still love, and are still sexually attracted to, each other. Their strong sense of family means Fester and Granny can live with them. Most importantly they give their children space to grow and learn and experiment without being smothered by parental guidance. Their values might not necessarily be what you or I would believe in. But they don't change them day to day on a whim. They believe in non-conformity and allowing people to exist in any way they wish as long as they aren't bothering somebody else. Isn't this the sort of family we should try to be? One we would all love to belong to?' Hmm . . .

After the nightmare of making the first film (the original production company, Orion, went bankrupt as they filmed and Paramount bought the movie and completed it, way over budget and time), Sonnenfeld originally refused to consider a second film. Then he read and liked the script and was offered a considerable raise in his salary, both of which overcame his objections.

The Animated Addams Family

Hanna Barbera first used the Addams Family as guest stars on their popular *Scooby Doo* show. Their appearances were so well received that the firm spun them off into their own show. In this, the Family is travelling about America in a special haunted wagon that can even dig a moat when they settle down for the evening. New characters include Abigail the bat, Ocho the octopus and Ali Gator.

1973 Series

Executive Producers	William Hanna and Joseph Barbera
Directed by	Charles A. Nichols
Produced by	Iwao Takamoto
Associate Producers	Paul Sommer and Maurice Pooley
Story	Bill Raynor, Bud Atkinson, Jack Mendelsohn, Miles Wilder, Dick Conway and Gene Thompson
Story Direction	Jim Carmichael, Carl Fallberg, Dave Hanan, Fred Crippen, Jan Green and Don Sheppard
Character Design	Takashi Masunaga
Animation Director	Carl Urbano
Animating Supervisor	James A. Pabian
Dialogue Director	Wally Burr
Background Styling	F. Monteniegre
Musical Director	Hoyt Curtin
Music Supervisor	Paul DeKorte
Unit Directors	Arthur Humberstone, Mike Salter and Terry Harrison
Production Manager	Dennis Gardiner
Supervising Editor	Mel Roberts
Layouts	Ted Pettingell, Toni Bailey, John Cooper and Mel Darsler
Backgrounds	Geoff Channell, Caird Green, Chris Collingwood, Jane Penning and John Dick
Animation Co-ordinators	Graeme Stubbings, David

	Thwaytes and Alma Sachs
Trace and Paint Supervisor	Sally Walls
Animators	Janet Nunn, Mike Pocock, Tom Barling, Peter Sachs, Bryan Foster, Joan Swanson, Mike Murphy, Rosemary Welch, Marie Szrnichowska, Lew Saw, Jim Waddell, Enrique Arnau, Marlene Robinson and Alan Simpson

A Hanna–Barbera Production

| Characters Created by | Charles Addams |

Voice Cast

Gomez	Leonard Weinrib
Mortitia and Granny	Janet Waldo
Uncle Fester	Jackie Coogan
Lurch	Ted Cassidy
Pugsley	Jodie Foster
Wednesday	Cindy Henderson

Additional Voices

Josh Albee
Howard Caine
John Carver
Pat Harrington, Jnr
Bob Holt
Don Messick
John Stephenson
Herb Vigran

There were 37 episodes, including the following released to video:

1) Left in the Lurch

Lurch's pen-pal, Bonnie Jo, thinks he's a big rock star heading a group named 'Freddie and the Frogs'. The Family helps to create this image for him, despite Lurch's attempts to run away from the travelling home.

Despite the fact that Lurch played the harpsichord in the original show, in this story he can't play anything. Gomez comments: 'After all that rehearsal, you can play as badly as any rock star.' 'Yes', agrees Mortitia, 'and sing even worse. You could be a superstar.' The promoter of a rock concert's verdict on the Family: 'I don't care how good they play, they just don't look weird enough for a rock combo.'

2) The Circus Story

Honest John's Old Tim Carnival is rightly billed 'The Worst Show on Earth', something only the Addams Family could love. With their help, however, it becomes a roaring success.

3) The Mardi Gras Story

Two crooks attempt to pin a robbery on the Family, and soon discover that crime really doesn't pay.

4) The Voodoo Story

The nasty Madame Hoodoo goes one on one against Granny, deep in the heart of the swamps.

5) Aloha Hoolamagoola

The Family is mistaken for a lost stone-age tribe when they visit Hawaii.

6) Ghost Town

Thieves after hidden gold try to terrify an old prospector, but they can't match the Family when it comes to chills.

7) Addams Go West

The Family find themselves up against legendary varmints like Wyatt Burp and Silly the Kid.

8) Follow That Loaf Of Bread

Thing is accidentally cooked into a loaf of Mortitia's Eerie Egg bread, and the Family have to track him down to get him back.

9) The Fastest Creepy Camper In The West

Uncle Fester invents a new super-fuel, but the results are as unpredictable as ever.

10) The Addams Family In New York

The Family is conned into buying Central Park, but they have a trick or three up their sleeves to prove that they really do own that park.

The most interesting aspect to the animated show was that Jodie Foster played Pugsley. Then a young actress working in shows like *Gunsmoke* and *The Courtship Of Eddie's Father*, she is now best known for her roles in films like *Silence Of The Lambs* and *Maverick*, as well as being a director (*Little Man Tate*). Both Jackie Coogan and Ted Cassidy reprised their vocal roles from the original show. Leonard Weinrib and Janet Waldo were both much-used on animated shows (she was Penelope on *The Perils Of Penelope Pitstop*, and Judy on *The Jetsons*).

1992 Series

Executive Producers	David Kirschner and Mark Young
Produced by	Ron Myrick
Story Editor	Bill Matheny
Creative Consultant	The Lady Colyton

Supervising Director	Ray Patterson
Directors	Robert Alvarez, Don Lusk and Carl Urbano
Animation Directors	Joanna Romersa, Frank Andrina, Joan F. Drake, Allen Wilzbach, Richard J. Bowman, Margaret Nichols, Art Scott, John Kafka, Kunio Shimarnura, Rebecca Bristow, Ed Love, Bob Kirk and Ken Southworth
Assistant to Producers	Karenia Kaminski
Storyboard Artists	Michael V. Bennett, Linda Rowley Blue, Barrington Bunce, Bwana, Greg Garcia, Drew Gentle, Gary Hoffman, Elaine Hultgren, Scott Jeralds, Peter Kingston, Brad Landreth, Tom Nesbitt, Philip D. Stapleton, Mario Piluso, Lane Raichert, Keith Sargent, Karl Toerge, Keith Tucker, Barbara Dourmashkin Case and Louis Scarborough, Jnr
Recording Director	Gordon Hunt
Animation Casting Director	Lynne Batchelor
Talent Co-ordinator	Jill Ziegenhagen
Music	Guy Moon
Theme	Vic Mizzy
Director of Music Production	Bodie Chandler

Graphics	Iraj Paran and Tom Wogatzke
Design Supervisor	Scott Jeralds
Character Design	Ginny Hawes, George Goodchild, Andre St. Amour and Emily Michels
Design Assistants	Dana Granger, Barbara Krueger and Jesus Rodriguez
Animation Supervisor	Chris Cuddington
Assistant Animation Supervisor	Nary Jamlig
Clean-Up Supervisor	Butch Orosa
Animation Checking Supervisor	Jan Adams
Animation Checking	Beth Goodwin
Background Supervisor	Al Gmuer
International Background Supervisor	Jonathan Goley
Background Layout Keys	Drew Gentle, Al Gmuer, Jim Hickey, Gary Mouri, Ronald Roesch, Swinton O. Scott III and Dean Thompson
Background	Bonnie Callahan, Jonathan Goley, Andy Phillipson, Patty Palmer-Phillipson, Leonard Robledo and Ron Roesch
Xerography	Star Wirth
Tracing Supervisor	Ros Mandi
Word Processing	Gail Prewitt and Linda Germain
Ink and Paint Supervisors	Alison Leopold and Stella Reyes

Colour Key	Brenda Burns
Production Managers	Kris Zimmerman and Catherine Peza
Assistant Production Manager	Benji Agoncillo
International Production Co-ordinator	Jo Harn
Production Co-ordinators	Vicki Casper and Rosanne Rodriguez
Production Assistants	Tori Pollock, Sandy Benenati, Debby Lathrop, Valerie Menk and Linda Moore
Programme Executive	Ellen Cockrill
Production Publicist	Joseph Swaney
Supervising Film Editor	Terry W. Moore
Film Editors	Gil Iverson, Tom Gleason and Tim Iverson
Sound Editor	Michele Douglas
Music Editor	Peter Collier
Track Readers	Jim Hearn, Kerry Iverson, Kay Douglas and Carol Iverson
Sound Direction	Ed Collins
Rerecording Mixers	Jim Aicholz and Ezra Dweck
Negative Consultant	William DeBoer, Jnr
Camera	Dan Bunn and Raul Salgado
International Production Executive	Paul Sabella
Executive in Charge of Production	Jayne Barbera
Produced in association with	Fil-Cartoons, Inc.
Production Supervisor	Jerry Smith
Based on characters created by	Charles Addams

A Hanna–Barbera Production

Voices

Gomez	John Astin
Mortitia	Nancy Linari
Wednesday	Debi Derryberry
Pugsley	Jeannie Elias
Uncle Fester	Rip Taylor
Granny	Carol Channing
Lurch	Jim Cummings
Cousin Itt	Pat Fraley
Mrs Normanmeyer	Edie McClurg
Mr Normanmeyer	Rob Paulsen
N.J. Normanmeyer	Dick Beals

Additional voices
Ruth Buzzi
Ernest Harada
Erv Immerman
Brian Mitchell
Marion Ramsey
Hal Rayle
Susan Silo
Marcelo Tubert
Renee Victor
Marcia Wallace
Anderson Wong
Anna Maria Horsford

This series is based mostly on the first *Addams Family* movie, with the same dark humour. Interestingly, though, John Astin returned to the role he had created for the original series.

1) Puttergeist

Written by   David Schwartz and
                                  Bill Matheny

On Halloween, Granny tells the story of the Puttergeist, a golfer from Happydale Heights who is looking for his lost head. Everyone believes it's just a myth until the ghost is sighted.

2) Addams Family PTA

Story by   David Schwartz and
                                  Billy Matheny
Teleplay by   David Schwartz

Mortitia is feeling rather desolate when the children seem to prefer working or playing with the other members of the Family, so she becomes more involved with their schooling.

3) N.J. Addams

Story by   David Schwartz, Bill
                                  Matheny and Lane Reichert
Teleplay by   David Schwartz

The Normanmeyers, being friends of the principal, are guest speakers in class (like every week). N.J. is so embarrassed by their talks that he runs away and wants to be adopted by the Addams Family instead.

4) Itt's Over

Story by   Earl Kress and
                                  Bill Matheny

Teleplay by	Earl Kress

Fester has started to grow hair, which he's scared will mar his good looks. The Family has to call in a specialist consultant – which can only be Cousin Itt.

5) Girlfriendstein

Story by	Earl Kress, Bill Matheny and Lane Reichert
Teleplay by	Earl Kress

Lurch is upset, and not attending properly to his duties. The children discover his girlfriend has jilted him, so Fester decides to build him a new one.

1993 Series

Executive Producer	David Kirschner
Produced by	Emory Ron Myrick
Story Editor	Bill Matheny
Creative Consultant	The Lady Colyton
Associate Producer	Karenia Kamenski
Animation Directors	Robert Alvarez, John Cataldi, Zeon Davush, Daniel De La Vega, Kateland Kobiack, Bob Nessler and Bob Tyler
Storyboard Artists	Glenn Hill, Michael V. Bennett, Scott Heming, Salli Hilborn, Elaine Hultgren, Mitch Schauer, Earl Kress, Gary S. Katona, Brad Landreth, Carol Lundburg, Lane Reichert,

	Karl Toerge and Roman Arambula
Recording Directors	Gordon Hunt and Ginny McSwain
Casting Director	Kris Zimmerman
Talent Co-ordinator	Jill Ziegenhagen
Supervising Recording Engineer	Edwin Collins
Recording Engineer	Alvy Dorman
Design Supervisor	Bob Onorato
Key Designer	Ginny Hawes
Designers	George Goodchild, Frank Rocco and Julian Chaney
Design Assistants	Steve Simone, Barbara Krueger, Donna Zeller and Jesus Rodriguez
Background Supervisor	Al Gumer
Background Layout Keys	Andrew Gentle and Ron Roesch
Backgrounds	Ron Roesch, Patty Phillipson, Andrew Phillipson and Maryann Thomas
Graphics	Iraj Paran
Music	Matt Muhoberac and John Zuker
Additional Music	Guy Moon
Theme	Vic Mizzy
Director of Music Production	Bodle Chandler
Ink and Paint Supervisor	Alison Leopold
Colour Key	Brenda Burns and Karen Gresli
Xerography	Star Wirth
Animation Checking Supervisor	Jan Adams

Animation Checking	Beth Goodwin
Post Production Supervisor/ Supervising Editor	Tom Gleason
Post Production Co-ordinator	Jeannine Roussel
Track Readers	James Hearn, Larry Cowan, Carol Iverson, Kenny Iverson and Kay Douglas
Sound Editor	Michelle Douglas, Three Rivers Editorial, Inc.
Music Editor	Peter Collier
Audio Post Production	Larson Sound Center
Rerecording Mixers	Anthony Constantini and Doug Gray
Negative Consultant	William DeBoer
Production Executive	Catherine Winder
Programme Executive	Jeff Holder
Unit Production Co-ordinator	Tori Pollack
Production Supervisor	Debby Hindman
Production Assistants	Michele Foruichi, Sandy Benanati, Valerie Menk, Linda Moore and Gail Prewitt
Animation by	Fil-Cartoons, Inc.
Overseas Layout Director	Tapani Knuutila
Overseas Animation Director	John Rice
Based on characters created by	Charles Addams
A Hanna–Barbera Production	

Regular cast as previous season. Additional voices
Michael Bell
Earl Boen
Julie Brown
Hector Elizondo
Dick Gautier

Peter Cullen
Candy Houston
Gordon Hunt
Nick Jameson
Vicki Juditz
Page Leong
Ian Monfette
Bob Ridgely
Pamela Sefall
Marcelo Tubert
Marcia Wallace
Marsha Warfield
Frank Welker
Charles Nelson Reilly
Robert Guillaume

1) Camp Addams

Story by   Bill Matheny and Ron
                                Myrick
Teleplay by   Bill Matheny

The children are forced to go to camp with . . . Mr
Normanmeyer in charge. They start by wishing they hadn't,
and he ends up wishing they hadn't.

2) A Girl And A Ghoul

Story by   Bill Matheny and Ron
                                Myrick
Teleplay by   Bill Matheny

Wednesday has a new idol: TV show host Graveyard Gary.
She wins a competition to meet him and discovers that her
hero isn't as disgusting as she'd hoped.

3) Color Me Addams

Story by	Bill Matheny and Earl Kress
Teleplay by	Earl Kress
Directed by	Emory Ron Myrick

Mortitia is painting portraits of Fester and Itt – in ghastly living (?) colour. Thing wants to help out, and is upset when Mortitia won't allow him.

4) No Ifs, Ands Or Butlers

Story by	Bill Matheny and David Schwartz
Teleplay by	David Schwartz
Directed by	Emory Ron Myrick

Lurch is feeling put-upon, bearing the brunt of doing chores for everyone, and without being thanked. Eventually, he's had enough and walks out, leaving the Family to fend for themselves.

5) Sweetheart Of A Brother

Written by	Bill Matheny
Directed by	Emory Ron Myrick

The Family is worried about Pugsley's eccentric behaviour. He's being too nice. Then they discover he isn't sick, but in love.

6) Double O Honeymoon

Written by   Bill Matheny
Directed by   Emory Ron Myrick

Double-O-Itt's nemesis, Thundermane, has escaped from jail, just when Itt has planned a much-needed vacation. Gomez and Mortitia volunteer to take on the maniac to help out.

7) Then Came Granny

Written by   Bill Matheny

Granny is doing a fortune telling business over the phone, but she's getting nothing by constant complaints. She's afraid that she's lost her abilities, and has to go to extreme lengths to get them back.

8) Jack and Jill and The Beanstalk/ Hand Delivered

Written by   (a) David Schwartz
                                      (b) Bill Matheny

Fester can't sleep, so he has Wednesday tell him a bedtime story. This involves mixed-up nursery rhymes in which the Family plays the various roles. In the short filler, the mail woman assigned to the Addams route refuses to let anything – or Thing – stand in the way of her delivery.

The Munsters

Background

The Munsters live in a mansion at 1313 Mockingbird Lane, in Mockingbird Heights, having recently moved in from Transylvania – not more than 20 years earlier. They used to live in Werewolf Junction, Transylvania, and still keep in touch.

Herman was built by Dr Frankenstein after earlier, less successful models went wrong. Work started on him around 1812, but he wasn't actually completed until about 1850. (Before being assembled, Herman spent six years at Heidelberg University – in different jars.) He is seven foot six inches tall and 150 years old. His shoe size is 26E, and he weighs three spins – the number of times the needle goes round the scales when he steps on them (i.e. 380 pounds). His pulse is 15, his blood pressure -3, his body temperature 62.8 – though it can drop to 55 and still be considered normal for him – and he has no discernible heartbeat. He has one brown eye and one chartreuse green. He wears a size 60 and 7/8 hat.

Herman has worked at the funeral home of Gateman, Goodbury and Graves for 17 years. Before that, he spent four years in the Army. He was stationed at Fort Banning for a year's training, then spent the next three overseas. His favourite food is cream of vulture soup. He never misses reading 'Little Orphan Annie'. He and Lily were married in 1865. His driver's licence number is V655034. He's a founder member of the Pat Boone Fan Club.

Lily (maiden name, Dracula) is over 400 years old – though she sometimes claims to be a girlish 137 – and has been dead several times. Her favourite seat is her electric chair. She sleeps in a shroud, with a lily in her hands. She calls Herman 'pussycat'.

Grandpa is Count Dracula, and, naturally, has a bat named Igor. He's 378 years old, and has died several times. He also has bat pills that can change him into a bat for short periods of time. He has had 140 (or 167) wives. His favourite magazine is 'Tomb And Garden'. He also reads the 'Vault Street Journal', 'Playghoul', and watches 'My Three Sons' (he thinks the family is bizarre). From time to time, he can change into a wolf. He sometimes has a hand in a bowl in the dungeon.

Eddie is 10, and has a werewolf doll named Woof-Woof, and a pet dinosaur named Spot, who lives under the stairs. Spot breathes fire and eats cars and such. They also have a black cat that roars like a lion. Eddie has a fireman's pole from his bedroom down to the kitchen, and he likes to hang around in cupboards and such. He sleeps in a casket.

Marilyn is a lovely blonde, but doesn't see herself that way: 'I'm the plain one in the family'. Everyone feels sorry for her deformity, and Herman is afraid they'll be stuck with her forever. She's attending Westbury College. She is the daughter of Lily's sister.

Instead of a cuckoo clock, they have a raven clock. The raven spouts off from time to time. It also has a tendency to pick the mailman's sack, and to collect shiny objects – like loaded guns. Their telephone is kept in a coffin.

Uncle Gilbert is the creature from the Black Lagoon. Herman has a twin brother, Charlie, who was raised in England, wears a monocle and is definitely the white sheep of the family. He's a con man with good manners and no morals.

Grandpa has a son, Lester, who is younger than Lily. He's got no head for business, but looks like a werewolf, which is presumably where Eddie gets his family features from.

The family doctor (who wishes he wasn't) is Dr Edward Howard Dudley, of 365 Grand Blvd., Mockingbird Heights. His home address is 4919 Woodbury Drive. Dudley is married, and has a son, Elmer, who is Eddie's age. Their postman is Warren Bloom. Their next-door neighbour is widowed Mrs Yolanda Cribbins. On the other side is widowed Mrs Cartwright. She quite likes Herman, who lends her a hand from time to time.

The family has three cars. The first is an old saloon (KJH 681), which is driven by an invisible chauffeur – possibly the same invisible person who always beats Grandpa at checkers. The second car is a modified sports hearse. Grandpa has his own car, the Dragula, which he built from organ pipes and a spare coffin from the funeral parlour.

Season One

Credits

Produced by	Joe Connolly and Bob Mosher
Production Executive	Irving Paley
Developed by	Norm Liebmann and Ed Haas
From a Format by	Al Burns and Chris Hayward
Script Editors	Norm Liebmann and Ed Haas (episodes 4, 7, 13)
Music	Jack Marshall
Director of Photography	Walter Strenge, ASC, Jack Marquette, ASC, Ray Rennehan, ASC, Lionel Lindon, ASC, Benjamin H. Kline, ASC, Fred Mandl, ASC, John L. Russell, ASC, Monroe Askins

Art Director	Henry Larrecq, Raymond Beal, Russell Kimball, Frank Arrigo, John J. Lloyd, Howard E. Johnson,
Film Editor	Bud S. Isaacs, Richard G. Wray, ACE
Assistant Director	Dolph M. Zimmer, Leo Burke, John Clarke Bowman, Frank Losee, Ronnie Rondell, Ray Taylor, Jnr
Set Decorators	John McCarthy and Robert C. Bradfield, James S. Redd, Ralph Sylos, Andrew Nealis
Costume Supervisor	Vincent Dee
Sound	Frank H. Wilkinson, Ralph E. Butler, Robert Bertrand, Corson Jowett, Lyle Cain, Melvin M. Metcalfe, Snr, Ed Somers, William Lynch, James T. Parker, A. Norwood Fenton
Recording Supervision	Waldon O. Watson (episode 1)
Editorial Department Head	David J. O'Connell
Music Supervision	Stanley Wilson
Makeup	Bud Westmore
Hair Stylist	Larry Germain, Virginia Darcy
Post Production Supervisor	Michael R. McAdam
Sound Effects Editor	George Ohanian, MPSE

A Kayro-Vue Production
Filmed at the Studios of Universal City

Cast

Herman Munster	Fred Gwynne
Lily Munster	Yvonne de Carlo
Grandpa	Al Lewis
Marilyn	Beverly Owen (to episode 13); Pat Priest (from episode 14)
Eddie Wolfgang Munster	Butch Patrick

The initial opening credits had Lily first and Herman last. This was reversed when Beverly Owen left the show and a new sequence was shot with Pat Priest. Then Herman was moved to the front of the credits, the obvious star of the show.

Since the show aired without titles, some episodes are known by more than one title. In those cases, both versions are given.

1) Munster Masquerade
24 September 1964

Written by	Joe Connelly and Bob Mosher
Directed by	Lawrence Dobkin

Cast

Tom Daly	Linden Chiles
Agnes Daly	Mabel Albertson
Albert Daly	Frank Wilcox
Mrs Morton	Lurene Tuttle
George Washington	Walter Woolf King
The Harem Girl	Nina Roman
1st Guest	Paul Bradley
2nd Guest	Berniece Dalton
3rd Guest	Roy Darmour

Marilyn's boyfriend, Tom Daly, is wealthy. His parents are giving a party, and he persuades them to invite the Munsters to the masquerade. Herman goes as a knight, Marilyn as a pilgrim, Little as Little Bo Peep – a horror costume! – and Grandpa tries changing himself into Mr Hyde. When the potion doesn't work, he decides to go as Napoleon. Meanwhile, the Dalys are worried about the Munsters causing problems. Mrs Daly is dressed as Juliet, while Mr Daly is dressed as Frankenstein's monster . . . Mrs Morton arrives to babysit Eddie, and the Munsters head off to the party. Herman thinks Mr Daly couldn't get a costume. The Dalys don't like the Munsters at all, and the feeling is reciprocal. However, Herman is awarded the prize for best costume, but Lily is scandalized when she realizes they think he's wearing two costumes. She insists that they go home. Marilyn is also upset, so Tom sees her home. He comes in for a cup of coffee, and sees the Munsters out of costume – and runs away. Marilyn thinks she's lost another boyfriend because of her looks – but his family was too weird, anyhow . . .

2) My Fair Munster
(Alternative title: 'The Munsters')
1 October 1964

Written by   Norm Liebmann and
                                    Ed Haas
Directed by   David Alexander

Cast
Warren Bloom   John Fielder
Yolanda Cribbins   Claire Carleton
Jack   Edward Mallory

Jack has been dating Marilyn, but when he finally sees

Herman, he panics and runs. The family all think it's Marilyn who's causing the problems, and Herman is afraid they'll be stuck with her forever. Grandpa decides to fix it by making a love potion for her. He adds it to her oatmeal, but she leaves without tasting it. Instead, Lily, Herman and Eddie accidentally get the dosage. The postman, Bloom, and Mrs Cribbins, the Munsters' next-door neighbour, both meet and complain about the family that's moved in. Meanwhile, Herman suggests to Lily that they should be nicer to the neighbours.

When Bloom arrives with a package for Lily, the love potion makes him fall in love with her. Mrs Cribbins, installing an electric fence, spots Herman and falls for him. At school, a horde of screaming girls chase Eddie home. That night, Bloom serenades Lily until Grandpa drops a flower pot on his head. Mrs Cribbins vamps Herman, and the poor Munsters have to run to escape the unwanted affections. Grandpa finally realizes what has happened, and retreats to his room as the potion wears off. Bloom and Mrs Cribbins come to their senses and beat a hasty retreat. Grandpa gets rid of the rest of the potion by throwing it over the fence. It lands on Mrs Cribbins' cabbages, which she cooks for a meal with Bloom . . .

This was the expanded version of the pilot sequence.

3) A Walk On The Mild Side
8 October 1964

Written by   Norm Liebmann and
                      Ed Haas
Directed by   Norman Abbott

Cast
Police Commissioner Ludlow   Barry Kelley
Police Chief Harris   Cliff Norton

Herman has trouble getting to sleep, and the only thing that helps is a walk in Midcity Park at night. The police are looking for a prowler there, and are disbelieving at first when people start turning up with reports of nine-foot high green monsters. Lily is worried about Herman's safety when she reads about these events in the newspapers. Grandpa is meanwhile working on an enlarging machine, and draining electricity from everywhere for it. Commissioner Ludlow thinks Police Chief Harris is cracking up when he orders his men to watch for the giant. That night, Herman goes for a walk in the park. Patrolmen Bell and Finkel see him, and jump him. Herman thinks they are the monster, panics, and flees home. They flee back to the police station.

Harris decides he has to set a trap to lure the monster out into the open – he dresses in drag and heads for the park that night. Meanwhile, Marilyn is out on a date, and aims to cut through the park. Herman finds out, and is worried for her safety, so he rushes off to help her against the monster. A purse snatcher attacks the disguised Harris, and Herman goes to help. Both Harris and the snatcher faint when they see him. Harris recovers first, and arrests the would-be thief. He's warmly commended for his actions – until he describes the man who helped him capture the crook . . . Ludlow then demotes him to pounding the beat – in Death Valley . . .

4) Rock-A-Bye Munster
15 October 1964

Written by   ·   Joe Connelly and
Bob Mosher

Directed by   Norman Abbott

Cast

Dr Dudley	Paul Lynde
Diamond Jim	Sid Melton
Mrs Dudley	Marilynn Lovell
Elmer	Peter Robbins

Herman and Grandpa overhear Lily and Marilyn talking about a new playmate on the way for Eddie, and jump to the conclusion that Marilyn is expecting. In fact, it's Dr Dudley's son – who Marilyn babysits – that's coming to stay for a week. Herman finds the doctor's card, and he and Grandpa go to see him. Dudley, without his glasses, thinks Grandpa is 'a tall penguin'. He does, however, confirm that the Munsters will be having a child next week . . . Meanwhile, as Herman's birthday is coming up, Lily visits Diamond Jim's auto dealership, looking for a car for Herman. She's in their old car, driven by an invisible chauffeur. She likes the look of a hearse, as well as a roadster, and agrees to buy both if he'll make a few changes.

Herman is trying to be thoughtful to Lily because of her 'condition'. Eddie thinks Herman's done something wrong, and he's feeling guilty. When Herman finally mentions a child arriving, Lily tells him that it's a boy, Elmer, who'll arrive at nine in the morning. Herman is amazed at what modern science can do. Next morning, Elmer arrives a little early, and Lily sends Herman in to see him. Herman goes, and sees a remote controlled Frankenstein's monster toy, and thinks it's his new son . . . which looks just like him!

Eddie tells him it's just a toy, and introduces Elmer. Thinking this 'ugly' boy is his new son, Herman faints. When he recovers, Lily explains the whole thing to him, and then gives him his birthday present – the customized hearse.

This episode introduced the well known Munster family car, the Koach.

5) Pike's Pique
22 October 1964

Written by	Norm Liebmann and Ed Haas
Directed by	Seymour Berns

Cast

Borden T. Pike	Richard Deacon
Fanny Pike	Jane Withers
Sonny Harkness	Pat Harrington, Jnr
The Mayor	Henry Hunter
1st Workman	Joe Brooks

The city gas department is building a new pipeline down Mockingbird Lane, and the only home they haven't got a right of way for is the Munsters. They elect to build the pipe deep, and figure 25 feet is plenty. This brings them right into the dungeon, face to face with Grandpa and Herman. Pike, on hearing the story from the panicked workmen, thinks it's a plot by the Munsters to jack up the price he'll have to pay. He goes to see them, though his wife, Fanny, thinks he's meeting a girl. Pike meets the family and nervously offers them $1500 for right of way. Grandpa objects, turns into a bat and flies off. Pike just flees. Herman calls him later to accept the offer. His wife thinks it's the girl again, so Pike decides to get his own back, and asks Herman to come and get the money. He aims to throw a

119

scare into his wife to shut her up. Herman has a cold, though, so he sends Marilyn instead.

When she arrives and asks for money from Pike, Fanny is furious, and slams the door on her. This infuriates Herman, who goes round to punch Pike for insulting his niece. Fanny answers the door and faints. Pike thinks Herman hit her, so he hits Herman, bloodying his nose. The next day, Pike comes round to apologize and to get the contract signed. Grandpa is suspicious, and gives Herman a pen with vanishing ink in it to sign with. After Pike has gone, Mrs Cribbins, their neighbour, calls to say she got $3500 from the Gas Company. Grandpa thinks they've been conned, but when Herman looks, the check is for $5,000. Pike adds in a note that Herman's cured his wife of being suspicious! Grandpa feels bad now, and uses his magic to restore the signature, just as the mayor is yelling at Pike for fouling up.

6) Low-Cal Munster
29 October 1964

Written by	Norm Liebmann and Ed Haas
Directed by	Norman Abbott

Cast

Dr Dudley	Paul Lynde
Nurse Fairchild	Caryl Rowe
Freddie	Ronnie R. Rondell
TV Announcer	Michael Jackson
Seymour Farber	Dick Winslow
Anna Farber	Monty Margetts
Arlene Farber	Diane Courtney
Lester Farber	Scott McCartor
Grandma Farber	Elsie Baker

Herman is on the rampage – and how did it all come about? He's on a diet. His old Army regiment is having a reunion, and he can't fit into the uniform, so he goes to Dr Dudley for a diet plan to help him lose weight in the ten days till the reunion. Dudley has sent his nurse with his glasses to be repaired, and without them he's practically blind. He gives Herman his physical more by error than anything else, then gets his glasses back – and faints. Herman gets his diet, which he sticks to scrupulously for the first eight days, then starts to weaken. Grandpa then catches him trying to raid the fridge. Herman refuses to give in, though, and gets to the final day – Thanksgiving. Grandpa details all the food he'll be missing, and Herman faints.

The family calls Dr Dudley, who examines Herman and decides he's dead. When Herman recovers, Dudley panics and flees. The family goes out for dinner, so as not to tempt Herman, leaving him tied up in the dungeon, watching TV. It's all about food, and he snaps. He goes berserk looking for something to eat, and breaks into the Farber house, where the Farbers are about to eat their Thanksgiving dinner. Herman eats the whole lot. The Farbers are amazingly understanding, but it's left Herman unable to get into his uniform, until he employs the help of one of Grandma's old corsets . . .

7) Tin Can Man
4 November 1964

Teleplay by	Norm Liebmann and Ed Haas
Story by	Robert Lewin
Directed by	Earl Bellamy

Cast

Mr Taggart	Arch Johnson

Mr Balding	Richard Simmons
The Wife	Kathleen O'Malley
The Man	Rand Brooks
1st Woman	Dee Carroll
2nd Man	Murray Alper

Taggart is an ex-prison guard, now working with the school about problem children. He wants Eddie expelled, and when principal Balding refuses, he aims to visit the family and see what's turning Eddie into a monster . . . Eddie has been given notes to bring home about his failing science grades, but he's been ashamed to show them to his folks. Finally, he confesses, and Herman is furious. He insists that he work on his science project, and Eddie is helped by Grandpa to build a robot out of old cans. Herman is busy, but he asks Marilyn to see Balding about Eddie. Impressed with her, Balding agrees that Eddie should have another chance. Meanwhile, Taggart visits the house and meets Grandpa. He's appalled at the house, and threatens to expel Eddie. Grandpa sets the robot onto him. Taggart runs back to school, but Balding won't listen to him, and threatens to expel him instead. Taggart decides he'd better make certain Eddie's robot fails at the science fair . . .

When the family arrive for it, Taggart slips a wrench into the robot, causing it to short out. Grandpa starts an emergency operation on it, and Herman faints at the sight of oil. It's Eddie's turn when Herman recovers, and Herman goes out to apologize and entertain the parents. They assume he's the robot, and when he starts telling jokes, everyone is laughing and cheering. The success goes to Herman's head. Grandpa finds the wrench, but the robot is beyond repair. Eddie has to go out to explain, and also to admit that his Grandpa helped him build the robot. Balding is impressed with his abilities and honesty, and commends him to the school. Later, at home, Eddie and Grandpa manage to reactivate the robot, and start teaching it some of Herman's jokes, hoping to revive Vaudeville . . .

8) Herman The Great
12 November 1964

Written by   Joe Connelly and
                                 Bob Mosher
Directed by   Earl Bellamy

Cast

Duke Ramsey	John Hubbard
Mr Hansen	Joseph Mell
Jerry	Johnny Silver
Strangler Murphy	Count Billy Varga
The Ring Announcer	Jimmy Lennon
The Referee	Tiger Joe Marsh
Killer Conklin	Matt Murphy
Genghis Cohen	The Great John L.
Tarzan McGurk	Gene Le Bell
Crusher Kowalski	Jay York
Wilbur	Teddy Eccles

To amuse Wilbur, one of Eddie's friends, Herman ties a knot in a steel bar. Wilbur's father, Duke Ramsey, is a wrestling promoter, and offers Herman a job. Herman is worrying about putting money aside for Eddie's college education, and agrees, as long as he can remain anonymous – afraid the family won't approve. Grandpa discovers the secret of who 'The Masked Marvel' really is, but agrees to keep quiet. That night, as the Marvel takes on Tarzan McGurk, Grandpa watches on TV. The family think that the Marvel is a bully, and cheer on his opponent. Herman is winning until Tarzan tells him a sob-story about needing the money, and then he deliberately throws the match, making everyone think he's chicken.

This is the way of all Herman's fights – Crusher Kowalski, Killer Conklin, Genghis Cohen – he is winning until they give him the sob-story, then he throws the match. Ramsey decides on a new scheme – he'll offer $50 a minute to anyone amateur who can stay in the ring with The Masked Marvel. Hansen aims to make certain that his man wins – by drugging Herman's water. The family watches the bout on TV, and Grandpa from the ringside. Lily and the rest finally realize that the Marvel is Herman, and start rooting for him to win. Herman is falling asleep, however. Grandpa smells trickery, especially when he realizes that the 'amateur' in the ring is none other than banned wrestler Strangler Murphy. He recharges Herman, who then wins easily. Meanwhile, a fire has broken out, and Ramsey asks Herman to clear the place. Herman removes his mask, and asks everyone to leave. One look at his face clears the place. Herman is given $1,000 reward, which he salts away for Eddie – and retires from wrestling.

9) Knock Wood, Here Comes Charlie
19 November 1964

Written by	Norm Liebmann and Ed Haas
Directed by	Lawrence Dobkin

Cast

Mrs Cartwright	Jean Willes
Leo 'Knuckles' Kraus	Mike Mazurki

Herman's twin brother, Charlie, arrives from England with presents for them all. He explains that he aims to make his fortune with his new invention which extracts uranium from sea water. Herman is avoiding his brother, knowing Charlie

124

is a twister and a con artist. Only Marilyn agrees with this estimate. Herman is convinced Charlie is here to con Lily out of the money her mother left her the last time she died. Knuckles Kraus calls Charlie for the $1,000 Charlie owes him on the fake uranium machine . . . Charlie offers to sell the machine to Lily for $5,000, but Herman utterly forbids it. Grandpa decides to test the machine to prove Herman wrong, and when it doesn't work, Grandpa comes to the only logical conclusion – he's broken it. He tries fixing it, but can only get it to produce gold. Lily mentions to Charlie about the widowed Mrs Cartwright next door, who likes Herman. Pretending to be Herman, he sells her the machine for $5,000.

When Herman finds out, he's appalled, and goes to buy the machine back. She doesn't believe Herman's story about having a twin, and Herman has to pay her $500 more for the machine back. Meanwhile, Grandpa tells Charlie that he's fixed his machine, and it's producing uranium again. The problem is that it's missing. Charlie rushes round to buy the machine back from Mrs Cartwright, only to discover Herman already has it. He returns to the house just in time to stop Herman from smashing it. He pretends to be overcome with remorse for what he's done, and buys back the machine from Herman. After he's gone, Grandpa returns and tells Herman about fixing the machine. Herman is furious, but Grandpa adds that the machine is rather unstable. Outside, Charlie is demonstrating the machine to Knuckles when it explodes . . .

10) Autumn Croakus
26 November 1964

Written by   James Allardice and
                                    Tom Adair
Directed by   Lawrence Dobkin

Cast

Lydia Gardner	Linda Watkins
Malcolm	Neil Hamilton
1st Policeman	Richard Reeves
2nd Policeman	Jerry Mann

Grandpa is feeling left out of family affairs, so when he sees an advertisement for the Kindred Spirits Matrimonial Agency, he decides to apply. Herman doesn't approve of that sort of thing, and will have nothing to do with it. Grandpa gets a reply from Lydia Gardner, who is then invited over to meet the family. She tries hard to find something nice to say about the house when she meets Marilyn and Lily. Grandpa makes an explosive entrance to impress her, and starts wooing her. This is exactly what Lydia wants – she and her partner, Malcolm, are actually working together to get Lydia married off to heavily insured old men, whom they then kill off to collect the insurance money. Grandpa has signed the papers, and he's next in line . . .

Herman won't even meet Lydia, and goes to sulk in his room. Lydia's first attempt to kill Grandpa with poisoned chip dip fails when Kitty knocks the bowl over. Her second idea is to create an 'accident' on the stairs with a roller skate and grease to make him break his neck. Herman goes down for a midnight snack, and misses seeing Lydia. On his way back up, he steps on the roller skate and simply crushes it. He's still annoyed with Lily over the Lydia business, and goes to sleep in the guest room, unaware of the fact that this is where Lydia is staying. Lydia sees him, and runs out in terror, triggering her own trap, and then shoots out of the door. The family is furious with Herman, convinced he frightened her off deliberately. Then the police arrive with her in tow. They've been arresting the gang, and explain what was in store for Grandpa. They think

126

Lydia's story of a monster was just concocted to get her an insanity plea . . .

11) The Midnight Ride Of Herman Munster
3 December 1964

Written by   Joe Connelly and
                                Bob Mosher
Directed by   Ezra Stone

Cast

Big Louie	Maxie Rosenbloom
Marty	Val Avery
Freddie	Lennie Weinrib
Al	Lee Krieger
Desk Sergeant	Joe Devlin

Herman is exhausted after a night at the drive-in, but he goes back to the car to fetch Lily her fur coat. There he falls asleep. Two crooks, Al and Freddie, steal the car for use on a bank job. They drive out to a small farm to pick up Marty. He is waiting for Big Louie, a punch-drunk ex-fighter, to arrive. He's to drive the car. Herman wakes up, and knocks on the door. The crooks think he's spent too long in the ring, and take him for Louie. Meanwhile, Lily has called the police to report Herman a missing person. They come across a drunk in the street who fits the vague description of Herman that Lily gave. They think he's Herman, and take him home, but in fact he's Big Louie, too confused to know who or where he is. The family is out looking for Herman, so the cops put Louie to bed to sleep it off.

Meanwhile, the crooks force Herman to drive to the bank to rob it. Then, when the alarm is sounded, Marty makes him drive off. The cops chase them, and Herman tries to obey all the traffic signs, driving the crooks crazy. Eventually, he has a bright idea, and deliberately crashes the car so that the police can arrest the crooks. The cops think he's all disfigured from the crash, but he assures them he's fine. He calls Lily, who's puzzled, since Herman is supposed to be safely in bed now. She and Grandpa check it out, and find Louie. Grandpa freezes him with a spell until the cops arrive with the real Herman. They cart Louie off to join his pals in jail.

12) The Sleeping Cutie
10 December 1964

Written by	James Allardice and
	Tom Adair
Directed by	Norman Abbott

Cast

Dick Prince	Grant Williams
Paul Newmar	Gavin MacLeod
George Spelvin	John Hoyt
Mr Hadley	Walter Woolf King

Grandpa has invented a gasoline pill that will change water to fuel. He writes with a sample to the Reliant Oil Company. Hadley gets the report and thinks it's from another lunatic, till he tosses a match into the pail of water, which explodes. He sends Dick to get a contract signed. Meanwhile, Marilyn has trouble sleeping, so Grandpa gives her a sleeping potion, which knocks her out. They can't wake her the next morning, and discover that Grandpa accidentally gave her a Sleeping Beauty potion. Now she can only be awakened by the kiss of a handsome prince – in rather short supply these days. Grandpa aims to burn the Sleeping Beauty formula, but burns his gasoline pill one instead. Dick arrives to get the contracts signed, but Lily sends him back, citing a family crisis.

Hadley thinks this is a ruse to get more money, and orders Dick to do anything to get the contract signed. Lily meanwhile places an ad in the paper for a prince. Two actors turn up, thinking it's for a role. When Herman comes up from the basement carrying Marilyn, however, both men flee. Dick returns, and Lily is about to send him off again when Herman reads his business card, and discovers he's Dick Prince . . . 'At last, our prince has come', Lily enthuses. He finds the family oddly likeable, and takes tea with them. Grandpa refuses to sign the paper unless Dick kisses Marilyn. They warn him she's the ugly one, and he steels himself. When it comes to the kiss, he wakes her up – then won't stop . . . Finally, Grandpa agrees to sign the contract, only to discover it's to keep his pill off the market, to avoid competition. Herman makes him sign without taking money, after what Dick has done. Dick then takes Marilyn off on a date.

13) Family Portrait
17 December 1964

Written by	James Allardice and
	Tom Adair
Directed by	Lawrence Dobkin

Cast

Chip Johnson	Fred Beir
Lennie Bates	Harvey Korman
Mr Morgan	Roy Roberts

Morgan, editor of *Event* magazine, has had a computer make up what it considers to be their average family, and the machine has picked the Munsters. There's a $5,000 prize, and a reporter and photographer are to stay with them for the weekend to do a profile. Grandpa is insulted at being called average, and refuses to co-operate, which could ruin the deal. He leaves a note with the raven saying that he and Igor have flown the coop. Herman and Lily go out searching for him in all his favourite haunts, without luck. While they are gone, Chip Johnson and Larry Bates arrive. Chip likes Marilyn, and begins heavy-handedly chatting her up. Larry, on the other hand, doesn't like the look of the house and wants to call it off. Morgan agrees when they phone him that if anything goes wrong, it can be called off. Meanwhile, Grandpa and Igor are actually hanging around in the attic.

Larry spots Grandpa when he's looking around, but Chip doesn't believe his story, thinking that Larry has been drinking again. Larry decides that it's definitely time to start drinking. He goes for a glass of water, and sees Herman getting ready for bed. Again, Chip won't believe him. Then Larry sees Lily, and Chip finally agrees to go with him and check out the house. Lily hears them moving about, and thinks they have burglars. She sends a reluctant Herman to investigate. They see one another, and everyone panics. Chip and Larry jump out of the window, and then Marilyn tells the family that they weren't burglars, but the men from the magazine. Chip and Larry call Morgan, who thinks they've both been drinking, and orders them not to come back without the picture. Larry breaks three cameras before he gets one – which Morgan thinks is a neat Halloween photo, and gives them a bonus. When the family see the picture and its caption, they think the caption was confused with another picture.

14) Grandpa Leaves Home
24 December 1964

Written by	Richard Conway and
	Roland MacLane
Directed by	Norman Abbott

Cast

The Manager	Robert Strauss
The Fellow	Bill Dungan
The Woman	Iris Adrian
The Friend	Nicky Blair
The Man	Bill Couch
The Dancer	Sarah Jane Ross

Herman is enjoying the jokes in *Murder In The Rue Morgue*, but is irritated by Grandpa's fidgeting and noise. Grandpa picks a fight with Herman, and then threatens to leave home, thinking no one cares about him. Eddie tries to stop him, and Grandpa plays up to it. Herman, however, thinks Grandpa is being childish, and won't go along with humouring him. By morning, Grandpa isn't home, and Lily starts to worry. Herman finally agrees to go looking for him, but can't find him. Then Eddie sees a picture of Grandpa, billed as The Count, doing magic tricks in the Domino Club. Lily calls him, and he says he's fine. In fact, the manager is getting annoyed with him, since most of his tricks don't work right. That night, Lily and Herman visit the place to check it out. Grandpa is supposed to do a trick of escaping from a locked trunk, but can't get out. Herman breaks it open, worried, but Grandpa is annoyed at him. He changes into a wolf, and the crowd loves the act. The manager offers Grandpa a big contract, but Grandpa realizes he's been foolish in thinking his family doesn't care, and goes home with them instead.

15) Herman's Rival
31 December 1964

Written by   Richard Conway and
                                  Roland MacLane

Directed by   Joseph Pevney

Cast

Ramon	Lee Bergere
Mr Haggerty	Chet Stratton
Lester	Irwin Charone
The Assistant	Tommy Farrell
Louisa	Karen Flynn

Lily discovers by accident that Herman is overdrawn at the bank. She aims to get a job to help out, without telling Herman, in case his pride is hurt. Actually, Herman has lent $5,000 to her brother, Lester, which Grandpa thinks was a stupid move, because Lester's a bum. He advises Herman not to tell Lily. Lily sees Mr Haggerty at the employment agency, who just happens to have an opening for a Gypsy palm reader at 'The Golden Earring' tea rooms. Lily can read palms with ease, and the owner, Ramon, is very pleased with her. Later that week, Herman comes home early, and is puzzled to find that Lily isn't there. Grandpa thinks she's seeing another man, and the next day he persuades Herman to go with him and follow Lily to see what she's up to.

To help attract customers, Lily reads Ramon's palm in the window. Grandpa and Herman think they're holding hands. Herman decides he'll take strong action – he writes to Dear Abby. When Lily won't explain where she's been, he gets even more worried, and decides to have it out with the home-wrecker. Lester calls after Herman's gone, and tells her about the loan. The job worked out, and he's coming over to pay the money back. Lily explains about her job to Grandpa, who tells her that Herman's gone down to have it out with Ramon. Lily calls Ramon, who is confident he can handle things. He takes one look at Herman, though, and faints. Lily and Grandpa arrive, and think Herman's punched his lights out. Lily is very touched. Lester arrives, just as Ramon recovers. Since Lester is a werewolf, Ramon faints again.

16) Grandpa's Call Of The Wild
7 January 1965

Written by	Joe Connelly and Bob Mosher
Directed by	Earl Bellamy

Cast

Willard	Ed Peck
Mr Haskell	Don Haggerty
2nd Ranger	Bing Russell
1st Ranger	Mike Ragan
1st Fisherman	Curt Barrett

Eddie wants to go camping, like the other kids, and Lily thinks it's a marvellous idea. Marilyn has to stay home to study, but Grandpa goes along. They head for Shadow Pine Park, where the rangers on duty think they're weird, and report their arrival to Supervisor Haskell. Herman sets up the tent, but Grandpa is disturbed by his pounding the tent stakes. To create some lovely shade, Herman moves a tree. Herman and Eddie go fishing, and Herman's long cast latches onto a fish frying in a camper's pan. He's puzzled when he catches a fried fish, and elated when his next catch is a barbequed chicken. That night, they hear wolves howling, and Grandpa gets nostalgic for the good old days. Lily won't let him go padding off with them, however.

In the morning, Grandpa is missing. They hear on the radio that the rangers caught a Transylvanian wolf in the night, and know what happened. Lily goes to claim her father, and meets Haskell and Willard. 'He's your wolf?' they ask. 'No', Lily replies, 'my father'. He's stuck as a wolf, and they won't turn him over to her, as they aim to ship him to the zoo the next day. Herman reluctantly agrees to break him out that night. The rangers think he's a bear, and scare him off, only to discover he's taken the wolf as well. In the morning, the rangers are checking all departing cars for the wolf. Lily manages to sneak Grandpa out as a hefty fur collar . . . Back home, they use one of his de-wolfing potions to change him back again.

17) All-Star Munster
14 January 1965

Written by   Joe Connelly and
                        Bob Mosher
Directed by   Earl Bellamy

Cast
Pop Mallory   Pat Buttram
Coach Denman   Frank Maxwell
Moose Mallory   Robert Easton
Jerry   Gene Blakely

Marilyn has a note from college – her tuition hasn't been paid, and she can't return until it is. It's very embarrassing, so Herman goes along to straighten it all out. Coach Denman and his assistant, Jerry, are expecting a new player, Moose Mallory, for their basketball team. He's supposed to be dumb, but great. Herman turns up to ask directions, and they think he's Moose. The coach loves his work on the field, since he can sink a shot from anywhere on the field, and sign him up. The real Moose and his father, real hicks from Kentucky, turn up, but the coach doesn't care – he's got his star, so he throws Moose out. Eddie finds the news about the coach signing up Herman in the news the next day, and the family realizes that Herman's blown it again. Moose and his father arrive, furious at what's happened, but Herman is determined to set matters straight. He goes back to see the coach and demands that the contract be torn up and Moose is to be signed. When he hits the desk to emphasize his point, he hammers it into the ground. The coach does as Herman wishes.

18) If A Martian Answers, Hang Up
21 January 1965

Written by	Joe Connelly and
	Bob Mosher
Directed by	Norman Abbott

Cast

Captain Halbert	Herbert Rudley
Mr Andrews	Dort Clark
Roger	Ronnie Dapo
Walt	Pat Rosson
2nd Man	Larry Thor
1st Man	Ray Montgomery

The FCC has granted Herman a ham radio licence, number W6XRL4. Grandpa prefers to use a crystal ball, but Herman is all fired up. Two of Eddie's friends, Walt and Roger, are playing spacemen using walkie-talkies. Herman picks up the message, and thinks he's contacted Mars. He's all excited, and lets Grandpa in on it. The next day, the kids are playing again, and claim to have landed on Earth. Herman and Grandpa go looking for their flying saucer with Grandpa's transistorized divining rod, which doesn't work too well. Eventually they find the kids in their space suits next to their toy saucer. The children are terrified and run, so Herman takes a picture of the ship. Grandpa shows it to the Air Force. Meanwhile, the next day, Herman communicates again with the 'Martians', who thought he was playing a nasty trick on them. Roger's father gets annoyed at Herman, and threatens to beat him up. When Herman says that the Martians don't know where he lives, Mr Andrews threatens to blow up the Earth. Grandpa returns home to find Herman hidden in the closet with Lily and Marilyn, convinced the world is coming to an end. Grandpa has discovered the truth and tells Herman that it was just a toy they saw. Herman is ashamed, and when he picks up another Martian call, he tells the caller to stop being so stupid. This time, it really is a Martian, who thinks humans are really rude creatures . . .

19) Eddie's Nickname
28 January 1965

Written by	Richard Baer
Directed by	Joseph Pevney

Cast

Dr Dudley	Paul Lynde
Miss Fairchild	Alice Backes

Eddie comes home upset, vowing never to go to school again. He's been given a new nickname, 'Shorty', because he's the shortest person in his class. Lily wants Herman to complain about it, and Grandpa wants to change everyone who calls Eddie names into a kangaroo. Herman prefers to tell Eddie to stand up to insults. Grandpa tries to teach Eddie how to box dirty to help out, but Herman stops this, since he disapproves of violence. Finally, Grandpa mixes up a potion designed to help Eddie grow overnight. It sort of works – Eddie wakes up with a beard . . .

Herman has to take Eddie to the doctor's, but he's embarrassed to be seen with such a hairy son. Dr Dudley is alerted by his nurse that Herman's there, and Dudley steels himself to see the son – who's got a paper bag over his head . . . He's astonished by the beard, but all he can suggest is that Eddie get used to a new nickname, 'Fuzzy'. Back home, the family isn't too happy, except Grandpa – who thinks he's found a cure for baldness. Then Eddie accidentally dips his beard in Lily's soup – which melts the beard away. Grandpa is crushed, but Eddie is restored. Herman hopes that this has taught Eddie that appearances aren't the most important thing in life. Eddie goes back to school, but that night is in tears again – this time for striking out at baseball . . .

20) Bats Of A Feather
4 February 1965

Written by	James Allardice and Tom Adair
Directed by	Jerry Paris

Cast

Mr Brubaker	Gilbert Green
Dr Grant	Alvy Moore
2nd G.I.	Allan Hunt
1st G.I.	Frank Gardner
Miss Guthrie	Barbara Babcock
Mr Hazlett	Thomas McBride
The Stewardess	Sally Mills
1st Boy	Ronnie Dapo
2nd Boy	Jimmy Mathers

There's to be a class pet show at Eddie's school, and Herman wants him to enter Spot. Spot, however, won't go. Lily thinks Eddie should take the kitten, but Grandpa suggests Igor. Eddie loves the idea, but Herman manages to insult the bat, who flies off in a huff. As Lily observes, 'he's a spoiled bat'. So that Eddie will have an entry Grandpa changes himself into a bat and pretends to be Igor. At school, the pets are being judged by Miss Guthrie and the principal, Mr Hazlett. 'Igor' does a few swoops about the room, but a squirrel wins. Eddie trades 'Igor' for the squirrel.

Back home, he learns it was Grandpa. Although the trade was only for the weekend, Timmy Brubaker sold the bat to his father, who works in a rocket lab in Washington DC. The family decides to fly out, and are amazed to have the plane to themselves. They think the stewardess is scared of flying, since she's in a state of shock. At the lab, Brubaker and Grant aim to send Grandpa up in a rocket, to test his radar. The problem is that they can't recover the rocket. They're astounded when the bat faints. They have a second bat, a female named Cleo, who fancies Grandpa. There are two new G.I.s on duty outside the lab, and when they see Herman, they think he's an experiment that's escaped, and take him in. Herman thinks they're just being polite. When the scientists see Herman, they jump out of the window. Herman grabs Cleo instead of Grandpa, and runs. When Brubaker and Grant return, they try testing Grandpa's radar, but he flies straight into a wall – then out the broken window. Back home, he surprises the family. Igor returns, and takes a liking to Cleo, so Grandpa tells Herman to explain to Eddie about the bats and the bees . . .

21) Don't Bank On Herman
11 February 1965

Written by   Douglas Tibbles
Directed by   Ezra Stone

Cast
Mr Grover   Maurice Manson
Mr Williams   Pitt Herbert
Fingers   Mousie Garner
Scotty   Jack Bernardi
The Woman Teller   Audrey Swanson

Marilyn is ill, so Lily is forced to send Herman and Grandpa
to the bank to draw out all of the money from their tax
account. At the bank, Mr Grover has received warnings
about a pair of thieves in Halloween masks robbing in the
area. Rather than endanger lives, the tellers are told to hand
over their money. When Herman arrives and asks for all the
money, the teller thinks he and Grandpa are the robbers,
and empties her drawer. Back home, they count it – $18,300.
Lily is furious because they've goofed again – there was
only $680 in that account. She insists that he return it the
next day. He can't sleep for thinking about it, and decides
to return it that night.

Grandpa goes along, and shorts out the alarms. Herman
pulls the door off its hinges, and they go to the vault. It's on
a time lock, but Herman prizes it out and resets it. When
they get into the vault, the door shuts behind them. They
find a phone, but can't get through. Grandpa hits the vault
alarm. Outside, Fingers and Scotty – the halloween mask
robbers – are varying their play, and raiding the bank at
night. They're amazed at how easy it is to get in, and blow
open the safe. When Herman and Grandpa emerge, they are
terrified. Thinking the thieves are rescuers, Herman hugs

them, knocking them out. Grandpa realizes they are crooks, and they beat a hasty retreat before the police arrive and capture the crooks.

22) Dance With Me, Herman
18 February 1965

Teleplay by	James Allardice, Tom Adair, Joe Connelly and Bob Mosher
Story by	James Allardice and Tom Adair
Directed by	Joseph Pevney

Cast

'Doc' Havermeyer	Don Rickles
Miss Valentine	Joyce Jameson

It's to be Parents' Night at Marilyn's school, but she hasn't mentioned it. Lily finds out, and wants to be subtle in asking, but Herman goes at it in his usual style. Marilyn explains that the night is a dance, and she knows how Herman hates dancing, and didn't want to embarrass him. Lily decides that it's time he learned, but he doesn't do too well with her. Grandpa wants to mix him a potion, but Herman decides to take lessons at the Happy Lands Ballroom. It's run by Happy 'Doc' Havermeyer, a con man, and his new instructress, Miss Valentine. He tells her to flatter her customers, and naturally Herman falls for it.

They get him to sign a ten-year contract. Grandpa reads it, and it's terrible, with all kinds of ways to gouge money out of Herman. Lily reports the school to the police, who decide to investigate. Doc gets a tip-off, and thinks that Herman is the planted police agent. He tells Herman that he's got no dancing talent, refunds his money, and tosses him out. Back home, Herman decides not to go to Parents' Evening, and sends Lily off with Marilyn. Lily pretends to sprain her ankle so she can stay with Herman – a sentimental gesture that disgusts Grandpa: 'This family's come a long way since Transylvania, when we used to pound stakes into one another.' Later, Herman takes up baseball, to do the father–son games at school. All he manages is to knock himself out.

23) Follow That Munster
25 February 1965

Written by	Joe Connelly and
	Bill Mosher
Directed by	Joseph Pevney

Cast

Mrs Andrews	Doris Singleton
Mr Kempner	Ken Lynch
Mike	Herb Armstrong
Her	Ronnie Haran
Him	Mike Winkelman

Herman has been going out in the evenings, and Grandpa discovers he's trying to be a detective, having enrolled in a correspondence course. Lily is annoyed with him, not knowing what he's up to. Herman practises his disguises and following people. Lily begins to suspect he's seeing another woman, and goes to the Kempner Detective Agency to have one of their men follow Herman. Kempner and Mike think the case is too weird, but when Herman calls in trying to get a job, they give him the assignment . . . He doesn't realize that they want him to follow himself, but Grandpa sees it instantly. He suggests that Herman go out as normal, then file a good report on himself. That way, everyone will be pleased. Herman does so, and when Lily reads it, she's all contrite – even though Herman overdoes the pathos in it a bit. The Agency is so pleased that they ask Herman to do another job – as a bodyguard for a Mrs Andrews, whose husband has been threatening her. She's impressed with him (after she's recovered from her faint). Meanwhile, Lily and Marilyn are out collecting for their favourite charity, Bundles for Transylvania. Lily rings the bell, and Herman answers . . . When Mrs Andrews calls out to get rid of her husband, Lily is furious, and floors Herman with one punch. Later, when she discovers the truth, she's apologetic, but Herman has lost his job. He's not discouraged – he's decided to take up being a barber, and open his own beauty salon . . .

24) Love Locked Out
4 March 1965

Written by   James Allardice and
                             Tom Adair
Directed by   Charles Barton

Cast
Dr Baxter   Elliot Reid
Winthrop   Norman Grabowski
Calvin   Bryan O'Byrne

There's an office party at the funeral home, and Herman stays there until after midnight, despite promises that he'd be home by six-thirty. Lily is furious, and locks him out of the bedroom. Herman is forced to sleep on the couch, which drives him crazy. There's a leaky faucet, which he finally ties in a knot. Then there's a mouse, which makes him terrified . . . Finally, he gets to sleep. In the morning, Lily is still furious, and this goes on for four days. Grandpa advises Herman to see Dr Harvey Baxter, a marriage counsellor and Marilyn gives Lily the same advice. Baxter finds Lily confusing, but advises her to apologize, to show how forgiving she is. She agrees to try. When Herman turns up, Baxter thinks he's been beaten by his wife, but eventually tells Herman to apologize to his wife and to be a peacemaker. Back home, both try to apologize at once, and both get further annoyed when the other insists on apologizing. Grandpa finally decides it's time for the ultimate weapon – fake measles. When Lily and Herman see Eddie in such a state, both fall over themselves to look after him, and make up their silly differences.

25) Come Back, Little Googie
11 March 1965

Written by	Leo Rifkin, Bob Mosher and Joe Connelly
Directed by	Joseph Pevney

Cast

Googie Miller	Billy Mumy
Mr Miller	Russ Conway

Googie Miller is an obnoxious child that Eddie goes to school with. When he visits the family to stay for the weekend, he makes fun of everyone there. In retaliation, Grandpa decides to change him into something more appropriate than a boy. Meanwhile, a chimp has escaped from the zoo and is hiding out at the house. Googie overhears Grandpa's plans and substitutes the chimp for himself, making Grandpa think his magic worked. Googie hides out, laughing at the credulity of the Munsters, who all believe the chimp is him. However, Googie isn't laughing so hard when everyone prefers the chimp to him – it has much better manners, for

143

one thing.

Guest star Billy Mumy is best known for his role on *Lost In Space*, but had been acting for several years on TV by this point in numerous guest roles. He's recently returned to acting and is appearing in *Babylon 5*.

26) Far Out Munsters
18 March 1965

Written by	Richard Conway, Joe Connelly and Bob Mosher
Directed by	Joseph Pevney

Cast

The Standells	Larry Tamblyn
	Gary Lane
	Tony Valentine
	Dick Dodd
Pops Murdock	Alex Gerry
The Hermit	Kelton Garwood
The Man With The Beard	Zalman King
The Bellboy	Frank Killmond
The Girl	Sue Winton
The Doorman	Tom Curtis

The rock group, the Standells, are due in town for a concert, and they need a place to stay. They don't want a hotel, because they always get mobbed, but they have a habit of wrecking houses they rent. Their manager, Pops Murdock, wants to hire the Munster house, figuring it's such a wreck they can't do more damage. Marilyn doubts that her family will agree, but Murdock offers $1500 for the weekend, plus a suite at the local hotel in compensation. Herman finally decides to go through with it, though he doesn't know who the house is being used by. The family goes to their luxury

144

hotel, but it's too clean and fresh for them, and they aren't comfortable. Finally, they decide to call it off and go home. The Standells, on the other hand, are thrilled with the Munster house, and start a swinging party. When the Munsters return, the party-goers think they're more guests, and like the weird threads. Herman is encouraged to recite poetry, which they find far-out, and Lily plays the harp and sings. The whole affair goes very well, and the family is popular. The Standells enjoy their stay, and give Eddie a signed picture of themselves. The Munsters enjoyed it, but are glad to be back to normal again . . .

Actor Zalman King went on to become a director of films such as *9½ Weeks* and *Wild Orchid*, as well as the series *Red Shoe Diaries*.

27) Munsters On The Move
25 March 1965

Written by	George Tibbles, Joe Connelly and Bob Mosher
Directed by	Joseph Pevney

Cast

Dennison	Bert Freed
Jerry	Joey Scott
Elmire	Lenore Shanewise
Poppa	Jan Arvan
Momma	Bella Bruck
Elderly Man	Charles Seel
Elderly Woman	Nydia Westman
Susan	Alma Murphy
Workman	Eddie Hanley

Herman has been offered a promotion when his firm decides to open a new branch office. But it will mean moving. Eddie isn't too happy about the idea because he's just been made captain of the school baseball team. Still, the family agrees to support Herman, even though it means leaving their lovely house. Now they just have to sell it.

28) Movie Star Munster
1 April 1965

Teleplay by	Joe Connelly and Bob Mosher
Story by	James Allardice and Tom Adair
Directed by	Jerry Paris

Cast

J.R. Finlater	Jesse White
Alfred Swanson	Walter Burke

J.R. Finlater and Alfred Swanson run an insurance racket. They create fake accidents to milk insurance companies of money. Their accomplice has been arrested, and they need a new accident victim. When they stop to ask directions and see Herman, they know they've found just the person. They convince him that they are movie producers filming a remake of 'Double Indemnity', and get him to sign their insurance policy. Herman shows up for 'filming' the next day, where he's supposed to be injured by a car driven by Alfred. After a few false starts, Alfred hits Herman – and smashes the car to pieces, injuring himself. J.R. thinks up a new accident, involving a ton of bricks being dropped on Herman's head. When Herman fouls up the 'scene', J.R. accidentally triggers the trap, and shooting has to stop while he's treated for concussion. Later, he tries again. This time, he sets up an office about four floors up, with a door leading outside. Herman is supposed to walk through the door, but has problems with the motivation of his character, then finally runs into the broom cupboard by mistake. J.R. demonstrates the right actions, and falls out of the door himself . . . Herman finally realizes what is going on, and gets nasty. Alfred jumps out of the door to get away. Later, both men try and get back at Herman, but are scared off by Spot.

29) Herman The Rookie
8 April 1965

Written by	Bob Mosher
Directed by	Jerry Paris

Cast

Himself	Leo Durocher
Himself	Elroy 'Crazylegs' Hirsch
Charlie	Gene Darfler

Leo Durocher, manager of the Los Angeles Dodgers baseball team is passing the Munster household when he's hit by a flying baseball. He's knocked out, and when he wakes up he heads for the person who hit the ball. Herman is worried that he's in trouble again, since he hit the ball, but he is astonished and delighted when Leo is interested only in signing him as a rookie player. Herman's strength enables him to hit drives way, way out, and he's entranced with visions of becoming a star. The other players aren't so happy, though, and eventually Herman realizes that baseball is fun as a game but not as a career.

30) Country Club Munsters
15 April 1965

Written by   Douglas Tibbles
Directed by   Joseph Pevney

Cast
Petrie	Woodrow Parfrey
Stubbs	Dan Tobin
Murdock	J. Edward McKinley
Bartender	Al Checco
TV Announcer	Johnny Jacobs

Herman wins a competition and the first prize is a family membership to the exclusive Mockingbird Heights Country Club. Petrie, the president of the club, is utterly appalled at the idea of letting in . . . well, *whatever* the Munsters are, and he tries to convince Herman not to accept. So does Lily, who thinks that the snobs at the club aren't really their sort of people. Naturally, Herman pays neither of them any attention and insists on taking part in the golfing and other activities, creating his normal brand of chaos, with Grandpa's help. Eventually, however, he realizes that Lily is right and they don't fit in.

31) Love Comes To Mockingbird Heights
22 April 1965

Written by   Bob Mosher and
                            Joe Connelly
Directed by   Joseph Pevney

Cast
Alan Benson	Charles Robinson
Uncle Gilbert	Richard Hale

A crate arrives for the family from Uncle Gilbert, and it's
filled with money. Ben and Alan, two con men, think that
they're onto a gold-mine here. Alan works in the bank
where the Munsters deposit the cash, and he agrees to
romance Marilyn to try and get his hands on the money.
Grandpa is suspicious of their motives, and is eventually
proven correct, much to Marilyn's chagrin. Uncle Gilbert
himself turns up to collect the money, which he wants to
invest in America.

Uncle Gilbert is actually the Gill-man from the Univer-
sal *Creature From The Black Lagoon* movies. Actor Richard
Hale, under the costume, is best known for playing *Cheyenne*
Bodie's Indian father on the Western series.

32) Mummy Munster
29 April 1965

Written by	Bob Mosher and Joe Connelly
Directed by	Ezra Stone

Cast

Dr Wilkinson	Philip Ober
Thatcher	Pat Harrington, Jnr

Dr Wilkinson announces to the press the discovery of a
great sarcophagus that he will open publicly. Meanwhile,
Herman's been having trouble sleeping, so Grandpa gives
him some extra-strength sleeping pills that will knock him
out for 24 hours. After taking one, Herman is struck by the
need to sleep while visiting the museum to collect Marilyn,
who's been studying there for school. He settles down in

the sarcophagus for a cozy snooze. Marilyn goes home alone, puzzled, and the family wonders what's become of Herman. They soon find out. Dr Wilkinson gathers the press and then opens the casket. Everyone is stunned by the 'mummy' inside it. Most stunned are the family, of course, when they see the pictures. That night, Wilkinson's nervous assistant, Thatcher, is on duty when Herman awakens. Thatcher faints, thinking the mummy has come to life and escaped.

Pat Harrington, Jnr is best known for his role on *One Day At A Time* (1975–84).

33) Lily Munster – Girl Model
6 May 1965

Teleplay by	Joe Connelly and Bob Mosher
Story by	Dick Conway
Directed by	Earl Bellamy

Cast

Laszlo Brastoff	Roger C. Carmel
Irving	Lois Roberts
The Beautiful Girl	Nina Shipman
Mr Franklin	John Alvin
The Little Girl	Kimberly Beck
Colette	Sally F. Morris
Millicent	Teke
The 1st Model	Susan Wedell
The 2nd Model	Tracy Butler

Lily is fed up with having nothing to do at home, and no one to do anything with, so she decides to get a job. She sees an ad for a girl model with Laszlo Brastoff. Brastoff is a top clothing designer, but bored with the usual line of models. When he sees Lily, he decides that she'll be the perfect lead for his upcoming fashion show. Meanwhile, Herman is annoyed that Lily has the job, and with the idea that men will be staring at her. Grandpa agrees, and decides to help out. The thing to do is to make Lily jealous, so he uses some of his pills on Herman to make him irresistible. The attempts to make him into Frank Sinatra and Richard Burton don't go too well, but Grandpa finally makes him into a rich Texas tycoon. To cement the likelihood of Lily being jealous, Grandpa changes himself into a beautiful girl, to fawn all over Herman. Herman and Grandpa go to the show, where the models can't stop talking about the Texas millionaire and the girl. Lily, while modelling, realizes that it's Herman, and is jealous all right – she knocks over the display onto her 'cheating' husband. Later, at home, Grandpa (now reverted) and Herman try and explain. Lily doesn't believe that Grandpa was the girl, and wants him to prove it. He can't, because his potion is gone. Eddie drank it, and is now a girl . . .

34) Munster The Magnificent
13 May 1965

Written by	Richard Conway, Bob Mosher and Joe Connelly
Directed by	Joseph Pevney

Cast

Teacher	Dave Ketchum
School Friend	Eddie Ryan

Eddie's school is having a talent show, and all the parents are joining in. Eddie is ashamed that there's nothing that Herman can do, but when he gets into an argument with other kids, he claims that Herman is a great magician. Unfortunately, Eddie's teacher then wants Herman to be the star of the show. Grandpa is offended, since he actually could do the magic involved. Lily is almost as appalled as Herman is when they hear the news, but Grandpa comes to the rescue with his magic. The problem is that Herman starts to love the applause and limelight and doesn't stick to doing the tricks that Grandpa has worked out for him, and eventually makes an utter fool of himself.

35) Herman's Happy Valley
20 May 1965

Written by   Richard Conway
Directed by   Ezra Stone

Cast
Barney Walters   John Hoyt
Curtis   Bartlett Robinson
Gil Craig   Richard Reeves

Con man Barney Walters sells Herman the deeds to the ten acres of worthless land, which includes the ghost town of Happy Valley – only to discover that gold really does exist there. With the aid of his henchmen, he decides that they'd better scare away the new owners and buy it back fast. The family, naturally, think Herman's been conned, but agree to try a vacation in his new purchase. To their delight, they discover that the ghost town apparently does possess real ghosts, and even Grandpa thinks Herman's made a smart buy. The 'ghosts' end up being terrified of the Munsters and giving up.

36) Hot Rod Herman
27 May 1965

Written by   Bob Mosher and
         Joe Connelly

Directed by   Norman Abbott

Cast

Leadfoot Baylor   Henry Beckman
Sandy Baylor   Brian Corcoran
Mechanic   Eddie Donno

The Baylors, father and son, are obnoxious rivals of the
Munsters. 'Leadfoot' is a great hot-rodder, and boasts that
his car can beat anything else on the road. Herman fool-
ishly rises to the challenge and bets that the Koach can take
him on. Baylor insists on the cars being put up as stakes on
the race – which Herman promptly loses. Grandpa is dis-
gusted with him and decides that the only thing to do is to
build his own car to beat Baylor. He constructs a modified
coffin that he calls the Dragula and provokes Baylor into
making the same bet with him. Baylor attempts to cheat to
win the race, but Grandpa wins out and regains the Koach.

37) Herman's Raise
4 June 1965

Written by   Douglas Tibbles, Bob
         Mosher and Joe Connelly

Directed   by Ezra Stone

Cast

Mr Gateman   John Carradine
Tom Fong   Benny Rubin

Herman is very nervous about asking his boss, Mr Gate-

man, for a raise. Lily explains that they really need more
money, so Herman screws up all his courage and tells
Gateman that he can't work without more money – and
Gateman agrees. Instead of giving him a raise, however,
Gateman fires him. Devastated, Herman then tries to find a
new job, but without any luck. He also has to prevent Lily
from finding out that he's actually lost his job. Eventually,
he gets his old job back because none of his replacements
could do the grave digging like Herman could, either.

Horror film star John Carradine made the first of several appearances as Herman's boss in this story.

38) Yes, Galen, There Is A Herman
10 June 1965

Written by	Bob Mosher and
	Joe Connelly
Directed by	Norman Abbott

Cast

Galen Stewart	Brian Nash
John Stewart	Walter Brooke
Mrs Stewart	Marge Redmond
Dr Leinbach	Harvey Korman

On his way home after work, Herman finds a youngster
named Galen with his head stuck in park railings. Herman
bends the rails to get Galen out, and the two become friends.
Problems arise when each tells of their adventures at home.
Grandpa thinks that Herman's just making the whole thing
up to make himself look good. The Stewarts think Galen is
making up the whole thing about a giant green guy who can
bend bars, and take him to a psychiatrist to convince him
that there's no such thing as a Herman Munster. Galen is
almost convinced until he meets Herman again.

154

Season Two

Credits

Produced by	Joe Connelly and Bob Mosher
Production Executive	Irving Paley
Developed by	Norm Liebmann and Ed Haas
From a Format by	Al Burns and Chris Hayward
Music	Jack Marshall
Director of Photography	Monroe Askins, Enzo A. Martinelli, Bud Thackery, Walter Strenge, ASC, William Margulies
Art Director	Henry Larrecq
Film Editor	Bud S. Isaacs, Danford B. Greene, George O'Hanion, Michael R. McAdam, ACE, Edwin H. Bryant, ACE, Richard M. Sprague
Unit Manager	James Hogan
Assistant Director	Dolph M. Zimmer, George Bisk
Set Decorators	John McCarthy, Robert C. Bradfield, James M. Walters, Julia Heron, Audrey Blasdel
Costume Supervisor	Vincent Dee
Sound	Lyle Cain, B.F. Ryan, Ed Somers, Roger Parish, Herbert Alberty, William Russell, James T. Porter, William H. Ford, Clarence E. Self, John L. Bury

Editorial Department Head	David J. O'Connell
Music Supervision	Stanley Wilson
Makeup	Bud Westmore
Hair Stylist	Larry Germain
Post Production Supervisor	Michael R. McAdam
Sound Effects Editor	George Ohanion, MPSE
Assistant to Producers	Keith Vincent

Cast

Herman	Fred Gwynne
Lily	Yvonne de Carlo
Grandpa	Al Lewis
Marilyn	Pat Priest
Eddie	Butch Patrick

39) Herman, The Master Spy
23 September 1965

Written by	Douglas Tibbles
Directed by	Ezra Stone

Cast

The Commissar	Val Avery
Valeiry	Leonard Yorr
Gregor	John Lawrence
Ninotchka	Bella Bruck
The Young Man	Edward Mallory
The Older Man	Henry Hunter
Charlie	John Zaremba
John	Howard Wendell
Roger	Robert Millar
The Russian Teletype Man	Jon Silo
The Announcer	Ed Reimers

The family has gone down to Paradise Cove to play on the

156

beach. Off the coast is a Russian trawler. Herman has taken up scuba diving, and heads off for a swim, while Eddie buries Grandpa again. At lunchtime, Herman is nowhere to be found. The reason is simple – the trawler has managed to bring him in with a catch of fish. The crew think Herman is a sea monster at first, but they realize he's a nice guy. They report him as the missing link to Moscow. Moscow doubts the story, convinced he's an American spy. US intelligence intercepts the messages, and gets worried. On the trawler, Herman is teaching the sailors to sing American songs, and is very popular. The US Director of Espionage issues a newspaper statement that the Russians haven't caught an American spy, so the Commissar orders the crew of the trawler to get rid of Herman. Lily and Grandpa have seen the news item and sketch of Herman and put two and two together. They head out to rescue him. To Lily's fury, the Russians are throwing a farewell party for Herman. She breaks up the party and marches him straight home, where she finally forgives him.

40) Dancing Bear
(Alternative Title: 'Herman's Child Psychology')
25 September 1965

Written by	Joe Connelly and Bob Mosher
Directed by	Ezra Stone

Cast

Big Leo	Gene Blakely
Charles	Michel Petit
Mr White	Bill Quinn
The Roustabout	Lee Henry

Eddie's friend Charlie aims to run away from his mean

parents, and wants Eddie to join him. Eddie discovers his folks are too nice to be mean, and he gets upset over that. He threatens to run away, but Herman just thinks he's after attention. When Eddie won't listen, Herman lets him leave, figuring he'll be back soon. After an hour, he's still not returned, and a worried Lily sends Herman to search the woods for him. Meanwhile, a bear named Olga and her cub have escaped from the circus, and are hiding in the woods. White sends Big Leo and his men looking for the bears. Herman finds the cub sleeping, and takes it home, thinking it's Eddie. When he gets home, he discovers that Eddie's been home for hours. Lily makes him take the cub back – and he runs right into Olga. Actually she's quite friendly, and just wants to dance, which pleases Herman. Lily and Grandpa go looking for Herman. When she sees him dancing with the bear, Lily gets furious and punches her. She then drives Herman home with a switch. Olga is relieved to see the men from the circus when they find her, and happily returns with them.

Herman: 'I don't understand what happened to my child psychology. It always worked on *Leave It To Beaver*.'

41) Bronco Busting Munster
30 September 1965

Teleplay by	Joe Connelly and
	Bob Mosher
Story by	Dick Conway
Directed by	Ezra Stone

Cast

Ted	Donald Barry
Hank	William Phipps
The Announcer	Dick Lane
The Cowpoke	Leonard P. Geer

There's a rodeo in town, and Eddie has proudly entered his father in the bucking bronco contest, confident he'll win. The prize is $500, and the organizers are worried at Eddie's confidence, so they plan to put Herman on their meanest horse, Volcano . . . Lily doesn't approve of Herman risking his neck, and wants Herman to persuade Eddie to withdraw his name. Herman tries, telling his son the fairy story about Sir Herman and the dragon, who doesn't slay the beast because he can't bear to leave his family. Eddie thinks the knight is chicken, so Herman daren't disappoint him by withdrawing. On the day of the event, he's so nervous, he goes to Grandpa for brave pills. Grandpa can't help there, but can help by changing himself into a horse for Herman. The labels have fallen off his pills, so it takes a few animals before he finds the right one.

At the event, Herman is assigned to chute 4. He tells Grandpa, who tries to slip into the chute. He's discovered, and the pill wears off. He's tossed out as a lunatic. Meanwhile, no one has stayed on their horse for the time to win the money. It's Herman's turn last, and he thinks Volcano is Grandpa. He stays in the saddle and wins the prize. Lily is really proud of him, and so is Grandpa, who turns up next to the horse Herman rode . . . Herman realizes he was risking his neck out there and faints.

42) Herman Munster, Shutterbug
7 October 1965

Written by	Dick Conway
Directed by	Earl Bellamy

Cast

Lou	Joe de Santis
Rod	Herbie Faye

Sgt. Baxter	Jess Kirkpatrick
The Officer	Robert Morgan
The Little Old Lady	Alma Murphy
Daniel Boone	Jefferson County

Herman has taken up photography. He annoys the family by taking forever to take their picture – then showering them with soot when the flash explodes. He heads into town to take photos, while Eddie practises his dirges. Meanwhile, two crooks – Lou and Rod – plan to rob the bank. Herman is having no luck taking pictures – even a statue of Daniel Boone runs away when it sees him. He goes to the bank to take a picture of it. When Grandpa develops the picture, he sees that Herman has actually unwittingly photographed the robbery in progress. The crooks find out from the papers that someone took a picture of the robbery, and they recall Herman's weird car. They start searching for it.

When they find the car, they try to con Herman into believing they're from the newspapers and want to buy the picture. Herman finally recognizes them, and they hold up the entire family. They hide out at the house. Lily smashes Herman's camera, annoyed at what has happened. Eddie practises his dirges. Herman feeds Spot. Grandpa plays cards with an invisible partner. The crooks are going crazy. Grandpa slips into the basement to make himself a potion to turn into a homing pigeon and fly to the police for help. The crooks spot this, and he claims it's his brand of cocktails. They drink it and are changed into birds. Grandpa calls the police to tell them the crooks are flying in to give themselves up. The sergeant can't believe this – until it actually happens. They even have Herman's photo with them as evidence against themselves.

43) Herman, Coach Of The Year
14 October 1965

Written by   James Allardice and
                                         Tom Adair

Directed by   Norman Abbott

Cast
The Husband   Henry Beckman
The Wife   Emmaline Henry

Eddie is upset at failing the track team – he's been nick-named 'Leadfoot' for his lack of speed. Herman decides to train him. Grandpa observes of Herman: 'Men like Herman are made, not born.' Herman tries pitching the shot, but goes too far. It demolishes a car a wife is driving – a story her husband won't believe. Then Herman tries the discus – and wrecks the wife's second car. Herman's pole-vaulting lands him through the upstairs window. Eddie isn't doing too well, and Lily is afraid Herman is overdoing things. Grandpa decides to help by making a speed pill. As he works, he observes to Igor: 'Quiet, stupid – you're not a bird. You're a mouse who joined the Transylvanian Air Corps.'

Grandpa offers Eddie his 'vitamins'. It speeds him up, and Herman thinks it's his training. Grandpa gives Eddie one a day until the track meet, when the pills are missing. He and Lily tell Herman, and all they can hope is that he's built up some reserves. At the meet, Eddie is winning all of his entries with ease. He asks Herman to talk to one of his team mates to speed him up – the boy takes one look at Herman and breaks all records. Back home, Eddie produces the missing pills. They tasted so terrible that he didn't take any after the first. Lily tosses them away, and realizes it was Herman's training that paid off, after all. A cat eats the pills, and chases a dog up a tree. The wife, driving her third car, crashes at the sight – and her husband grounds her.

44) Happy 100th Anniversary
21 October 1965

Written by	Douglas Tibbles
Directed by	Ezra Stone

Cast

Jack Poyer	Noam Pitlik
Mr Parker	Robert Cornthwaite
Mr Walpole	Jack Grinnage
The Bank Manager	Vinton Hayworth
The Bank Clerk	William O'Connell
The Admiral	Foster Brooks

Lily and Herman's 100th wedding anniversary is coming up, and both plan to surprise the other. Each tries to take a check for $1000 from their account, but both are bounced, since there is only enough for one in the account. Grandpa suggests to Herman that he get an evening job to make the money to buy a gift. Lily also thinks of this. Both unwittingly apply at the Cleaver Employment Agency. Herman's interviewer thinks he's correct to apply for a night job. Both Parker and Walpole are horrified by their clients, but both have the same solution: welders, since they are totally covered up. Both Herman and Lily get jobs at the Crosby Ship Yard, not knowing the other has also. Grandpa and Marilyn are in on the secret and realize they'll be working at the same place. Since it's large, they doubt the couple will meet.

Actually, they are both teamed up. Each starts flirting with the other on the job, writing messages in soot, since

162

the place is so noisy. Neither realizes who they are flirting with. Then they are staggered by the fact that the other likes what they do. They finally start to suspect the truth about who they are working with. An Admiral comes to inspect the work they've been doing, and they are forced to unmask. When they see one another, they're furious that the other has been flirting on the job. They start fighting, and are fired. Back home, they won't talk to one another. Grandpa settles the problem, pointing out that they were attracted to one another even when dressed in masks, showing how strong their love is. They make up again. Even if they don't have expensive gifts for one another, they have each other.

45) Operation Herman
28 October 1965

Teleplay by	Joe Connelly and
	Bob Mosher
Story by	Dick Conway
Directed by	Norman Abbott

Cast

Dr Willoughby	Dayton Allen
Dr Elliott	Don Keefer
Miss Hazlet	Marge Redmond
The Doctor	Justin Smith
The Attendent	Bill Quinn

Eddie is home from school, having eaten a note he was supposed to give his parents. This annoys Herman, who hates Eddie to eat between meals. It seems that his tonsils are in bad shape. Herman looks, and faints. Later, he takes Eddie to Dr Willard Willoughby, a terribly short-sighted doctor, who finally manages to deduce that they'll have to

163

come out. 'You're a kind boy', he tells Eddie. 'The kind I don't need.' He insists on Eddie going to hospital, and Herman faints again. After the operation, he forbids Herman to see Eddie, afraid he'll faint in the hospital. Marilyn and Lily visit him, and he's doing fine. Grandpa is annoyed, and he and Herman decide to sneak out that night to see Eddie.

At the hospital, the nurse thinks Herman is a crash victim, and goes for an attendant. Lily meanwhile discovers Herman missing, and she and Marilyn start to worry. At the hospital, the men discover it's after visiting hours, and only authorized personnel are allowed in. Grandpa disguises himself as a doctor, and Herman as a patient. While Grandpa's getting dressed, the nurse wheels Herman into the operating room. The doctor there is appalled, and has Herman given laughing gas so he can be operated on. While they go for another doctor, Grandpa finds Herman, and sneaks him out, giggling the whole way. When they arrive home, Lily hears them, and thinks Herman is drunk. Grandpa manages to explain, however. Later, Eddie returns home, with his tonsils in a jar – and Herman faints again.

46) Lily's House Guest
(Alternative Title: 'Lily's Star Boarder')
4 November 1965

Written by   Douglas Tibbles
Directed by   Ezra Stone

Cast
Chester Skinner   Charles Bateman
Mr Leonard   Buddy Lewis

The family has decided to let the guest room, despite Herman's tantrums. They have 27 applicants, none of whom even come in, before Chester Skinner accepts the place. He works nights, and has a confidential job. He calls his boss to confirm he's in the house. He's very charming and friendly, and the family takes to him right away – except for Herman, who's very jealous of him. He hasn't even met him, so he stays outside after he supposedly went to work to spy on him. Lily spots him and is furious. That evening, Herman and Grandpa look in Chester's room – and find a gun, cameras and a map of the neighbourhood. They believe he's a gangster.

There's a pair of binoculars on a tripod, looking over Mr Leonard's house. Herman sees he has a lot of furs in his house, and thinks Chester is going to rob him. Lily can't believe his ideas. Actually, Leonard is the crook, and when Herman calls him to warn him, he starts packing to get out. Meanwhile, Grandpa sets a trap for Chester, which works perfectly. Herman then ties him up in the cellar. Then he and Grandpa finally realize that Chester is a policeman, watching Leonard. They have to tell Lily, and she sets Chester free. Herman and Grandpa make up for their error – they set Spot loose, and he jumps on Leonard's car and they catch the gang.

47) Herman's Amnesia
(Alternative Title: 'John Doe Munster')
11 November 1965

Written by   Richard Baer
Directed by   Earl Bellamy

Cast
Desk Sergeant   Frank Maxwell
The Judge   Willis Bouchey
The Bailiff   Olan Soule
1st Workman   Barry O'Hara

2nd Workman	Peter Dawson
Police Officer	Joe Quinn
1st Child	Michael Blake
2nd Child	Monica Bush

Herman is shopping when he's hit on the head by a falling safe. The workmen think he's been badly injured, but he's just lost his memory. The family is worrying when they see a police message of a John Doe – Herman. Lily and Grandpa go to claim him, but he doesn't recognize them. The police need a court order to release him, so Lily has to apply to adopt Herman. The judge initially thinks he's on *Candid Camera*, but agrees to the adoption finally. Herman is happy, and enjoys playing with Eddie. He's having so much fun that Grandpa wonders if he's somehow faking it. The family tries to jog his memory back, but after ten days they've seen no change. Marilyn suggests they hit him on the head again, which always seems to work in the movies. Grandpa has a better idea – make him jealous of a suitor for Lily. Maybe the shock will make him recover. He takes a pill to become the film-star suitor, and ends up as Rudolph Valentino, complete with whip. Herman isn't in the slightest bit jealous, so that plan falls through. Then Eddie tries flying his kite from the roof. Herman, worried about Eddie, reverts to normal, catching him as he falls. He's recovered, but Grandpa still has a problem getting back to normal. The pills are all unlabelled, and he's now changed into a French noble . . .

The Judge in this story was played by Willis Bouchey, familiar to most viewers as one of the more frequent judges hearing cases in *Perry Mason*.

48) Prince Charming
(Alternative Title: 'The Man For Marilyn')
18 November 1965

Written by	James Allardice and
	Tom Adair
Directed by	Ezra Stone

Cast

Ted Bradley	Roger Perry
Frank Colson	Don Edmonds
Al	Dick Wilson
Harry	Dave Willock
The Boy	Jackie Coogan, Jnr
Linda	Jan Barthel

Marilyn has been to another wedding, and comes home with a boy – who flees when he sees Herman. Everyone thinks it's because of Marilyn's terrible looks, but Grandpa has a plan. He's aiming to turn a frog into Prince Charming for her to marry – a near-sighted frog, so it won't mind Marilyn's looks. Grandpa feeds the frog the potion as a fly, but nothing happens. The family goes to the movies, but Marilyn stays home. She accidentally locks herself in her room. Passing the house is architect Ted Bradley, and Frank. Ted stops to look at the weird house, and hears Marilyn calling for help. He thinks that she's being kept prisoner, and is convinced of it when the family arrives home. He heads off for help. Grandpa and Herman think he's the frog transformed, and capture him, not wanting Marilyn's groom to escape. They tie him up in the dungeon, and go to break the news to Marilyn, who's dressed in bridal black.

   Ted talks Eddie into letting him go as a joke on Grandpa, and he runs off. When Grandpa goes into the dungeon, he finds the frog, and thinks the Prince has changed back.

167

Meanwhile, Ted reports the incident to the police. Al and Harry come to investigate, but are convinced the whole thing is a student prank. They believe that the family are all students in masks playing about, and leave, chuckling. Everyone thinks they were really pleasant. Grandpa gives the frog a double dose of his potion. The next day, Marilyn and her friend Linda see Ted and Frank. Marilyn is offended when Ted calls Herman and Grandpa ugly, and she walks off on him. When Grandpa sees Linda, he thinks his double dose of the potion changed the frog into a girl . . .

49) Herman's Driving Test
25 November 1965

Written by	Dick Conway
Directed by	Ezra Stone

Cast

Charlie Wiggens	Charlie Ruggles
Mr Howell	Irwin Charone
Mr Foster	Francis DeSales

Herman has been promoted to driving the firm's hearse. Lily discovers his driving licence expired 20 years ago, and sends him to take his test again. He flunks it. Grandpa coaches him for his next attempt, which takes him four and a half hours just to complete the written test. Fred Howell takes him on the practical, which Herman does first at high speed, then in reverse. Howell passes him, but Herman is so excited that he backs into Howell's car, and gets his permit torn up.

Grandpa suggests that they go to a small town so he can try again. He selects Groverville, which is just a few houses, and the court. In charge is Charlie Wiggens, a short-sighted, forgetful old man. He initially thinks that Herman and

Grandpa want to get married. When he's corrected, he accidentally sounds the fire alarm, then starts to head out in his capacity as fire chief. They get him back on the case, and he tests Herman. After a drive of about ten feet, he passes Herman – he hates traffic, and won't go any further. Herman goes to work in high spirits, to return driving the hearse – the economy model, pulled by horses.

This episode is brilliant, mainly due to the comedic genius of Charlie Ruggles, playing his role to the hilt, and beyond.

50) Will Success Spoil Herman Munster?
9 December 1965

Teleplay by	Lou Shaw, Joe Connelly and Bob Mosher
Story by	Lou Shaw
Directed by	Ezra Stone

Cast

Dick Willet	Gary Owens
Bill	Frank Evans
The Judge	Nolan Leary

Eddie has been playing with a tape recorder a friend left, and Herman can't resist singing into it, a very idiosyncratic version of 'Dem Bones'. Eddie returns the tape recorder the next day, and Bard's father hears it. He's a disc jockey named Dick Willet, and he decides to give the song a try on his show. The family hear it, and think it sounds almost as bad as Herman singing in the shower. The audience response, however, is terrific, and that station keeps playing it. They offer a five-year contract to the unknown singer, and the family is amazed to discover that it's Herman. He goes in to make the record, which shoots to Number 3 in the charts and the success goes to Herman's head.

He gets a chance to sing on TV, and spends hours getting ready for it. Lily is wondering: 'Will success spoil Herman Munster?' She dreams about him being a big star, making movies, winning Oscars – and getting worse all the time. Finally, he even divorces her in the dream, because his ego demands fresh wives all the time. When she wakes, the family gets together for a council of war, hating the egomaniac Herman has become. Grandpa decides to fix him with batch of Nothin' Muffins – that turn anything good into nothing. Herman is on a diet and won't eat one, so Grandpa fires one down his throat from a cannon. Herman's voice goes all squeaky, and he's forced to cancel the TV show. He's very depressed, so the family explain why they've done it, and he realizes that they were right. He was becoming a monster! He decides it's time to quit showbiz.

51) Spot Is Missing
(Alternative Title: 'Underground Munster')
16 December 1965

Written by	Joe Connelly and
	Bob Mosher
Directed by	Don Richardson

Cast

Mayor Handley	J. Edward McKinley
Ted	Warren Parker
1st Workman	John Mitchum
2nd Workman	Buck Kartalian
1st Reporter	Jimmy Joyce
2nd Reporter	Hoke Howell
The Photographer	Bob Harvey
1st Woman	Helen Kleeb

2nd Woman	Elsie Baker

Grandpa is working on a machine to fix the city elections
and get rid of Mayor Handley. Spot has been bad, and
tracked mud through the house. Herman taps him with a
rolled-up newspaper, and Spot runs away from home. Workers in the sewers report seeing a monster down there, and
the family realize that it's Spot. Marilyn goes to City Hall
to ask for help, and reporters after a story take her to the
Mayor. He thinks it's a plot to embarrass him, and throws
her out. That night, Herman goes down into the sewers
after Spot. In the morning, workmen see him, and panic.
They report back to the Mayor, who's now on the spot. He
decides to use dynamite to get rid of the monsters in the
sewers. Lily and Grandpa hear of it, and dash over, afraid
Herman might get hurt. They arrive as the Mayor drops the
first stick. Herman finds it, and thinks it's the work of a
litterbug – and tosses it back. It plasters the Mayor and
Grandpa. Spot finds Herman and takes him home. The next
day, the Mayor arrives, hoping to win the Munsters' support for the election. Instead, he runs off at full speed when
he sees them, which doesn't surprise Herman – he always
figured the Mayor was shifty. Grandpa tries his voting
machine, but it's a literal washout – it's a converted shower,
and soaks Herman.

52) Morgan's Treasure
(Alternative Title: 'The Treasure Of
Mockingbird Heights')
23 December 1965

Written by	George Tibbles
Directed by	Charles Rondeau

Regulars only

When the lights go out during a storm, Grandpa and Herman head into the dungeon looking for the fuses. What they find instead is a secret chamber, and on the wall the clue: 'Morgan's treasure's in this valley; look behind the noble sally'. Inspired with the thought of a fortune in gold in the house, they check Grandpa's library, and discover that Morgan was in Mockingbird Valley in 1672, and reputedly buried gold there. Grandpa finds a carved salamander on the wall, and behind it a genuine pirate map. They follow it to the yard. They have to take eight paces from an oak – but the oak isn't there. Eddie points to a stump, and they start off. After eight paces, they dig. Eventually, they uncover a box, which is filled with treasure . . . The problem is that Herman and Grandpa get highly suspicious of one another, and start rigging traps to the box. Yelling and screaming, they start feuding. Lily tries to get them back together, without luck. That night, both try sneaking down to the treasure, and end up caught in bear traps – set by Lily. She tells them that the treasure was wrecking their lives, so she gave it away to the rescue mission. Poor once again, Herman and Grandpa make friends again.

53) Eddie And The Bully
(Alternative Title: 'Herman's Peace Offering')
30 December 1965

Written by   Doug Tibbles
Directed by   Ezra Stone

Cast
Mack McGinty   Jackie Minty
Uriah   Bryan O'Byrne
Clyde Thornton   Chet Stratton

Eddie is being picked on at school by bully Mack McGinty.
Grandpa wants him to fight back, but Herman is a devout
believer in pacifism – until a practical joker at work named
Uriah starts picking on him, and it's all Herman can do to
avoid starting a fight.

54) Gambling Fever
(Alternative Title: 'Herman Picks A Winner')
6 January 1966

Written by   Dick Conway
Directed by   Ezra Stone

Cast

Big Roy	Barton MacLane
Lou	Joyce Jameson
Vic	Sammy Shore
Lefty	Charlie Callas
The Announcer	Joe Hernandez

Eddie's been sent home for pitching pennies, so Herman
decides to teach him a lesson about the follies of gambling
– by betting all of Eddie's money on a horse certain to lose.
He's heard of a dry cleaners that also takes bets, and heads
down there to wager on Bluebell. The joint is run by Big
Roy, with his men Vic and Lefty. The horse starts last, but
actually wins, netting Eddie $300. Herman tries again to
lose, this time picking Sad Sam. Again it wins, netting
$14,364. Big Roy thinks Herman has a system, and wants
him to work for them. He uses Lou to get to Herman – but
she demands a big bonus for this. She vamps Herman, and
pretends to have car trouble, so he takes her home. Lily gets
worried when Herman doesn't show up, and Grandpa admits that he's been using magic to make the horses win. He

wants to teach Herman a lesson, since he makes such a big
fuss out of small matters. Herman can't pick a winner to
save his life . . . Big Roy demands a winner from Herman,
so Herman picks Royal Flush. The gang will kill him if it
doesn't win. The next day, Grandpa attempts to track
Herman down. The race is on, and Royal Flush comes in
last, losing Big Roy wads of cash. He and the boys go to
kill Herman. Grandpa slips Herman an anti-gravity pill, so
he can walk down the outside of the building to safety.
They then call the cops, and turn the gang in.

55) Herman, Disfigured
(Alternative Title: 'Just Another Pretty Face')
13 January 1966

Written by   Richard Baer
Directed by   Gene Reynolds

Cast
Dr Dudley   Dom DeLuise

Grandpa has built another mysterious machine in the basement, and Herman can't resist peeking. He turns it on, and
accidentally gets zapped by the artificial lightning. Grandpa
is forced to show the family what has happened – Herman
is disfigured. He looks (shudder) handsome. Herman and
the family are most upset, and have trouble getting ad-
justed. Lily takes Herman to Dr Edward H. Dudley, the
family doctor. He thinks Herman's face is an improvement,
and can't imagine why he wants plastic surgery to change it
back. He says no one would do it. Meanwhile, Grandpa has
found Herman's original blueprints, and feels sure he can
duplicate the original conditions again and restore Herman.
Lily isn't sure, but Herman wants to do it. It sort of works
– Grandpa gets Herman his face back, but he now has a

female body and curls . . . He gets a job as a cocktail waitress, and heads out. There's a storm, and Herman is hit by lightning, which restores his old form back again.

For the 'disfigured' Herman, Fred Gwynne played the role without his usual heavy makeup

56) Indian Herman
(Alternative Title: 'Heap Big Herman")
20 January 1966

Written by	Joe Connelly and Bob Mosher
Directed by	Ezra Stone

Cast

Wonga	Ned Romero
Manikoo	Len Lesser
Powatuma	Felix Locher
The Man	Richard Jury
The Indian Girl	Sally Frei

It's vacation time again, and the family – minus Marilyn, who has tests – is off to Buffalo Valley . . . as usual. Herman's only booked two berths on the train, so they have to double up. A nervous passenger reading a ghost story at night leaps off the train when he sees Lily. The rest of the passengers flee when they see Herman. This leaves them a car to themselves. Herman bores the family to sleep reading them legends about lost Indian tribes. The train stops at Indian Flats, and Herman gets off to look for a magazine. The train leaves without him, so he heads for the nearest village. It's an Indian one, which Herman takes for the lost tribes. Actually, they're just waiting for the tourists to come back, and when they see Herman they have ideas. He looks just like their totem pole Manitoba, so Powatuma decides

175

that Herman must have been sent from the gods. He wants
Herman to marry an Indian girl and bring prosperity to the
tribe. How can Herman refuse? The family has meanwhile
returned to Indian Flats to look for him. Lily is furious
when she sees Herman playing about and ready to get
married. She hauls him off, and the Indians resign themselves to wait longer. Back home, when Herman explains it
was a mock wedding to help the tribe, Lily forgives him.

57) Lily's Beauty Shop
(Alternative Title: 'The Most Beautiful Ghoul
In The World')
28 January 1966

Written by	Ted Bergman
Directed by	Ezra Stone

Cast

Mrs Harkness	Elvia Allman
Mr Holmes	Charles Lane
The Secretary	Adele Claire
Dorothea Harkness	Mary Mitchell

The family receive a special delivery letter from
Transylvania. When Herman hears ticking, he soaks the
package in a pail of water for 20 minutes, only to discover
he's been hearing the clock, not the package. It's a scroll
from Cousin Wolverine's lawyer, saying that their cousin is
dead again, and has left them $10,000. When there is dis-
agreement on what to do with the money, Marilyn suggests
that Herman and Lily both share it equally. Lily uses her
half to open a beauty parlour. She and Marilyn prepare the
old recipes for use, and Mrs Harkness and her daughter are
their first customers. Herman invests his half in an invention of Grandpa's to transmit power by radio waves. The

176

machine works, but they blow all the street lights when they use it. Meanwhile, the Harknesses faint when they see each other – they look like ghouls.

They head straight for their lawyer, Edgar Z. Holmes, to sue. He orders Lily to restore his clients to the way they looked before. Lily can't understand why, but reluctantly agrees. Grandpa, meanwhile, is fined $1,000 for his destruction of municipal property. He then tries to use the machine to power Lily's shop, without telling her. It affects the hair driers, and renders both of the Harknesses bald. They go back to Holmes, who sues for $10,000 in damages. Herman gloats, since he never thought the beauty shop would work, but Grandpa realizes that it was the power machine's fault. The Harknesses turn up, their hair having been restored even better than before overnight. They want to finance Lily's invention now, and not sue her after all. The problem is that Grandpa and Herman, in remorse, have smashed it. When Grandpa tries to rebuild it, it starts growing hair on bowling balls . . .

58) Grandpa's Missing Wife
(Alternative Title: 'Grandpa's Lost Wife')
3 February 1966

Written by   Douglas Tibbles
Directed by   Ezra Stone

Cast
Pamela Thornton   Jane Withers
Clarence   Douglas Evans

Herman is reading *Startling Detective Stories*, when he sees an ad for Grandpa, with $1,000 reward from Pamela Thornton in Sioux City. Herman writes a letter to collect the reward, but Lily insists on talking to Grandpa first. He

177

can't recall ever being in Sioux City, so Herman calls Pamela up. She says that Grandpa is her long-lost husband who ran out on her. They confront Grandpa with this, but he can't remember a wife in Sioux City. Then they find Eddie has been helpful and mailed the letter and Grandpa is in trouble. Pamela shows up, looking for him, and she's boiling mad. She threatens legal action unless Grandpa visits her at her hotel. He goes, aiming to have it out with her, but she is sweet to him, and talks of all their money. Grandpa likes the sound of that, and signs a form for Clarence J. Wedge, her lawyer. Then he goes home to pack, insulting Herman. When he returns to the hotel, Pamela explains that they are not married – she is coming into a big inheritance only if she's married. She found Grandpa's picture in an old magic magazine, and thought he'd be dead. The 'reward' was to convince the courts she was sincere. When he came over, he signed a paper that they were married, and she no longer needs him. They throw him out, and he has to return and apologize to Herman. Herman throws him out, then hears him plotting murder . . . Actually he's just reading the latest issue of *Startling Detective Stories*.

59) Cursed Ring
(Alternative Title: 'The Fregosi Emerald')
10 February 1966

Written by	Richard Baer
Directed by	Ezra Stone

Cast

Henry J. Fregosi	Paul Reed
The Telephone Operator	Louise Glenn
The 1st Secretary	Joan Swift
The 2nd Secretary	Marilyn Bell

It's Marilyn's birthday, and Eddie's given her a ring he found in the attic. Grandpa faints when he sees it – it's the Fregosi Emerald, and it's cursed. Herman refuses to believe in such superstition. Marilyn arrives home from her date with Roger Davis in terrible shape, everything having gone wrong. Herman thinks it was just coincidence, and insists that Lily wear the ring in the morning to prove this. When she does, her oatmeal turns to glue, and her popovers really pop. This stops when she takes off the ring, and she refuses to put it back on. Herman does, determined to prove the curse is nonsense. He's almost brained when the water heater collapses and just misses him. He finds he can't get the ring off, so the family isolate him. Lily suggests that they try to get the curse taken off. Grandpa agrees, but has to track down a Fregosi descendant. He calls Werewolf Junction, Transylvania, where the telephone operator recognizes his famous name and is awe-struck. There's just one Fregosi left, who lives in Detroit – Henry J. Fregosi.

They fly out to see him. His secretaries think they're some odd advertising agents. Fregosi denies even being from Transylvania, until Herman shows him the ring. Then he panics, telling them he has to deny his origins, afraid he'll be exposed and thrown out. He agrees to take the curse off the ring, and takes them into his well-equipped private lab. It's from here that he puts curses on competitor's cars – the last one he really cursed being the Edsel . . . He removes the curse, and the ring falls off Herman's finger. It's now safe for Marilyn to wear it. Back home, Eddie has found the Nathanson Ruby – so cursed that it makes the Fregosi Emerald look like a good-luck charm. Herman accidentally swallows it . . .

60) Zombo
17 February 1966

Written by   Dennis Whitcomb
Directed by   Ezra Stone

Cast
Zombo   Louis Nye
The Director   Digby Wolfe
Frank   Mike Barton
Billy   Jimmy Stiles
Tommy   Jackie Minty

Eddie is watching his favourite show, 'Zombo', about the keeper of a haunted house. Herman is annoyed, because Eddie looks up to Zombo as a real neat guy. Eddie wins a competition, and receives a whole load of prizes, plus a trip to appear on the show. The neighbourhood kids admire Eddie, and form a Zombo fan club, which adds to Herman's irritation. When Marilyn and Lily make a fuss about Zombo's good looks, Herman becomes intolerable. Grandpa gives Herman a secret potion, which makes Herman grow straggly hair, a hump and fangs like Zombo. The kids are not impressed, and Eddie is embarrassed.

On the day of the show, Lily takes Eddie to the studio, while Herman stays home and sulks. Eddie meets the real Zombo, an actor, not the ghoul he expected. He watches in disappointment as he prepares for the show. Marilyn and Grandpa meanwhile force Herman to watch the show. Eddie realizes that Zombo's haunted house is just special effects, and not the real thing, and he's heart-broken. On the air, he pulls off Zombo's wig, and exposes the whole thing as a fake to the viewers. The show is cancelled, and Zombo is happy – he can get out of his stupid contract and go on to act in better things – 'Hamlet' or 'My Mother The Car'.

180

Herman is happy to be Eddie's hero again, but a trifle disappointed to discover Zombo was a fake all along. He's losing his faith in television.

61) Herman Munster, Poet
(Alternative Title: 'Cyrano de Munster')
24 February 1966

Written by	Douglas Tibbles
Directed by	Joseph Pevney

Cast

Clara Mason	Joan Staley
Clyde Thornton	Chet Stratton
Ann Carter	Eileen O'Neill

Lily is painting a picture of Grandpa, while Herman composes poetry for the 'Morticians' Monthly'. Clyde, one of Herman's co-workers, is shy around girls, and he admires Herman's poetry. He asks Herman to write him a love letter to win the heart of a girl he fancies, and Herman agrees. Despite Grandpa's warning, Herman composes several drafts, and then gives the final one to Clyde. Lily discovers one of the early drafts, and gets annoyed, thinking Herman is writing the letter for himself. Clyde has meanwhile got his date with Clara, but she wants to hear more of his poetry. He has Herman sneak in to feed him lines. When it works, he tells Herman to go home. Then Clara wants another poem, and Clyde has to tell her the truth. Struck by the beauty of Herman's poetry, Clara is convinced that he must be the man for her. Meanwhile, Lily goes to see Clyde, to check up that Herman was telling Grandpa the truth. Herman – not having seen Clara – thinks that Lily is the girl he's been helping Clyde to woo. Lily and Clyde both think that Herman is making time with Clara, and rush

181

back to confront him. Clara arrives just before them, and goes to throw herself into her sensitive lover's arms. When she sees Herman, though, she screams and runs. Eventually, everything is explained, and Lily confesses that she actually liked some of Herman's poems.

62) Tone Deaf Eddie
(Alternative Title: 'The Musician')
3 March 1966

Written by	Richard Baer
Directed by	Ezra Stone

Cast

Mr Gateman	John Carradine

Herman discovers that Mr Gateman is fond of music, so he hits on a scheme to get a raise: he'll have Eddie become a musical prodigy and impress the boss! The problem is that Eddie is dreadful on every instrument he attempts, driving the family to distraction and Grandpa to his basement to whip up a potion to cure his troubles.

63) Missing Link Munster
(Alternative Title: 'Prehistoric Munster')
10 March 1966

Written by	Douglas Tibbles
Directed by	Joseph Pevney

Cast

Professor Fagenspahen	Harvey Korman
Professor Hansen	George Petrie
The Young Doctor	Richard Poston

Eddie enters Herman in the 'Father of the Year' contest, which Herman is convinced he will win. Marilyn has Herman model for a clay sculpture for her art class, which does nothing to lessen Herman's ego. When her teacher, Professor Fagenspahen, sees the result, he's astounded, thinking it's her idea of primitive man. She tells him that it's her uncle, and he goes to see Hansen in Anthropology, and the pair of them invite Herman to the school, aiming to exploit him for fame and money. Herman thinks the invitation is for the 'Father of the Year' contest, and goes along. He's a bit puzzled when the two lecturers have a doctor examine him, but they play along with his delusion, privately gloating over their rediscovery of prehistoric man. Meanwhile, Eddie discovers that a Mr Jordan has won the 'Father of the Year' contest, and thinks it's because he sent in his entry too late. When Herman arrives home again, he throws a tantrum when he finds out he hasn't won. Everyone wonders who the people were that interviewed Herman. The next day, they find out – the papers report the firing of three Professors attempting to pass off Herman as the missing link. The family think it failed because no one could believe such a handsome figure as Herman could be a monster. In fact, the University thought no one like that could possibly exist!

64) Johan
(Alternative Title: 'A Visit From Johan')
17 March 1966

Written by   Joe Connelly and
                        Bob Mosher

Directed by   Gene Reynolds

Cast
Dr Frankenstein IV   John Abbott

| The Motel Manager | Forrest Lewis |
| The Manager's Wife | Helen Kleeb |

The great-grandson of Dr Frankenstein is visiting the US with Johan – a double for Herman. He calls Herman to drop by. Herman does, greeting him with: 'Dr Frankenstein, I presume?' Frankenstein shows him Johan, and asks him to keep quiet about the creature. He was one of the original Frankenstein's less-successful pilot models before he built Herman. Johan's been living in the woods since 1815, and is imperfected, unpolished. The Doctor asks Herman to take Johan home and teach him how to live in polite society. Herman agrees, and he and Grandpa secrete Johan in the dungeon, and attempt to teach him to talk. Meanwhile, Lily is getting ready to go away for the weekend with Herman. While Herman is out, Johan escapes, and Lily thinks he's Herman, with laryngitis, and takes him off for their romantic vacation.

When Herman returns, Grandpa thinks he's Johan at first. Then the truth dawns. Grandpa calls up Lily, who thinks he's just joking, and trying to spoil Herman's weekend. Herman and Grandpa visit Frankenstein, who exerts his telepathic control over Johan to bring him back to his hotel room. Lily follows, and freaks out when she sees two Hermans. Dr Frankenstein explains, and thanks them for their troubles. He's decided to take Johan back to a private tutor in Germany with him. Once he's gone, Herman settles down to finish his 1st grade reader – he wants to see how the story will end . . . Lily wonders if they've been left the wrong monster, but Grandpa thinks there's no real difference between them anyhow.

65) Boris The Robot
(Alternative Title: 'Eddie's Brother')
24 March 1966

Written by   Dick Conway
Directed by   Ezra Stone

Cast
Boris The Robot   Rory Stevens
Sally   Wendy Kottler

Eddie wants a baby brother to play with, a thought that makes Herman and Lily faint. Herman decides Eddie wants companionship, and tries to be his pal. He (naturally) fails rather miserably. Eddie still wants a baby brother. Grandpa suggests a subtle hint for Lily – putting out Eddie's old baby clothes. Herman can't find them, but finds his own. When Lily comes in, Herman's dressed in his old bonnet, with his rattle. She thinks he's going into second childhood. When Herman explains, she tells him that having another baby won't help – by the time he's old enough for Eddie to play with, Eddie will be too old to play. Grandpa has worked on a solution – he's built a robot playmate for Eddie, Boris.

Boris is very helpful and popular. He even likes Herman's awful jokes. Eddie resents him, and is very jealous, so he runs away. Herman uses Spot to track Eddie down, and he's hiding up a tree. Eddie tries to explain to Herman how he feels, and Boris overhears. Feeling he's splitting up the family, Boris decides to leave. Eddie apologizes, and they make up. Boris finally leaves to live with the Munsters' relatives in Death Valley. Eddie gets a new friend at school – a weird kid named Sally, who loves bugs and icky things.

66) Fair Deal Dan
(Alternative Title: 'Herman The Tire Kicker')
31 March 1966

Written by	James Allardine and
	Tom Adair
Directed by	Ezra Stone

Cast

Fair Deal Dan	Frank Gorshin
Corbett	Rian Garrick
Blinky	Johnny Silvers
Spangler	Pat McCaffrie
Sgt. Stockwell	Dennis Cross
Beasley	Jimmy Cross
1st Drunk	Saul Gorss
2nd Drunk	Jack Perkins
3rd Drunk	Fred Carson
The Driver	Jack Wilson

Marilyn has to spend ages getting to college on the bus, so Herman decides to spend his bonus on a car for her. He visits Fair Deal Dan's, where the cars are in terrible shape – especially when Herman has kicked the tyres. Dan cons him into looking at a convertible by making him think he can't have it. As soon as he drives off in it, Dan and his men pack up the place and leave, fast. Back home, the car falls apart on Herman. Lily makes him take it back, and Grandpa goes along for moral support. What they don't know is that the police have the car listed as stolen.

The lot is empty when they arrive, but they are stopped by police officers. Grandpa turns into a bat and flies off. The police think Herman is drunk, and arrest him. He's allowed to call home, but has forgotten the number. He's tossed in jail with the drunks, who immediately swear off the booze. Lily and the family turn up to bail him out, and he spots Fair Deal Dan, who's been brought in for being drunk. He sees Herman, and confesses to everything, thinking Herman is out to get him. Herman gets his money back, and puts it in a college fund for Eddie. Marilyn no longer needs a car – she gets rides both ways from the police now . . .

67) A House Divided
7 April 1966

Written by   Dick Conway
Directed by   Ezra Stone

Regulars only

Eddie's birthday is coming up, so Herman and Grandpa hide out in the garage to make him a present. Eddie tries to sneak a peek, but falls into a trap they've dug. They continue like this for a while, and Lily gets annoyed. She goes to tell them off, and is caught in another trap. That doesn't improve her mood. They've been building a go-cart, which Herman then tests. He can't control it, and crashes. Grandpa is furious, and the two of them have a blazing row. Herman is so annoyed that he paints a white line down the middle of the house, and both men are to stay on their own side of it. Eddie is puzzled, and Lily and Marilyn are annoyed at the pettiness of the males. The phone, for example, is on Herman's side, and he cuts the cord rather than let Grandpa use it. Even Spot is divided, though Herman is unhappy about the fact that he's got the half that eats.

Lily decides to fight back, and she marks the table into portions – with Herman and Grandpa getting the parts that have no food on them. Neither of the men will give in first, and set about making their own food instead. On the night before his birthday, Eddie goes to bed. Lily has had enough,

187

and orders both Grandpa and Herman to work together on a present for Eddie – or else. With no option, they work together, and build him a soap-box aeroplane. Eddie is disappointed, until he discovers that it can really fly. Herman and Grandpa then head back to the garage and fall into the traps that they set themselves. The girls won't let them out until they promise to make up and behave. Herman then has the task of erasing the line he's painted . . .

68) Fraternity House
(Alternative Title: 'Herman's Sorority Caper')
14 April 1966

Written by	Douglas Tibbles
Directed by	Ezra Stone

Cast

Phil	David Macklin
Jim	Michael Blodgett
John	Ken Osmond
1st Girl	Vicki Fee
Janice	Bonnie Franklin
Cindy	Vicki Draves
2nd Girl	Hedy Scott
Campus Policeman	Mike Ross
Janitor	William Fawcett
Ralph	Frank Gardner

Students aim to use the Munster House for a freshers' initiation, thinking it's abandoned. Herman has developed hiccups, wrecking the place. When nothing else works, Grandpa uses the Transylvanian brain freezer on him. It pole-axes Herman, and turns him into a statue. That night, two students arrive, and think that the family – all fast asleep – are props rigged to scare them. John decides that they should take Herman and place him in the hall of residence for a joke. In the morning, the family discover Herman is missing. Grandpa reluctantly wakes him from his trance. Herman can't understand how he got there, but he's horrified to discover he's in a girl's wardrobe on campus . . . He keeps hiding from the various girls, terrified of what they'll do to him if they find him. He calls home, and Grandpa sets out to help him. He flies out as a bat, scaring the girls long enough for Herman to sneak out. When the caretaker and policeman arrive, Grandpa has reverted again, and is arrested as a lunatic. Later, he's back home, and Herman starts hiccupping again . . .

Lily: 'Herman has a very mechanical brain. In fact, I think it used to belong to an old mechanic.'

Guest star Bonnie Franklin later went on to star in *One Day At A Time* (1975–84), and also to direct episodes of *The Munsters Today*.

69) Herman's Car Crash
(Alternative Title: 'Herman's Lawsuit')
21 April 1966

Written by   Douglas Tibbles, Joe
                                Connelly and Bob Mosher
Directed by   Ezra Stone

Cast
Marge Kingsley   Dorothy Green
Ted Thatcher   Jerome Cowan
The Movie Director   Monroe Arnold
Wilbur Kingsley   Simon Scott
The Legionnaire Captain   Than Wyenn
The Foreman   Fabian Dean
The Man   Eddie Marr
The Customer   Bob Harvey

189

Herman is crossing the street when he is hit by a car driven by Marge Kingsley. He faints when he sees the damage he's done. She thinks he's badly injured, and goes for an ambulance. He thinks she's gone for the police, and rushes home to tell the family. She finds his licence, and her husband decides they'd best have their lawyer, Thatcher, offer Herman $10,000 to settle out of court. Herman receives the letter, but thinks that they want him to pay them $10,000, which he cannot afford. When Herman doesn't reply, Thatcher visits the family. He's astonished by the place, and thinks they are poverty stricken. Lily tells him that Herman is 'down at the mortuary, getting an estimate'. He thinks she means he's on death's door, when actually she means he's pricing the building of a new wing. She tells him that $10,000 is out of the question, so he calls Kingsley and suggests he raise the amount to $20,000, fast.

Herman again thinks he has to pay, and panics – he runs away from home. He tries to find a new job, but is fired from the steel mill after dropping hundreds of pounds of ingots through the floor. His next attempt is as a target in a fairground for people to throw balls at. The balls bounce off his head, though, with such force that they knock the customers out. Grandpa tracks him in his crystal ball, and sees him joining the Foreign Legion. They race out, just as he's about to be shot for cowardice. They don't realize it's just a film set until they manage to get him fired. They explain that the whole affair with the money has been settled, and he comes home with them again.

70) An Average American Family
(Alternative Title: 'A Visit From The Teacher')
12 May 1966

Written by   Joe Connelly and
                                   Bob Mosher

Directed by   Ezra Stone

Cast
Mr Bradley   Willis Bouchey
Miss Thompson   Pat Woodell

Herman is fixing the toaster as Grandpa starts up his new invention – a machine to generate electricity to power the house. It zaps Herman. Eddie is working on a school assignment, a paper about his parents, 'the average American family'. Grandpa's project needs a few problems ironed out, but Eddie at least finishes his task. When he reads it at school, his teacher, Miss Thompson, has him read it to the principal, Mr Bradley. Neither can believe the weird things Eddie has written, and they think he has problems at home. They decide to visit the family to discuss Eddie's problems.

They're astonished at the state of the house, and the vulture in the garden. They think that Lily is green due to malnutrition. Grandpa pops up to say hello, then returns to his experiments. As the teachers are discussing Eddie's composition, Grandpa blows the lights. Herman arrives home, and Miss Thompson and Bradley just see a hulking shape, and have had enough. They try to leave, but take a wrong turn and end up in the coffin phone booth. When the lights come on, they both see Herman for the first time, and take a very polite and nervous leave. After that, they leave Eddie alone. Grandpa gives up with his electrical experiments, and starts working on the water supply. He manages to create one – but it comes via the electrical wiring . . .

Munster, Go Home!

1966

The Munsters was proving to be a huge hit on TV during the first season, and the decision was made to produce a full-length movie based on the characters, which would be aired on TV. The big difference – aside from the length – was that it would be shot in colour, rather than black and white. At the last minute, however, the decision was made to switch the film to the cinema, since it was felt that it was possible to capitalize on the success of the show. In many of the markets abroad, the series had no airing, so the film didn't do very good business. Even in the US, where the show was hot for its first season, the film played to less than packed houses. The general feeling seemed to be that the show didn't translate well to the screen. One problem had to be that the movie looked like it had been filmed on a TV budget on the backlot – which it had.

Written by	George Tibbles, Joe Connelly and Bob Mosher
Directed by	Earl Bellamy
Music	Jack Marshall
Produced by	Joe Connelly and Bob Mosher
Director of Photography	Benjamin H. Kline, ASC
Art Directors	Alexander Golitzen and John Lloyd
Set Decorators	John McCarthy and Julia Heron
Sound	Waldon O. Watson and Corson Jowett
Unit Production Manager	James H. Hogan
Film Editor	Bud S. Isaacs

Makeup	Bud Westmore
Hair Stylist	Larry Germain
Costumes	Grady Hunt
Assistant Director	Dolph Zimmer
Stunt Co-ordinator	Carey Loftin
Matte Supervisor	Albert Whitlock
Associate Producer	Irving Paley
Assistant to Producers	Keith Vincent

Cast

Herman Munster	Fred Gwynne
Lily Munster	Yvonne de Carlo
Grandpa	Al Lewis
Eddie	Butch Patrick
Marilyn	Debbie Watson
Freddie	Terry-Thomas
Lady Effigie	Hermione Gingold
Roger	Robert Pine
Cruickshanks	John Carradine
Squire Moresby	Bernard Fox
Joey	Richard Dawson
Grace	Jean Arnold
Millie	Maria Lennard
Herbert	Cliff Norton
Mrs Moresby	Diana Chesney
Alfie	Arthur Malet
Hennesy	Ben Wright

Herman's Uncle Cavanaugh, the 4th Earl of Shroudshire, has died and left everything to Herman – the new Lord, and inheritor of Munster Hall. The family heads for England, but Herman is terribly seasick. Marilyn meets a British racing driver, Roger, and they start a romance. In England, Lady Effigie Munster and her two children aren't taking the news well. Freddie, the spoilt, homicidal son, wants to be

193

Lord Munster, and the daughter, Grace, wishes the Munsters dead. Lady Effigie has contacted the mysterious Griffin for instructions, and Griffin suggests scaring them away. They plan this with the aid of the battered old butler, Cruickshanks. Freddie has started things his way – he's sent Herman a basket of fruit with a bomb in it. Lily throws it overboard, thinking there are loud worms in the fruit. Grandpa accidentally takes a wolf pill instead of a seasickness pill, and changes. He's caught and locked in quarantine – and it's six months for pets in England.

Herman recovers from the seasickness, and Lily sends him to set Grandpa free. Roger is romancing Marilyn when he sees Herman and panics. She thinks Roger's making up stories of monsters to avoid a shipboard romance. Herman frees Grandpa, and the wolf changes back to his 'normal' form. When the boat docks, they head for Shroudshire. The local pub contains Millie, the barmaid, Hennesy, the owner and one-time stablehand at the Hall, and Alfie and Joey, two handymen who pick up coffin-sized boxes from the Hall regularly. Grandpa asks directions to the Hall, and the family finishes the trip. That night, Lady Effigie tries the scare tactics, but the spooks and noises just make them all feel at home. Freddie, on the other hand, panics when he sees his new relatives.

Freddie and Grace think they should kill the newcomers, but Lady Effigie is sticking to the Griffin's plans. Squire Moresby, in the pub, suggests that all the Munster family should be shot. On his way home, he and Marilyn collide. She apologises, and he takes her home to meet his son – Roger again. The romance starts up again. Meanwhile, everyone finds out that the local road race is a grudge match between the Moresby and Munster families. When the Squire discovers Marilyn is a Munster, he orders her out of his house. Meanwhile, the rest of the family discovers that the locals hate the Munster family, and fear the Hall

– but why? That night, Herman and Grandpa investigate. They discover a secret passage, and a counterfeiting press. Alfie and Joey arrive for their latest shipment of money, but are scared off. Herman, wanting the police, yells: 'Car 54, where are you?'

He tells Lady Effigie, who promises to contact the authorities – but since she's the head forger, naturally she does nothing of the sort. The Griffin aims to kill Herman in the race, and to make it look like Roger's doing. Herman loves the idea of entering the race for the family's honour, but crashes his car on the first attempt. Grandpa builds a new one from spare parts and a coffin. Herman sets off for the race, and Marilyn takes Eddie along to watch. Lily and Grandpa discover that there's a plot to kill Herman, but they are caught by Freddie and tied up in the secret tunnels. They escape when Alfie and Joey arrive for the boxes – which contain not money but two vampires . . . The race is going crazy, since the Griffin has knocked out Roger and taken his place. Herman thinks that he's subject to a lot of accidents, but they are attempts by the Griffin to kill him. Despite everything, though, Herman wins the race, and goes to collect his prize. The Griffin tries to run him down, but the car smashes on contact with Herman. The Griffin is dazed, and unmasked by the police – as Millie, the barmaid. She's actually Cruickshanks' daughter, and has been promised she can be Lady Munster when Freddie inherits. Freddie, Grace, Lady Effigie and Cruickshanks are all also arrested. Herman and the others are homesick for America, so they decide to go home, and donate the Hall to the public. Roger decides he'll make sure he does more racing in America from now on, and kisses Marilyn a lingering goodbye.

This movie was originally shot as a TV film, but released to the cinema instead when it was seen how well other made-for-TV films were doing there – notably the spin-offs from *The Man From UNCLE*. It is the only time that we see what the family looked like in colour. Despite being ostensibly set in England, it was (naturally) filmed on the backlot at Universal Studios. The only concessions made to the English were in the casting.

Terry-Thomas was spending a good deal of time in the US at this point, capitalizing on playing British cads and bounders in films like *It's A Mad, Mad, Mad, Mad World* (1963). Hermione Gingold appeared in *Gigi* and *Bell, Book And Candle* (both 1958) among her numerous films. Robert Pine was a regular on *CHiPs* (1977–83).

The Munsters' Revenge

(1981) TV

Written by	Arthur Alsberg and Don Nelson
Directed by	Don Weis
Executive Producer	Edward J. Montagne
Co-Producers	Don Nelson and Arthur Alsberg
Director of Photography	Harry L. Wolf, ASC
Art Director	James Martin Bachman
Film Editor	Frederic W. Barrata, ACE
Based on Characters developed by	Norm Liebmann and Ed Haas
From a Format by	Al Burns and Chris Hayward
Music	Vic Mizzy
Set Decorator	Morey Hoffman
Sound Recordist	Coye Vanover
Casting	Joe Reich

Cast

Herman	Fred Gwynne

Grandpa	Al Lewis
Lily	Yvonne de Carlo
Eddie	K.C. Martel
Marilyn	Jo McDonnell
Cousin Phantom of the Opera	Bob Hastings
Glen Boyle	Peter Fox
Dr Diablo	Sid Caesar
Igor	Howard Morris
Chief Boyle	Herbert Voland
Commissioner McCluskey	Charles Macaulay
Michael	Colby Chester
Pizza Man	Joseph Ruskin
Dr Lichtliter	Ezra Stone
Ralph	Michael McManus
Patrolman Pete	Sandy-Alexander Champion
Patrolman Larry	Gary Vinson
Shorty	Billy Sands
Warren Thurston	Barry Pearl
Prisoner	Al White
Slim	Tom Newman
Elvira	Anita Dangler
Mrs Furnstrom	Dolores Mann
The Girl	Hilary Horan
The Boy	Kenny Rhodes
Loader #2	Read Morgan
Loader #1	Mickey Deems

The family is visiting the waxworks museum, and discover that they're in there also. After closing time, though, the waxworks come to life. They're really robots, built by Dr Lichtliter and Ralph for their boss, Dr Diablo. The robots go on a crime wave, stealing items for Diablo's masterplan. Naturally, the police think that the robots of Herman and Grandpa are the real people, and they are arrested by Chief

Boyle. His son, Glen, thinks they might be innocent – especially since he's smitten with Marilyn. Herman accidentally breaks himself and Grandpa out of jail, and they head for the waxworks. There they see Michael and Ralph bring the dummies to life, and they substitute themselves for their robots.

Diablo has the robots run to the pizza parlour, where they hand over a fortune to the owner. Grandpa and Herman tip Glen off, and he leads a raid on the museum. Diablo manages to hide all of the evidence, though, and no one believes Glen. Grandpa and Herman dress as waitresses 'Estelle' and 'Marie' to work in the pizza parlour. They see the owner buying blueprints, which he then takes on to Diablo. Glen attempts to arrest Herman, but a couple of customers come to his rescue, thinking Glen is fresh. Grandpa and Herman head for the museum, where they are mistaken for their own robots again. Diablo now explains his plan – the National Gallery is holding a Halloween Party, and his robots will attend and steal the treasures of the mummy. He says he's the mummy's brother, and he wants the amulet it wears to seal his claim to the throne.

Grandpa has an idea – he wants to bring the mummy to life, using his revitalizing potion. Glen arrests them, though, and Grandpa has to change to a bat to escape with Herman. They make it to Transylvania, and find the old castle, guarded by Igor. The villagers are aiming to burn the place down, and in his panic, Igor collapses and dies. Grandpa tests the potion on him, and it works. It even makes him handsome, and he defects to the villagers' side. Meanwhile, Marilyn and Glen attempt to sneak into the waxworks to find proof that Herman and Grandpa are innocent. They are caught, and placed under a big belljar to suffocate to death. Herman and Grandpa return home, and learn that Marilyn is missing. Grandpa heads for the National Gallery to bring the mummy to life, while Herman and Cousin Phantom of the Opera head out to find Marilyn. Phantom's glass-shattering voice saves the suffocating pair, and Herman and Glen head for the Gallery. Marilyn steals the robot controller, and stops them working. Diablo tries to grab the necklace, but the mummy grabs him. It's not a mummy, but Herman. Grandpa's potion made the mummy into a baby! Having cleared their names, the Munsters can return home for their favourite holiday – Halloween!

This was a very unsuccessful attempt to revive the old series, proving to be another ratings flop. It had taken a great deal to persuade Fred Gwynne to return. He felt that his career had suffered as a result of doing the role, and he'd struggled hard to overcome this. To return to the part might wash away all he'd accomplished. On the other hand, he wasn't working so much anyway, so eventually he gave in and agreed.

The script wasn't exactly compelling, and seemed to suffer most from a confusion about whether the story was for *The Munsters* or *The Addams Family*. Writers/producers Arthur Alsberg and Don Nelson are best known for *Bridget Loves Bernie* (1972–73), an amiable sitcom. Executive Producer Edward Montagne's TV credits stretch back to *Man Against Crime* (1949–56), and his comedy experiences include *McHale's Navy* (1962–66) and *The Misadventures Of Sheriff Lobo* (1979–81).

Guest star Sid Caesar is a true legend of American TV, with his *Your Show Of Shows* (1950–54) being one of the best-loved series ever produced. His career faded considerably in the late sixties and he was reduced to making guest shots in nostalgia-driven shows such as this.

The Munsters Today

Twenty years after the original series finished, Universal decided that an updated version was a viable proposition. They 'explained' in the opening credits of the new show that (for no apparent reason) the Munsters went into suspended animation for twenty years after the original show in a machine Grandpa invented, and have now returned. (They obviously ignored *The Munsters' Revenge*, pretty much as everyone else tried to do.) The show was produced strictly as a videotaped stage production to keep costs down, and by a company experienced at low-budget work (they had produced a fourth season of *Airwolf*, for example, when the network cancelled the show to make up sufficient episodes to allow the series to enter syndication).

John Schuck was tapped as the new Herman. He was best known then for his witless Sgt Enright role on *McMilland And Wife* (1971–77) and later as the robot half of *Holmes And Yoyo* (1976). He has since appeared as a Klingon ambassador in *Star Trek IV* and *Star Trek VI*. 'When I was first called about this part, I recoiled', he admitted to *TV Guide* (27 August 1988). He then agreed to the part, provided that he didn't have to wear all the heavy makeup that Fred Gwynne had suffered through. The producers agreed, making him a less monstrous Herman. 'I'm a lot more user-friendly', he joked.

Taking the role of Lily was Lee Meriwether. She was best known from her role in *Barnaby Jones* (1973–78) and *The Time Tunnel* (1966–67), but she was Miss America in 1955 (she used her winnings to take acting lessons) and also played Catwoman in the *Batman* show. Jason Marsden, the new Eddie, has made a career out of playing obnoxious kids, notably on *Eerie, Indiana* (1992–93). Hilary van Dyke is the niece of actor Dick van Dyke. Howard Morton is best known from *Gimme A Break* (1981–86).

Season One

Credits

Produced by	Lloyd J. Schwartz (to episode 9, 21), Bryan Joseph (from episode 10)
Supervising Producer	Patricia Foss Palmer
Executive Producer	Arthur Annecharico
Executive Story Editors	Ann L. Gibbs, Joel Kimmel
Executive Story Consultant	Bryan Joseph (to episode 9, 20)
Story Editors	Bill Rosenthal, Noah Taft (to episode 8, 10, 20)
Associate Producer	Dustin Nelson
Art Director	Richard Johnson, Jimmy Cuomo
Casting	Kim Dorr, CSA
Based on Characters developed by	Norm Liebman and Ed Haas
From a Format by	Al Burns and Chris Hayward
Original Theme Music	Jack Marshall
Theme Song Arrangement and Original Music	Wintermoon Music
Additional Scoring	L.A. Arpino, Bill Fulton (episode 14 on)
Associate Director	Susan Straughn Harris, Cindi Annecharico, Don Sullivan
Stage Managers	John Marsh, Jerry Sarcone,

	Chris St. Marie, Garrett Cohen, Sean McNamara, Deborah Jones, Stephen Goepel
Booth P.A.	Bonnie Morley
Lighting Director	Dan Kuleto
Special Effects	Chris Hill, Jim Rudenski, Rick Rakowski, Ted Haler
Post Production Manager	Tom Buel
Property Manager	Bill Lawrence
Assistant Property Manager	Patty Schmidt, Carol Canada
Set Decorator	Debbie Madalena
Costume Designer	Valeria Watson
Costume Assistant	Robin Bell, Sharon Pencille, Nancy Hubbard
Makeup Design	Larry Abbott, SMA
Makeup Artists	David Abbott, Gil Mosko, Robert Scribner
Prosthetics and Makeup	Bill Munns (episode 23)
Hair Stylist	Debbie Stein (to episode 22); Jaklin Muns (episode 23)
Technical Director	Cliff Miracle, Sam Orender, Dave Buchanan
Audio	Bill Kennedy III, Miles Weiner, Ira Leslie
Senior Video	Bobby DaSilva, Roy Fusco, Randi Johnson, James Malone, Andy Dickerman, George Palmer, Bob Vinson, Ross Elliott
Camera	Steve Casaly, Victor Gonzales, Lee Rizor, Greg

	Grouwinkle, Dave Heckman, Gary Sager, Joe Bertschi, Ed Nelson, Tom Faigh, Lee Grover, Doug Ritt, Malcolm Bhone, Don Davis, Lewis Friant, Phil Neely
Engineering Supervisor	Dave Radford, Jim Rudenski
Editor	Craig Anderson
Assistant Post Audio Supervisor	Steve W. Barton
Rerecording Engineer	Michael E. Lawshe, Lisa Arpino, Bill Fulton, Jnr
Production and Post Production Facilities	The Arthur Company's 'One Take' and 'The Last Stop'
Shot on Location at	Hollywood Center Studios
Executive in Charge of Production	Mike Fierman
The Arthur Company	
MCA TV	

Cast

Herman	John Schuck
Lily	Lee Meriwether
Eddie	Jason Marsden
Marilyn	Hilary van Dyke
Grandpa	Howard Morton

Note: As the series was syndicated, the episodes were not shown in the same order or on the same date in all markets. The dates given here are for the first airing in New York. None of the episodes carried on air titles.

Episode 1
8 October 1988

Written by   Barbara Berkowitz
Directed by   Norman Abbott

Cast

Dee Dee Nelson	Mary Cadorette
Dustin Nelson	Scott Reeves

Marilyn has fallen for a boy at school, Dustin Nelson. His mother, Dee Dee, is to judge the Mockingbird Heights cookery contest. Herman decides to enter this, but first he has to learn to cook. The family is not looking forward to tasting his attempts, but Lily braves it. His soup sticks her mouth together. Even Herman realizes he's a lousy cook. Grandpa suggests using Momma Medusa's Transylvania Surprise recipe, which even Herman can't foul up. For once, Grandpa's right, and it tastes perfect. Grandpa has this nagging feeling he's forgotten something, though. Herman enters the contest, and a rather frazzled Dee Dee tries his recipe, and is astonished at how good it tastes. Grandpa has finally remembered what it was he'd forgotten – the cake turns people into ducks, unless they drink bats' milk. Dee Dee changes into a duck, and they have to give her the milk to change her back. Dustin and Marilyn meanwhile hit it off together rather well.

Dustin Nelson is actually the name of the show's associate producer. Director Norman Abbott directed a number of episodes for the original show. Mary Cadorette was a regular on *Three's A Crowd* (1984–85), the American version of *Robin's Nest*.

Episode 2
15 October 1988

Written by   Lloyd J. Schwartz and
                                       Hope Juber

Directed by   Dick Harwood

Cast

Svetlana Rambova   Natasha Pavlova

Grandpa has won three wishes in the Transylvanian sweep-stakes, but doesn't know what to use them on. He misses dinner while he's thinking, and becomes hungry. He wishes he had a tarantula burger and Russian dressing. The first two wishes come true – he gets his burger and a young Russian girl, who is getting dressed. She's Svetlana Rambova from Kiev, and wants to go home. He tries to hide her, but is detected by Lily. Grandpa claims she's his fiancée, a belly dancer, which Herman likes the sound of. While Grandpa is thinking of a way to get her home, Lily discovers the truth. She makes Grandpa realize that he's got to use his last wish to return Svetlana home, which he does.

Episode 3
22 October 1988

Written by   Bryan Joseph
Directed by   Bob Claver

Cast

Headlock Henderson   Daniel Riordan

Eddie is being bullied at school by Butch Henderson. Lily and Herman advise him to talk to Butch about it, and try to straighten out the problem. This gets Eddie a black eye, so he asks Grandpa for help. Grandpa makes a potion to give him super-strength. Eddie then tosses Butch onto the school roof. Butch's older brother, Headlock Henderson, is a weight-lifting contender, and comes to see Eddie – to thank him for showing Butch that bullying doesn't pay. Eddie starts getting big-headed about the strength, and decides to cream Headlock in the weight-lifting contests. Herman and Lily try to make him realize this is wrong, but he insists. On the day of the contest, the strength potion will run out in 30 minutes. Eddie overhears Headlock talking to his brother about how much training he's done, and how he's worked all his life for this competition. Feeling guilty for his ego problems, Eddie deliberately blows the contest so Headlock wins. Having learned his lesson, Eddie returns to school – only to come home with another black eye . . . from a girl . . .

Episode 4
29 October 1988

Written by	Adele Styler and
	Burt Styler
Directed by	Peter Isacksen

Cast

| Howie Buchanan | Richard Horvitz |
| Miss Foster | Vernee Watson-Johnson |

Miss Foster, Eddie's teacher, calls Lily in to see her. She thinks Eddie is weird, and needs help. Lily thinks it's Eddie's spelling. Miss Foster thinks Lily is from California. Meanwhile, Marilyn has decided she wants to be a film director, and make a movie with the family in it. They all have their own ideas about it, which annoys her. Miss Foster gives

Eddie a psychological test, and Herman goes along as well. He can't keep his mouth shut, and he fails the test. Back home, Howie Buchanan, a school friend of Marilyn's, arrives with his video camera to shoot the film. He starts freaking out in the house, especially when he finds that Grandpa won't photograph. Nevertheless, they start making the film, a spoof of 'Star Wars'. Miss Foster arrives as they're finishing, and thinks this is why Eddie was acting odd – he was getting into his role for the film. Miss Foster is impressed with the family togetherness. When they watch the film, though, Howie was so nervous, he shot it all in fast motion, and they fairly zip through their lines.

Episode 5
6 November 1988

Written by	Bill Rosenthal and Noah Taft
Directed by	Peter Isacksen

Cast

Mr Maurice	Norman Fell
Chanel	Yvonne Erwin
Taffy	Julie Silliman

Lily has been sneaking out at night, which worries Herman, who thinks she may be seeing another man. Actually she is working on fashion designs, and applies for a job with Mr Maurice. He likes her weirdness and humour, and hires her to design for his show, two weeks off. She breaks the news to the family, but Herman doesn't like it, since he has to do more chores. He stays home to work in the house and watch soap operas. Lily is working long hours for the show, and on the day, Herman and Grandpa visit her. This scares off her two models, so she compels Grandpa and Herman to stand in for them. Maurice approves of the idea of 'ugly models', and the show begins. They overact terribly, and Herman ends his display by falling through a wall. The whole show is a big hit, and Maurice wants to go on the designer road with it. Lily decides, however, to give it up and go back home with her family.

The best joke so far in the show is in this story – Herman sees everyone off in the morning, in a twisted version of the initial opening credits from the old show. Norman Fell is a veteran actor best known for his role in *Three's Company* (1977–79), the American version of *Man About The House*.

Episode 6
13 November 1988

Written by   Elroy Schwartz
Directed by   Peter Isacksen

Cast
Dan Steinburg   Gregory Sierra
William Wickham   Ron Kuhlman
Mayor Huntley   Jay Fenichel
The Punker   Kenny Rhodes

Herman can't stop sneezing. Steinburg and Wickham of the INS arrive – Immigration and Naturalization. They want to see Vladimir Dracula, because he has no immigration record, and is an illegal alien. Grandpa simply forgot to do it the last few hundred years. He's called in to have the information taken down. He gives his profession as 'bloodsucker', to which Steinburg responds: 'A lawyer, eh?' They discover that they can't take his picture. He's jailed, along with a punk, and the local mayor. Herman brings him a lunch from Lily – chicken in a casket. He breaks the door accidentally, and he and Grandpa run for home. Lily is furious, knowing the INS agents will come for them both. Grandpa makes himself and Herman invisible so they can hide. Steinburg and Wickman arrive and start looking for them. Herman sneezes, and they return to normal. Eddie is dressed as a mockingbird for the football mascot. Lily makes the agents realize how stupid their report will sound if they put in invisible men, giant chickens and so forth. They decide instead to make Grandpa an official American. Herman sneezes the top off the mockingbird, making it into a bald eagle . .

Episode 7
20 November 1988

Written by	Bill Rosenthal and Noah Taft
Directed by	Bonnie Franklin

Cast

Ms Finster	Ruth Buzzi
Mr Carswell	Charlie Brill
Sherman	Peter S. Palmer

The Mockingbird Heights Father/Son Sports Day is coming up, and Herman promises to go with Eddie. He then learns of his old investment in Ant Ranch, Inc. – which has experienced a blossoming due to a new toy craze for ant ranches. He attends the AGM, run by Douglas Carswell, helped by Ms Finster, his secretary. Herman manages to object to everything, and the meeting is postponed for two weeks. Carswell then discovers that Herman – who bought his stock in the sixties – is now the majority stockholder. Herman thus becomes an executive, with a terrified Ms Finster as his secretary. Eddie is very unhappy with his father's new job, since it stops him from practising. Herman has problems with the job, and dreams that the family has a new father, Sherman. The next day in work, he resigns his job, to the delight of Carswell and Ms Finster. At the sports day, he and Eddie quite literally demolish the competition.

Ruth Buzzi was a regular on *Rowan & Martin's Laugh-In* (1968–73). Charlie Brill is a regular on *Silk Stalkings*, one of Stephen Cannell's late night adventure series

Episode 8
27 November 1988

Written by   Danny Morris
Directed by   Doug Rogers

Cast
Dr Sandy Brown   Nancy Dussault
Himself   Gordon Cooper

Herman has passed a physical at work with an impressive score on his stress test – so impressive that astronaut Gordon Cooper calls him. He and Dr Sandy Brown want Herman to come in to NASA. When he does, after initial reluctance, they test him, and then ask him to volunteer for the civilian space programme. Herman is over the moon with the idea of going to Venus with Dr Brown. It'll be a three year round trip, though, and all the family except for Grandpa are against it. They go with him for the final tests, and Lily is even less happy when she sees Dr Brown. Herman passes everything but the intelligence test. Then it's the final test, the flying one, and Herman is flunked on it – he's scared of heights. Back home, he receives another call, this time from the submarine service . . .

There's one section where Herman is sitting in a room heated to 450 degrees, and a pitcher of water starts boiling.

It should have boiled considerably before that!

Gordon Cooper is, of course, a real Gemini astronaut.

Episode 9
4 December 1988

Written by	Ted Bergman and Kathy Joseph
Directed by	Peter Isacksen

Cast

Freddie Wonder	Allan Fawcett
Rick	David Coburn
Ron	Joey Green
Ralph	Rob Garrison

Marilyn has news – the rock group the Lizards is appearing on the TV show 'Rock Fever' and needs somewhere to rehearse, so she's invited them over. They trash hotels, so can't stay there. Meanwhile, Lily makes Grandpa help to make Herman a 275th wedding anniversary present, making gold with an electron modulator. Grandpa makes cheese, then a chicken instead. The Lizards – Rick, Ron and Ralph – love his lab, and ignore his instructions not to touch anything. They play with the modulator, and turn themselves into real lizards. Grandpa needs the right sound to change them back, and they're still lizards at show time. The family goes along to the studio to explain the problem, and the 'Rock Fever' host, Freddie Wonder, takes them for the Lizards. Lily gives Herman his present – gold neck bolts for dress occasions. Freddie introduces the 'group', which becomes a hit singing 'The Munster Rap'. The last note is the right one to change the Lizards back to people, but the Munsters are big hits. Later, at home, the family wheels out an anniversary cake, and Spot lights all the candles.

211

Episode 10
11 December 1988

Written by	William Cyr
Directed	by Lee Lochhead

Cast

Professor Forbes   Jack Fletcher

Grandpa is moaning about preferring the old ways of doing things, but Marilyn suggests he take chemistry classes at Mockingbird Heights University. He goes along, but staid Professor Forbes bores the class to sleep. He doesn't like Grandpa, who takes over the class when Forbes leaves, and teaches the students to make rain. Forbes won't believe in alchemy, and laughs when Grandpa fails to turn his watch into lead. He throws Grandpa out of the class. The rest of the family is decorating, and Grandpa feels sorry for himself, and old at last. Herman and Lily pretend they've booked him into an old folks' home, and he likes the idea. It takes Eddie to make him to realize it's Forbes who is old, not him. Grandpa faces Forbes again, and this time pulls off the trick of turning the watch to lead. He also gives Forbes a potion that turns him into a razzle-dazzle science showman.

Episode 11
18 December 1988

Written by	Bryan Joseph
Directed by	Doug Rogers

Cast

Dr Dugan   David Byrd
The Patient   Gene Castle

Eddie has a sore throat, so Herman takes him to see Dr
Cutter, who is on vacation. Dr Dugan is filling in, and he
thinks Herman has had the accident. He X-rays him, and
sends Eddie home cured – but takes Herman to the hospital
to remove the huge spring from inside him. Eddie relays
the news to Lily and Grandpa, who are appalled – the
spring is keeping Herman together. Disguising themselves
as staff, the family sneak into the hospital to rescue Herman.
Meanwhile, Herman has been accidentally torturing a fel-
low patient. Dr Dugan tries to keep Herman, but the family
breaks him out. Later, Herman aims to take the hearse
racing, but Mrs Goodbury is using it for shopping.

Episode 12
29 January 1989

Written by	Steve Baum and
	Neil Alan Levy
Directed by	Peter Isacksen

Cast

Skinner	Paul Williams
Himself	David Horowitz
Regina Avalon	Suzanne McCambridge
Misha Goss	Paul 'Mousie' Garner
Jimmy	Kenny Ford

Herman saves Jimmy Elkin from a falling branch, and is
written up as a hero in the 'Mockingbird Mirror' for it. Ad
man R.M. Skinner and his assistant, Regina, arrive at the
house, wanting to use the hero to promote their new product, Liquorice Puffs. It's non-nutritional, but Grandpa convinces Herman to do it for the money and fame. He acts as
Herman's agent. The family can't stand the Puffs, but they
give Spot a sugar high – onto the roof. Herman realizes that

213

his endorsement of them is probably a bad thing, but again Grandpa talks him out of quitting. Consumer advocate David Horowitz invites Herman onto his show 'Fight Back'. Misha Goss is called on the carpet for a non-working trash compactor – which Herman promptly trashes. Horowitz challenges Herman about Liquorice Puffs, and Herman starts to read the prepared speech Grandpa gave him. Then he realizes this is wrong, and he's setting a terrible example to Eddie. He trashes the script, and admits that the cereal is disgusting and non-nutritional. Skinner fires him, but expresses an interest in Grandpa's pet rat, Stanley, who's an excellent liar. Grandpa expresses an interest in becoming Horowitz's agent.

Paul Williams is a singer/actor of short stature. David Horowitz really did host a show called *Fight Back* (he also appeared on the sitcom *Alf* in his own persona).

Episode 13
5 February 1989

Written by	Hope Juber and
	Kim Mortensen
Directed by	Lee Lochhead

Cast
Dottie	Nanette Fabray

Grandpa is left home alone as usual on a Saturday night. Everyone seems to have a partner but him, so he answers a lonely hearts' advertisement on TV. It's for a video dating service, which raises a problem since he can't be photographed. He does the video anyway, figuring it'll make him seem mysterious. He receives a fast reply, from an adventurous lady named Dottie. She takes the house and the family into her stride, and they start dating. She's impressed

214

with him, especially that he can sky-dive without a para-chute. Lily is upset about his staying out all the time partying. She discovers that Dottie has had a dozen husbands, all of whom died on the dancefloor. A few days later, Lily and Herman discover that Grandpa and Dottie have gone to a dance marathon. Fearing the worst, they rush over – to discover that Grandpa outlasted her, and that they took second place. Dottie proposes to Grandpa, but he's not ready for marriage. She agrees to look him up when she's back in a few years from her safari expedition.

Nanette Fabray was a star on Broadway in the forties and fifties, and appeared on *One Day At A Time* (1979–84). She's the aunt of actress Shelley Fabares (*Coach*).

Episode 14
12 February 1989

Written by	Joy Grdnic and
	Patty Gordon
Directed by	Doug Rogers

Cast

Mr Talbot	Paul Wilson
Barney Morley	Donald Most
Rosemary Morley	Desiree Boschetti

Herman is put on commission when the funeral business is dying down, and they need more income. Grandpa comes up with the idea of turning the house into a bed and break-fast place. They do have problems getting customers to stay – most run off screaming. Herman thinks the house must look too expensive for them. Grandpa discovers a hotel critic is doing the rounds incognito, and believes this could be their big chance. When Mr Talbot arrives, Grandpa thinks he must be the critic, and insists that everyone go out

215

of their way to please him. Mr Talbot is obnoxious and complaining, and has them running around like crazy trying to please him. A couple checks in – Mr and Mrs Morley – Mrs Morley is expecting. Morley is the real critic, and is not impressed initially. Lily then discovers that Talbot is a birdseed salesman, and Grandpa is furious. He spooks Talbot so badly that he flees. Rosemary Morley is spooked, too, and has her baby early. Later, Grandpa reads a kind review by Mr Morley, who thinks the house is a great theme place to stay at.

Donald (Donnie) Most is most noted for his role as Ralph on *Happy Days* (1974–80).

Episode 15
19 February 1989

Written by   Ann L. Gibbs
Directed by   Lee Lochhead

Cast
Mrs Cousins   Dr Joyce Brothers

Lily tells Marilyn off for spending too much time on the phone with Dustin and neglecting her chores. She thinks she's being picked on. Meanwhile, Lily is coming down with the 'flu, with the mortuary party coming up on Friday. Marilyn, sulking, ruins Grandpa's tassle on his Save the Bats cap. Fed up with criticism, she runs away from home. Eddie is pleased, and wants her room. Grandpa flies off to look for her. Marilyn goes to see Mrs Cousins, the school guidance counsellor, and discusses her problems. She calls the family, and Herman goes to collect Marilyn. Mrs Cousins thinks Marilyn has only normal teenage stress – until she sees Herman. Then she runs for her life. Herman tells Marilyn that the family loves her, and convinces her to come home – even if she does have chores to do. Lily recovers from her 'flu, but Grandpa and Herman both catch it.

Dr Joyce Brothers is a real psychologist who often hosts counselling shows for American TV. Her career actually took off after she was a contestant on *The $64,000 Question*, which she won twice (answering questions on boxing).

Episode 16
26 February 1989

Written by	Bill Rosenthal and Noah Taft
Directed by	Peter Isacksen

Cast

Louie Schecter	Robert Clary

The mummy, Louie Schecter, is due to wake up for his one week every 300 years. He's an agent, who helps make someone a star. Last time, he helped Lily to win the Miss Transylvania contest. When Louie wakes, Lily updates him, and he decides that she can win the Mrs Transylvania contest – with his help. He starts practising with her, and Herman begins to get very jealous. Grandpa, for once, thinks he's right, and suggests Herman takes his revenge. Herman then tries to pretend he's seeing another woman, which goes right past Lily. When she finally realizes what Herman's been saying, she has a talk with him and realizes Herman feels totally left out. She persuades Louie to work with Herman as well. Louie reluctantly agrees, and discovers that Herman is totally without talent. Louie tells Lily that the only way she'll win the contest is without Herman. Lily decides that it isn't worth it, and Louie falls asleep for another 300 years.

217

Episode 17
5 March 1989

Written by   Michael Davidoff

Directed by   Bob Claven

Regulars only

Grandpa aims to enter again for the Houdini Open Classic, wanting to earn his own trophy to join those of the rest of the family. When he tries to escape from a straight-jacket, however, he's trapped, which amuses Herman. Later, a box arrives – and Grandpa's in it, chained up – another failure. Lily tries to get him to stop, but he refuses to listen. Herman insults him, and Grandpa leaves home. Herman then manages to lock himself in the straight-jacket, and forgets where he put the key. Lily goes for Grandpa, who refuses to return home unless Herman apologizes. Herman is forced to, and they still have trouble. Even Grandpa can't find the key. Herman then remembers it's in his pocket! Eddie falls in the moat and is attacked by one of the monsters. Herman breaks out of the jacket and goes to Eddie's rescue. Grandpa, seeing how Herman escaped, decides to give up the escape artist bit. The family clubs together and buys him a special trophy – a bat-shaped one for the world's best Grandpa.

Episode 18
12 March 1989

Written by   Anne L. Gibbs and
                                  Joel Kimmel

Directed by   Peter Isacksen

Cast

Dee Dee Nelson   Mary Cadorette

Roger Nelson   Greg Mullavey
Dustin Nelson   Scott Reeves
Howie Buchanan   Richard Horvitz

Clothing provided by Fila
Shoes provided by Diodora

Lily and Herman are involved with a fund-raising dance for
the medieval museum, and Marilyn is excited that she has a
date with Dustin Nelson. Lily suggests that she invite him
to the dance. When Dustin arrives to take Marilyn out,
Herman invites his parents in. Dee Dee owns a boutique,
while Roger is a plastic surgeon. To Dee Dee's disgust,
Roger takes a professional interest in Herman's face. His
wife freaks out when they're invited to dinner, and is appalled when she discovers that she'll be attending the dance
with the Munsters. She flatly refuses to allow Dustin to
date Marilyn, though. Marilyn is heart-broken, and Herman
tries to help out by recruiting Howie to take her to the
dance, to Howie's delight. Marilyn, however, won't go
without Dustin. On the night of the dance, things go as well
as they can with Herman present. Marilyn decides to support her relatives and turns up. So does Dustin, ignoring his
mother, and the youngsters have a great time. Dee Dee just
freaks as usual.

   Greg Mullavey was a regular on the sitcom *Mary
Hartman, Mary Hartman* (1976–78).

Episode 19
7 May 1989

Written by   Bill Rosenthal and
                              Noah Taft
Directed by   Norm Abbott

Cast

Dee Dee Nelson	Mary Cadorette
Roger Nelson	Greg Mullavey
Dustin Nelson	Scott Reeves
Slim	Barry Dennen

Herman has been watching TV, and is convinced he has the legs of Stanislaw the Dancer. Whenever he hears music, he starts uncontrollable tap-dancing. Meanwhile, the family have new neighbours – the Nelsons. When Dee Dee learns they're moving in next to the Munsters, she freaks. The only thing that keeps her there is the promise by Roger of a designer pool by Mr Frank. Dustin likes being close to Marilyn. Dee Dee bricks up the window facing their house. Mr Frank's design turns out to be too large for their garden, so they have to talk the Munsters into letting them use part of their property . . . which means making friends . . . Lily and Herman arrive to welcome them to the neighbourhood. When Dee Dee puts on some music, Herman tap-dances through the window. Roger manages to convince Herman that they are friends, but Grandpa thinks it's just a trick. Lily throws a welcoming party for the new neighbours. Dee Dee doesn't want to go, but Roger insists. He's grown to quite like Herman. At the party, Roger manages to convince Herman that his legs aren't dancing legs, and it's all in his head, thus curing him. When Herman asks Dee Dee for a dance, though, she faints.

Episode 20
8 August 1989

Written by	Lloyd J. Schwartz
Directed by	Peter Isacksen

Cast

Wolfgang	Jerry Houser
Bert	Kip King
Howie Buchanan	Richard Horvitz

Bert Fearman and his brother, Fingers, are crooks just released from jail, after robbing a bank ten years earlier. They
had hidden their loot inside a clock in what they had thought
was a deserted house. It was the Munster home, and the
family were sleeping. To try to recover the money, Fingers
dons a werewolf mask, and poses as a fictional 'Cousin
Wolfgang'. Though the family is suspicious at first, they
then welcome him in, and insist he stay with them. They're
always about, so he can't get at the clock. Instead, he starts
pocketing valuables. The family ask him to join their bowling team for the evening, and he's touched. They do well
against their opponents, but Bert plants a bomb in a bowling ball to blow the Munsters up. They can then recover
their money without interference. Fingers discovers that he
can't let the family down, and disposes of the ball by bowling it – blowing up the frame and winning the game for the
family. Back at the house, he confesses to his imposture.
Lily is touched, realizing that he does care about them.
Herman insists on taking the money back to the bank, and
Fingers turns over everything he's pocketed.

Episode 21
27 August 1989

Written by	Bob Destri and
	Billy Riback
Directed by	Peter Isacksen

Cast

Mr Higashigawa	John Fujioka

| Tiffany | Danya Winston |
| Heather | Kimberlee Kramer |

Eddie has been given two days to improve his voice or be thrown out of the Glee Club. Worried about a series of neighbourhood robberies, Herman decides to take up Kung Fu to be able to defend his family. Mr Higashigawa isn't too thrilled with Herman, who proceeds to terrify the class and then break all of the bricks with one finger. When Marilyn arrives home, she finds Herman has booby-trapped the place. Meanwhile, Grandpa manages to improve Eddie's voice – but it is running at the wrong speeds . . . Herman is wrecking the Kung Fu hall in his enthusiasm, and giving the instructor broken limbs. Worried that someone may be attacking his family, he rushes home. Meanwhile, two of Marilyn's friends, Tiffany and Heather, arrive at the house. Eddie sings, in a Michael Jackson style, and they mob him. Herman arrives, and thinks they're assaulting Eddie, until Marilyn explains. Eddie is elated – he's back in the Glee Club again.

Episode 22
14 May 1989

| **Written by** | Marc A. Brown |
| **Directed by** | Lee Lochhead |

Cast
| Gill | Peter Isacksen |

Herman is fed up with Melvin at work bragging about his son's sporting prowess. Eddie, overhearing, thinks Herman wishes he was a sports star, so he takes up basketball. Herman is overjoyed, but Eddie is pretty bad at the game. To improve his game, Herman calls on his cousin Gill, the

222

fish-man, who's a professional basketball player in Transylvania. Gill swims over, but even he can't help Eddie's lack of skill. Herman thinks it's all Gill's fault, and then, suddenly, Eddie is hitting every shot. Lily discovers it's not Eddie's skill at work, but Grandpa's telekinesis. Eddie admits to his father that he's terrible at the game, and doesn't even like it. Herman wants to know why he's playing, and Eddie admits it's to make him happy. Herman explains that he doesn't care about the sports at all, he just wants Eddie to be happy. Gill now decides it's time to head home. Grandpa starts making things vanish now, and goes looking for Herman . . .

Episode 23
4 June 1989

Written by   Bryan Joseph
Directed by   Peter Isacksen

Cast
Ms Jessica Bowton   Lois Nettleton

Ms Jessica Bowton, of the City Council, arrives. The Munsters own property on the outskirts of town – a swamp, to be exact – that the town wants to buy and turn into an art museum. Herman refuses to sell, but Ms Bowton won't give up. Grandpa is trying to wither a plant using his plant food, and spills some on Herman. It's actually a love potion. Ms Bowton calls up, threatening to have the Munster property condemned. Herman goes to try to talk her out of it, and she instantly falls for him. Herman panics and runs home. Lily has Grandpa start working on an antidote. Ms Bowton calls again, claiming she's fine, and wants to talk business. Herman goes back, but she's lying – to be alone with him. She offers him his swamp back for a kiss. Grandpa arrives just in time with the antidote, and she's once again finding Herman repulsive. Lily blackmails her into tearing up the condemnation order by offering to leave Herman for her.

Season Two

Credits

Produced by	Bryan Joseph
Supervising Producer	Patricia Fass Palmer
Executive Producer	Arthur Annecharico
Co-Executive Producer	Craig Kellem
Story Editors	Bill Rosenthal and Noah Taft, except: Michael Davidoff (episodes 28–41)
Associate Producer	Dustin Nelson
Art Director	Jimmy Cuomo
Casting	Kim Dorr, CSA; also Joey Paul (episode 27 on)
Based on Characters developed by	Norm Liebermann and Ed Haas
From a Format by	Al Burns and Chris Hayward
Original Theme Music	Jack Marshall
Theme Song arranged and Additional Music	Wintermoon Music
Additional Scoring	L.A. Arpino
Associate Director	Don Sullivan
Stage Managers	Ted Ray, Jerry Sarcone, Deborah Jones, Dennis Capps
Booth P.A.	Peter Field
Lighting Director	Dan Kuleto
Special Effects	Hank Andrusick, Thomas

	Reichardt, except: Michael Buenfil and Michael Canepa (episode 28 on)
Post Production Manager	Tom Buel
Properties	Bill Lawrence
Assistant Props	Patty Schmidt
Set Decorator	Debbie Madalena, except: Ted Berner (episode 28, 34); Adam Falehi (episode 45)
Costume Designer	Gregory Smith, except: Jennifer Michaud (episode 28)
Costume Assistant	Pikke Allen
Makeup Artists	David Abbott, Gil Mosko
Hair Stylist	Jody Lawrence
Technical Director	Karl Messerschmidt, except: Brad Keys (episode 36); Robert Tubb (episode 37)
Audio	Myles Weiner, William Kennedy III
Senior Video	George Palmer, Bob Vinson
Camera	Malcolm Bhone, Bob Cambell, Don Davis, Lee Rizor, Joe Burchi, Steve Casaly, Rocky Danielson, Victor Gonzales, Jim Rohrig, Ron Tosches, Doug Rutt, Arnold Garth Wilson, Matin Goldstein, Jim Velarde, Elizabeth Bailey, Joey Bertshi
Engineering	Dave Radford,

	Jim RuDenski
Videotape Editor	Craig Anderson, Michael Lorenzo, Mary Holland
Rerecording Engineers	Chris Brosius, Craig Porter, Greg Hedgepath, Brian Buel
Clothing Provided by	Surf Fetish
Production and Post Production Facilities	The Arthur Company's 'One Take' and 'Last Stop'
Videotaped at	Universal Studios, Universal City, CA
Executive in Charge of Production	Mike Fierman
The Arthur Company	
MCA TV	

Cast

Herman	John Schuck
Lily	Lee Meriwether
Grandpa	Howard Morton
Marilyn	Hilary van Dyke
Eddie	Jason Marsden

Episode 24
8 October 1989

Written by	Bill Rosenthal and Noah Taft
Directed by	Bonnie Franklin

Cast

Herself	Zsa Zsa Gabor

Lily thinks that her marriage is in a rut, after watching Oprah. She and Herman recall how they dated 300 years ago in the local cemetery. They decide to have Grandpa look after Eddie for the weekend, and then have a romantic weekend together. Grandpa aims to take Eddie to Universal Studios, but Eddie is convinced it's going to be a boring weekend with Grandpa's same old stories. Meanwhile, Herman and Lily are having worse problems as they try to relate. Herman refuses to believe that they even have a problem, until 'marriage expert' Zsa Zsa Gabor assures him that they do. He then reads up about it, and he and Lily make up a list of what annoys them about each other. It just makes them worse. Meanwhile, Grandpa and Eddie solve their lack of communication – Grandpa starts talking about his baseball memories, and Eddie is fascinated. Lily and Herman meet again at the cemetery, and apologize to each other – not knowing that Eddie and Grandpa are watching . . .

Zsa Zsa Gabor is best known for being married several times and simply being herself. She was arrested and convicted of striking a policeman, and threw public tantrums during the trial, which was taking place as this story aired.

Episode 25
15 October 1989

Written by   Leslie Eberhard and
                         Barbara Hobart
Directed by   Lee Lochhead

Cast
Inspector   Alan Blumenfeld
Real Estate Agent   Beverly Sanders

The house is flooded after a storm, but the family insurance will cover the repairs. But they have to move out in the meantime. They are moved into a very yuppified apartment, which the kids love, but the adults hate. Herman and

Lily finally start to enjoy it, and even buy new clothes. They're fast becoming yuppies, and aim to sell the old house and move in here permanently. Even the kids now think they're overdoing things, and Grandpa loathes the whole thing. Lily and Herman even start throwing cocktail parties, and enjoying the social round. When the old house is finished, they return to it, and memories start coming back to them. Getting bored with the yuppy life style, they all prefer to return to their old way of life.

Episode 26
22 October 1989

Written by	Jeffrey Sachs
Directed by	Scott Redman

Cast

Claudia	Laura Mooney

Eddie is having problems dealing with being a teenager, and is running into trouble on his first day in a new school. Lily disapproves of his up-to-date clothing, and wants him back in his old purple suit. At school, Eddie asks out Claudia, and then gets all nervous. Back home, Herman puts his foot down, insisting Eddie wear his old suit. Eddie changes as soon as he's out of the house, but is picked on by bully Sean. Claudia is kept in class, and she misses her date with Eddie. Disillusioned, Eddie tries to explain to his father that he just wants to fit in with the other youngsters. Grandpa manages to cheer Eddie up by telling him of his problems at school. Back at school, Eddie and Claudia make up, and then Eddie fights it out with Sean. Lily and Herman can't understand their son, but they decide they had better simply try and tolerate the new Eddie.

Episode 27
29 October 1989

Written by   Ron Jarvis and
                                Philip A. Scorza

Directed by   Bob Claver

Cast

Delores Heath   Leslie Easterbrook
Dean Heath   Michael Bell

The family have new neighbours, Dean and Delores Heath. They invite the new people over for a murder mystery party. Dean loses the invitation, and they don't realize that it's a game. They think that the whole thing is real, and start to panic when Marilyn is 'killed'. Then her body disappears. A clue tells them that Herman is really an undercover policeman, but he doesn't seem helpful. Lily asks Dean to kill her 'husband', Grandpa. Dean panics, and confesses to the murder to try to get arrested and out of the house. Delores faints. Grandpa tells Dean that it's just a game, but he doesn't tell Delores. He plays along, accusing Delores of the killings. She starts yelling back about her affairs. The family thinks it's all fun, and wants them back. Dean thinks there'll be a better murder next time . . .

Leslie Easterbrook was a regular on *Laverne & Shirley* (1980–83). Michael Bell has appeared on many shows including a stint on *Dallas* (1980–81). He was also in the pilot story for *Star Trek – The Next Generation*.

Episode 28
5 November 1989

Written by   James Pieroni and
                                Bruce Teicher

| **Directed by** | Bonnie Franklin |

Cast

Sam Hawkins	Shelley Berman
Sonny Scales	Steve Susskind
Judge	Alex Finlayson

Herman saves Sam from choking in a restaurant, and Sam visits the next day – to thank him, and then to serve him with a summons. Sam is a lawyer, and is suing for 'illnesses' brought on by Herman's ham-fisted help. Grandpa hires Herman a nasty lawyer, Sonny Scales, but Sonny seems to be just out to fleece them also. In court, Sam accuses Herman, twisting the facts. Sonny claims Herman is incompetent and a Communist to boot. Herman fires him, and Grandpa takes on the case. His attempt to bribe the judge almost gets Herman convicted. Herman (in his Jimmy Stewart persona) then pleads for justice, without much effect. The judge starts to choke, and Grandpa urges Herman to let him die, so they can get a mistrial. Herman saves him, however, and wins his case.

Shelley Berman is a stand-up comedian who guests on numerous shows, including *The Girl From UNCLE*.

Episode 29
November 2nd, 1989

| **Written by** | Michael Davidoff |
| **Directed by** | Bruce Bilson |

Cast

| Gordon Fenway* | John Sanderford |

*credited as 'Fenwick'

Herman's old assistant at the funeral parlour, Gordon Fenway, is in town. He's taken his exams, and is a wealthy coroner. Herman is embarrassed, and thinks that he is a failure, for not having done better. He wishes he'd never been made. Grandpa builds a machine to show him what life would have been like if he hadn't. Herman goes through the process, and wakes up where he doesn't exist. The house is bright, cheery and expensively decorated. Lily in this life married Gordon. She's fat, lazy and addicted to chocolates and her own way. Marilyn's a valley girl, dumb and obnoxious. Eddie's a yuppy, and has a nasty streak. Spot is a poodle. Herman manages to break through, and tries to tell them off, but they won't listen to him. He decides that he's happy he's been made after all, and Grandpa restores him to the right dimension. Herman realizes that he's a success where it counts – with his family.

Director Bruce Bilson later went on to be a co-creator and producer of both *The Flash* and *Viper*.

Episode 30
19 November 1989

Written by   Mark R. Cassutt
Directed by   Scott Redman

Cast
Mr Grubbs   Ernie Sabella
Brad Penman   Casey Ellison

During a school test, Brad Penman copies from Eddie, but it's Eddie who is caught and given a failing grade. Grandpa decides to boost Eddie's confidence by teaching him how to do the Evil Eye and cause bad luck to fall on Brad. Eddie tries it out on Herman, who comes home from work in bandages after an accident. Then Eddie hears that Brad was expelled for cheating, and he's convinced he's got the power. The family is terrified of him, giving in to his every whim. Only Grandpa thinks it's all nonsense, but is hurt standing up to the Evil Eye. At school, Eddie finds Brad is still there – the story of his expulsion was his idea of a joke. He tries again to copy from Eddie, but this time Eddie tells the teacher, Mr Grubbs. The rest of the class backs Eddie up, and Brad finds he really is expelled. Back home, Eddie apologises to everyone for his bad behaviour.

Episode 31
26 November 1989

Written by   Bryan Joseph
Directed by   Bonnie Franklin

Cast
Willy Loomis   Dann Florek

The new gravedigger, Willy Loomis, is so gloomy that he's grating on Herman's nerves. Lily invites Willy to dinner to try to cheer him up. He's incredibly depressing, though, and even gets a bone in the mashed potatoes. He's accident prone and miserable, and affects the whole family. His apartment burns down, and he manages to soft talk Lily and be invited to stay. It looks like he'll never leave, so Herman suggests that they out-gloom him. Whatever he says, they try and top in misery – and he enjoys it. Lily has finally had enough of all the gloom, and cheers up. She makes everyone look on the sunny side of things, except Willy – he's depressed at their optimism, and finally leaves.

232

Episode 32
3 December 1989

Written by   Andrew Borakove
Directed by   Bonnie Franklin

Cast
Louis   Teddy Wilson
Sam   Leslie Eberhard

It's the anniversary of the Munsters' arrival in America. As every year, they write down their wishes for the coming year and put them in the 'melting pot'. Grandpa is usually the most voluminous, but puts nothing in – he's disillusioned and dissatisfied with what he's achieved. Sam, his computer, tells him his only option is to make a deal with the Devil, who promptly arrives: he's a cool black guy named Louis. He offers Grandpa whatever he wants, a price to be named later. Grandpa accepts, and the deliveries start rolling in. The problem is that he's soon dissatisfied. Louis returns, knowing Grandpa wants out of the contract. He agrees to a hand of cards; if Grandpa wins, he goes free – otherwise the Devil takes his price, which is Herman. Needless to say, both he and Grandpa cheat like crazy, but eventually Grandpa outcheats even the Devil, and wins.

Episode 33
10 December 1989

Written by   Bill Rosenthal and
                              Noah Taft
Directed by   Bonnie Franklin

Cast

Katja   Jo deWinter

Lily's mother, Katja, arrives, bearing gifts, including a voo-
doo doll of herself for Herman. Grandpa is still trying to
avoid her, since she left him 350 years ago. She decides to
stay for a while, and tries to win him over. Though she
constantly contradicts him, she makes his favourite foods,
and tells him she wants them to get back together. He
reluctantly agrees to a date, and promises to be pleasant.
She admits that she was wrong to have left him and Lily.
He refuses at first to forgive her, but admits he's still in
love with her. They have a wonderful evening. She promises to return after she's been to Transylvania to pick up her
things, but Grandpa knows better – she's too fond of her
freedom to return permanently.

Episode 34
17 December 1989

Written by   Robert Schechter
Directed by   Peter Isacksen

Cast

Lt. Reynolds   Floyd Levine

There's a copycat Jack the Ripper killer in Mockingbird
Heights. The ID picture looks like Grandpa, and Herman
becomes paranoid. One sign is a scent of liverworst – which
Grandpa feeds to his rat, Stanley. He also has taken to
carrying a small black bag, which he won't let anyone
open. Then a man Grandpa has a grudge against is the next
victim, so Herman calls the police. Lt Reynolds comes
down, and thinks Herman did it. Herman convinces him
otherwise. He confronts Grandpa, who admits he's been

234

taking night classes in knitting, and was too ashamed to admit it. Reynolds catches the real killer – a dead ringer for Grandpa.

Episode 35
4 February 1990

Teleplay by	Leslie Eberhard and Barbara Hobart
Story by	Daryl Rowland and Lisa de Benedictis
Directed by	Scott Redman

Cast

Ygor	Foster Brooks
Frank	Peter Schuck
Yetta	Yetta
Bella	Angelina Fiordellisi
Boris	Loren Freeman
Damien	Christopher Fielder

Aunt Yetta's infamously ugly daughter, Bella, is going to marry Boris, son of the invisible trapeze artist. Yetta decides to hold it in the Munster home, with Ygor, the family hunchback, officiating. He arrives drunk. Damien, their creepy cousin, also arrives, and the rest of the family is just plain cranky. Bella and Boris are having problems, and then Herman's estranged brother, Frank, arrives. The two start bickering, and Boris decides to leave. Frank is jealous of Herman, thinking that he was an unwanted model. Herman smooths things out, and finally Boris arrives for the ceremony. As soon as they are married, Bella turns beautiful and Boris turns visible.

Episode 36
11 February 1990

Written by   Andrew Boracove
Directed by   Peter Isacksen

Cast
Mr Graves   Graham Jarvis

Lily is on a cleaning binge, and wants help. The family all use various lies to get out of it and to go to the ball game. Grandpa even agrees to lie for Herman's boss, Mr Graves, who also wants to go. They all meet up accidentally at the game, and their lies become more complex – and when they return home to Lily, things become even worse. Finally, she tells them that she knows they've all been lying, and are put on extra chores – Grandpa ratted on them.

Episode 37
18 February 1990

Written by   Bill Rosenthal and
                            Noah Taft
Directed by   Lee Lochhead

Cast
Annie   Holly Fields
Kyle   Randy Kaplan
Lloyd   Larry Spinak

Eddie has been watching his favourite TV show, 'Those Terrible Teens', which his parents have forbidden. It's about Annie, Kyle and Lloyd who live together and do whatever they want, without adults. Grandpa fixes the remote control, which should stop Eddie watching the show– but in-

stead zaps him into it. Grandpa can't get him out, and
accidentally pulls a pretty girl from it instead, who gets
along with his skeleton, Leonard. The family head for Universal Studios and go onto the set. Eddie refuses to come
home, so the family stays, trying to fit in. The Terrible
Teens find them weird, and Eddie gets offended. He'd
rather go home with his folks.

Episode 38
25 February 1990

Written by   Michael Davidoff
Directed by   Bonnie Franklin

Cast
Ivan   Marty Ingels

Leonard has been savaged by a pack of poodles, and as he
tries to save him, Grandpa remembers how they met. He
was a student with a dungeon he shared with Ivan Gladstock,
who was studying to be a jester. He brings Leonard, who
gets locked in the wall chains. Ivan's a slob, who really irks
Grandpa. They deliberately annoy one another, but finally
get along. Ivan is killed in a chariot crash, and there's no
one to look after Leonard but Grandpa. Back in the present,
Leonard makes a full recovery, and even gets a female
skeletal girlfriend.

Episode 39
4 March 1990

Teleplay by   Scott Redman
Story by   Larry Carroll and
                      David Carren

237

Directed by   Scott Redman

Cast
Dr Fierman   Milt Oberman

The family discovers Spot is pregnant. To distract a worried Eddie, Herman tells him the story of how he was born.
Lily had problems with the Stork plant, which couldn't
make up its mind. She was pregnant, but Transylvanian
pregnancies last only 24 hours. She suffers violent mood
swings, not helped when Grandpa can't locate a
Transylvanian midwife. Herman finally takes Lily to Dr
Fierman at the local hospital. Stunned by the oddness,
Fierman aims to call in a news crew to record everything,
and throws Herman out. Herman is annoyed, and tosses
Fierman out. Eddie is born, and to console the doctor, they
name the baby after him – Edward Wolfgang. Back in the
present, they find Spot was only suffering from indigestion.

Episode 40
22 April 1990

Written by   Bryan Joseph
Directed by   Bonnie Franklin

Cast
Mr Gateman   Andrew Bloch
Lance Gateman   Moosie Drier

Mr Gateman convinces Herman to look after his son, Lance,
by offering to promote him to foreman. Gateman has been
divorced nine years, and hasn't seen Lance since then.
Lance arrives, and he's a total foul-up, constantly running
into trouble. He comes on to Marilyn, and to a widow at a
funeral. He accidentally kills Lily's pet parrot. Gateman,

meanwhile, is hiding out to avoid the boy. Finally, the family can take no more, and aim to throw Lance out. He's used to it, and tells them they lasted longer than most. Lily, feeling sorry for the boy, decides they must reunite the family, and they force Gateman to come over for dinner. Reluctantly, the two of them start opening up, and finally are reconciled. Herman doesn't get the promotion, but he's not bothered – the man who did has to look after Gateman's daughter, who's just out of Leavenworth . . .

Episode 41
29 April 1990

Written by   Paul Lander
Directed by   Bonnie Franklin

Cast
Mr Goodbury   Stanley Ralph Ross

Herman is elected spokesman for the gravediggers, and tries to persuade Mr Goodbury to lower the quotas. Instead Herman is fired, and decides to start his own parlour, the House of Herman. Grandpa doesn't believe in him, but at Lily's insistence tries to help. Goodbury spends most of his time gloating at Herman's lack of success, and fights every move he makes to put him out of business again. Herman even tries advertising on TV, but is outclassed. Finally, everything is repossessed, and Goodbury comes round, waiting for Herman to beg for his old job back. Herman refuses – and Goodbury ends up begging him to come back, because the crew can't work without him.

Stanley Ralph Ross is a writer/actor, who has done both on shows from *Batman* to *The Man from UNCLE*.

239

Episode 42
6 May 1990

Written by	Michael Davidoff and Andrew Boracove
Directed by	Lee Lochhead

Cast

Count Strimpkin	Bill Daily

Count Strimpkin is in hiding after writing 'Thicker Than Water', a book that mocks many of the old vampire traditions. The other vampires, led by Count Vlad the Impaler, want him dead. Grandpa is an old schoolfriend of Strimpkin's, but is on the Impaler's side. When the Count arrives, looking for a hiding spot, Lily helps, but Grandpa wants to turn him in. Nothing can change his mind until he hears that thirty people have been killed when vampire extremists have bombed a bookstore carrying Strimpkin's work. Then he helps the Count to run from the assassination squads.

This was an incredibly unfunny and tasteless attempt to turn the Rushdie affair into a comedy. Bill Daily is best known for his roles as Roger on *I Dream Of Jeannie* (1965–70) and Howard on *The Bob Newhart Show* (1972–78).

Episode 43
20 May 1990

Teleplay by	Bill Rosenthal and Noah Taft
Story by	Laura Glendinning and Donna Blinder
Directed by	Bonnie Franklin

Cast

Dr Frankenstein   Charlie Brill

Herman's feeling ill, so the family calls in a specialist to help – the great-great-great-grandson of Dr Frankenstein. Unfortunately, he's a podiatrist now, calling himself Ken Schaefer, and not a very good one. He's brought Herman's blueprints with him, and his cures seem to accentuate the characteristics of various parts of the original people whose bodies make up Herman. Finally, however, Herman is restored, and Frankenstein gains a certain measure of respect for his own talents. The family receives a whopping house-call bill.

Episode 44
3 June 1990

Written by   Robert Schechter
Directed by   Lee Lochhead

Cast

Foster Newkirk   Barry Dennen

There's a gravedigger's strike, so Herman is off work. Grandpa is on the management's side, being anti-union. After a couple of weeks, Eddie is bored of going to baseball games with his father, and Herman's cleaned everything in the house he can. When money starts running out, Grandpa takes a job as a shoe salesman, and keeps on at Herman. Foster Newkirk, another of the gravediggers, suggests that he and Herman scab, but Herman refuses to compromise on his ideals. The strike is finally over, and Herman's first spending is on new shoes – which he makes Grandpa fit him for.

Episode 45
10 June 1990

Written by   Michael Davidoff
Directed by   Bonnie Franklin

Cast
The Widow Jurgeson*   Herta Ware

*Listed as Johansen

The widow Jurgeson tells the parlour she can't afford a funeral for her dead husband. Herman feels sorry for her, and offers to conduct one from his home for her. Initially, she seems to be a sweet old lady in a wheelchair, but she begins to make increasingly absurd demands on the family, and even convinces Herman to have her as a house guest. Finally, she admits that she hated her husband, and is doing this simply because she wants her revenge on him. Then they discover she's not even poor – she inherited millions from him.

Herta Ware is probably best known to TV viewers for playing Picard's mother on *Star Trek – The Next Generation*.

Season Three
Credits

Produced by	Bryan Joseph
Supervising Producer	Dustin Nelson
Executive Producer	Arthur Annecharico
Co-Executive Producer	Craig Kellem
Co-Producer	Craig Anderson; also Mark Miller (from 6.1.91)
Production Executive	David Buelow

Production Consultant	Tracey Hivner
Production Manager	Peter Field
Art Director	Jimmy Cuomo
Casting	Kim Dorr, CSA, Joey Paul
Based on Characters Developed by	Norman Liebman and Ed Haas
From a Format by	Al Burns and Chris Hayward
Original Theme	Jack Marshall
Arranged by and Additional Music	Wintermoon Music
Additional Scoring	L.A. Arpino, Bill Fulton
Associate Director	Gene Leong
Stage Managers	Jim Mancuso and Jerry Sarcone
Booth P.A.	Allison Cole
Lighting Director	Dan Kuleto
Special Effects	Michael Buenfil and Michael Canepa
Post Production Supervisor	Tom Buel
Properties	Patty Keck
Assistant Properties	Marty Maltos, R. Brandt Daniels
Set Decorator	Sally Bedding, Debbie Madalena
Costume Designer	Jennifer Michaud, Terry Hunter
Costume Assistant	Terry Hunter, Mary M. Flemming
Makeup	David Abbott, Gil Mosko, Carlos Yeggy
Hair Stylist	Jody Lawrence
Technical Director	Nina Wolfson
Audio	William Kennedy III, Thom Wilson

243

Senior Video	Robert Vinson, Jack Palacio, Jnr
Camera	Rocky Danielson, Hector Gonzalez, Jillayne Pautsch, Jim Rohrig
Engineering	Dave Radford and Jim Rudenski
Videotape Editors	Cindi van Winkle, Clifford H. Coburn, Richard L. Roberts
Rerecording Engineers	Brian Buel, Dave Schultz, Linda Keim
Clothing Furnished by	Surf Fetish
Production and Post Production Facilities	The Arthur Company's 'One Take' and 'The Last Stop'
Executive in Charge of Production	Mike Fierman
The Arthur Company MCA TV	

Cast

Herman	John Schuck
Lily	Lee Meriwether
Grandpa	Howard Morton
Marilyn	Hilary Van Dyke
Eddie	Jason Marsden

Episode 46
4 November 1990

Written by	Mark Miller
Directed by	Russ Petranto

Cast

Genghis Khan	Richard Moll
Grandpa's Mother	Ruth Buzzi
Yorga	Sandy Baron
Shirley Zlebnick	Yetta

When Grandpa is depressed at his approaching 400th birthday, the family decides to throw him a party and invite all his old – very old – friends.

Richard Moll is best known for his role as Bull on the sitcom *Night Court*.

Episode 47
2 December 1990

Written by	Mark Miller
Directed by	Russ Petranto

Cast

Mrs Thomas	Lana Schwab
Rob	Dustin Diamond

After drinking one of Grandpa's potions, Eddie discovers he is now telepathic.

Episode 48
30 December 1990

Written by	Robert Schechter
Directed by	Russ Petranto

Cast

Alicia	Terry Ivens

Eddie meets an Italian model and falls in love. When she wants him to get married and move to Europe with her, he agrees.

Episode 49
6 January 1991

Written by   Mark Lyons and
                                 Kimberley Wells
Directed by   Russ Petranto

Cast
TV Announcer   Greg Lewis
Mrs Traynor   Simone Gad

Herman, Grandpa and Eddie are settling down to watch their favourite team on TV, all wearing their lucky mascots – when they are suddenly left to watch the Traynor baby instead.

Episode 50
27 January 1991

Written by   Jeffrey Russel
Directed by   Jerry Ross

Cast
Delivery Man #2   John David Conti

Eddie decides he wants a credit card, but his parents are convinced he'll misuse it.

Episode 51
3 February 1991

Teleplay by	Alan Moskowitz
Story by	Robert Schechter
Directed by	Russ Petranto

Cast

Little Andy	Michael Oliver
Mrs Graves	Kathryn Kates
Big Andy	Moosie Drier

Lily is left an obnoxious kid to babysit, and there's trouble when Grandpa becomes involved with an ageing machine.

Episode 52
10 February 1991

Written by	Bryan Joseph
Directed by	Russ Petranto

Cast

Genie	Billy Barty

While she is cleaning up, Marilyn rubs a magic lamp that makes a genie appear. He has one wish left to give, and everyone in the family wants it.

Episode 53
17 February 1991

Written by	Bryan Joseph
Directed by	Russ Petranto

Cast

Stephanie	Julie McCullough
Jack	Troy Shire
Al	Cal Gibson

Eddie has a serious crush on Stephanie, who in turn is hooked on Jack – a bully who always beats Eddie at video games.

Episode 54
24 February 1991

Teleplay by	Alan Moskowitz
Story by	Craig Kellem
Directed by	Scott Redman

Cast

Slash	Michael Kopelow
Hope	Julia Milaris
Faith	Jennifer Rade

Eddie gets involved with a rock group, and records a hit single.

Episode 55
3 March 1991

Written by	Andrew Borakove
Directed by	Russ Petranto

Cast

Mrs Hummer	Darlene Kardon

Marilyn exposes a career guidance person at her school who's getting kickbacks from a local burger joint to find them workers.

Episode 56
17 March 1991

Teleplay by	Bryan L. Joseph and Andrew Borakove
Story by	Ann L. Gibbs and Joel Kimmel
Directed by	Russ Petranto

Cast

Aunt Lucretia	Camila Ashland
Aynsworth	Kenneth Danziger
Mr Tolliver	Loren Freeman

Aunt Lucretia leaves a treasure trunk to the family – but she's a notorious practical joker, and the trunk is empty . . .

Episode 57
24 March 1991

Written by	Mark Cassutt
Directed by	Scott Redman

Cast

Grandma	Kathleen Freeman
Linda Melcombe	Cathy Lind Hayes
Barry Melcombe	Daniel Doty
Yorga	Sandy Baron
Manny Glicksteen	Dick Gautier

Herman wins a promotion – but he must move to California. The family put the house up for sale, and Grandma decides it had better stay in the family.

This was an uncredited remake of one of the original series, 'Munsters On The Move'.

Episode 58
31 March 1991

Written by   Janice Pieroni and
                             Bruce Teicher
Directed by   Marlena Laird

Cast
Bo   Jim Doughan
Frank Thresher   Roy Stuart

After Grandpa mocks him, Herman decides he's going to
stop being such a sap – and begins by making Grandpa find
a job. Then he moves into big business, and makes a real
killing in the funeral game.

Episode 59
7 April 1991

Written by   Andrew Borakove
Directed by   Russ Petranto

Cast
Natasha Jones   Lucy Lee Flippin
Kyle   Jack Armstrong
Nelson   Lance Wilson-White
Derek   Anthony Palermo

Marilyn is depressed about her lack of a love-life, but when
Derek Anderson asks her to the dance, she turns him down.
Grandpa thinks she's being too picky.

250

Episode 60
14 April 1991

Written by	Howard Friedlander and Ken Peragine
Directed by	Russ Petranto

Cast

Dr Carver	George Furth

Grandpa builds a recycler to help with waste disposal, and it accidentally recycles Herman into a normal human being.

This was another uncredited remake of an episode of the original series, this time of the 'Herman Disfigured' episode.

Episode 61
20 April 1991

Written by	Andrew Borakove
Directed by	Russ Petranto

Cast

Jack	Robbie Rist

Grandpa has a visit from Jack, the surfboarding angel, who tells Grandpa that unless he does a lot of good deeds fast, it's the downward trip for him when the last wave hits.

Episode 62
28 April 1991

Written by	Mark Miller
Directed by	Russ Petranto

Cast

Mother Earth   Kaye Ballard

It's Global Awareness Month, and Mother Earth is convinced that Herman isn't ecologically aware, so she arrives to check up on him.

Episode 63
5 May 1991

Written by   Mark Cassutt
Directed by   Peter Isacksen

Cast

Agent Williams   Dan Conway
Mr Watanabe   Pat Morita

Chain letters cause all kinds of misfortunes at the Munster house, starting with Herman getting a pink slip, and deteriorating from there.

Episode 64
19 May 1991

Written by   Janice Pieroni and
                                  Bruce Teicher
Directed by   Russ Petranto

Cast

Brois   Mel Johnson, Jnr
Betty   Janis Ward
The Policeman   Mark Neely

Grandpa's dishonesty catches up with him when he bets Eddie that he can con Herman into committing a dishonest act.

Episode 65
12 May 1991

Written by   Mark Miller
Directed by   Russ Petranto

Cast
Dr Susan Evans   Marcia Wallace
Okra Dimpley   Francesca Roberts
Larry   Paul Scolardi

Lily's old sorority sister, Susan, arrives for a visit, and tries to make Lily uncomfortable with her life.

Episode 66
16 June 1991

Written by   George Tricker and
                             Neil Rosen
Directed by   Marlene Laird

Regulars only

Money is tight for the family, but Eddie wants a pair of expensive sneakers, and Marilyn wants to go to Fort Lauderdale with her friends.

Biographies

Note: A helpful reference source for some of the following entries was *The Complete Actors Television Credits* (1948–88) by James Robert Parish and Vincent Terrace (The Scarecrow Press, 1989).

John Astin

John Astin was born in Baltimore, Maryland, on 30 March 1930. His father, Allen V. Astin, was Director at the Bureau of Standards in Washington, DC. He was educated at Washington Drama School and Johns Hopkins before attending the University of Minnesota Graduate School. He began his acting career on the New York stage before making the transition to television and movies at the end of the fifties, with the help of Tony Randall. His first wife was actress Suzanne Hahn, with whom he had three children. They divorced during the filming of *The Addams Family*. He branched out into directing TV shows in the seventies, and remains a popular comedy actor to this day. He married actress Patty Duke after they lived together in the sixties, in 1972, and the couple were divorced in 1983. They have a son, Mackenzie, born in 1973, who is also an actor. He is now married to his third wife, Valerie.

I'm Dickens – He's Fenster (1962–63)
The Addams Family (1964–66)
The Pruitts Of Southhampton (1967)
Operation Petticoat (1977–78)
Mary (1985–86)
Eerie, Indiana (1992)
The Addams Family (1992–94) [voice only]
The Adventures Of Brisco County, Jr (1993–94)

254

Maverick: 'The Town That Wasn't There' (2.10.60)

Peter Loves Mary: 'Wilma's Phantom Lover' (1960)

The Twilight Zone: 'A Hundred Yards Over The Rim' (7.4.61)

The Donna Reed Show: 'Mouse At Play' (5.10.61)

Hazel: 'The Investment Club' (1962)

Hennessey: 'Remember Pearl Harbor' (1962)

87th Precinct: 'King's Ransom' (19.2.62)

Route 66: 'Go Read The River' (12.3.62)

Ben Casey: 'Preferably, The Less-Used Arm' (30.4.62)

Dennis The Menace: 'A Quiet Evening' (1962)

77 Sunset Strip: 'Dress rehearsal' (25.5.62)

Route 66: 'Journey To Nineveh' (28.9.62)

The Greatest Show On Earth: 'An Echo Of Faded Velvet' (11.12.63)

The Farmer's Daughter: 'Bless Our Happy Home' (19.2.64)

Destry: 'The Infernal Triangle' (1.5.64)

Occasional Wife: 'I Do, We Don't' (11.10.66)

The Wild, Wild West: 'The Night Of The Tartar' (3.2.67)

Batman: 'Batman's Anniversary/A Riddling Controversy' (8.2, 9.2.67)

Hey Landlord: 'Czech Your Wife, Sir?' (9.4.67)

Sheriff Who (25.9.67) [Unsold pilot]

The Flying Nun: 'Flight Of The Dodo Bird' (12.10.67)

Gunsmoke: 'Hard-Luck Henry' (23.10.67)

He And She: 'The Coming Out Party' (15.11.67)

Death Valley Days (1968)

CBS Playhouse: 'The Experiment' (25.2.69)

Bonanza: 'Abner Willoughby's Return' (21.12.69)

Love, American Style: 'Love And The Intruder' (4.12.70)

Night Gallery: 'Pamela's Voice' (13.1.71)

The Odd Couple: 'Oscar's New Life' (5.3.71)

The Doris Day Show: 'The Father-Son Weekend' (8.3.71)

Men From Shiloh: 'Jump Up' (24.3.71)

Night Gallery: 'Hell's Bells' (17.11.71)

Insight: 'Death Of An Elephant' (1972)

Love, American Style: 'Love And The Intruder' (25.2.72)

McMillan & Wife: 'Night Of The Wizard' (24.9.72)

Night Gallery: 'The Girl With The Hungry Eyes' (1.10.72)

Temperatures Rising (10.10.72)

Love, American Style: 'Love And The Happy Medium' (27.10.72)

McMillan & Wife: 'Cop Of The Year' (19.11.72)

Insight: 'Truck Stop' (1973)

Circle Of Fear: 'Graveyard Shift' (16.2.73)

The Partridge Family: 'Diary Of A Mad Millionaire' (23.3.73)

McMillan & Wife: 'Two Dollars On Trouble To Win' (1.4.73)

Insight: 'The One-Armed Man' (1974)

Afternoon Playbreak: 'Miss Kline, We Love You' (27.2.74)

Insight: 'Out Of The Depths' (1975)

Get Christie Love!: 'Our Lady In London' (29.1.75)

Police Woman: 'Nothing Left To Lose' (14.2.75)

Marcus Welby, MD: 'Unindicted Wife' (25.2.75)

The Bob Crane Show: 'A Case Of Misdiagnosis' (8.5.75)

Insight: 'For The Love Of Annie' (1976)

Police Story: 'Firebird' (6.2.76)

Philip And Barbera (13.8.76) [Unsold pilot]

Welcome Back, Kotter: 'The Museum' (28.10.76)

Lannigan's Rabbi: 'Say It Ain't So, Chief' (17.4.77)

Insight: 'Second Chorus' (1978)

Love Boat (16.9.78)

Fantasy Island: 'The Beachcomber/The Last Whodunnit' (30.9.78)

Facts Of Life: 'Summer Of '84' (26.9.84)

Diff'rent Strokes: 'A Haunting We Will Go' (29.9.84)

Murder, She Wrote: 'Hooray For Homicide' (28.10.84)
Night Court: 'Inside Harry Stone' (29.11.84)
Simon & Simon: 'Revolution #9½' (13.12.84)
Riptide: 'Baxter And Boz' (22.1.85)
Otherworld: 'Mansion Of The Beast' (9.3.85)
Murder, She Wrote: 'Joshua Peabody Died Here' (6.10.85)
Murder, She Wrote: 'A Lady In The Lake' (10.11.85)
Murder, She Wrote: 'Sticks And Stones' (15.12.85)
The Love Boat: 'Egypt' (8.2.86)
Mr Boogedy (20.4.86) [Unsold pilot]
Night Court: 'The Next Voice You Hear' (2.10.86)
Neat And Tidy (15.12.86) [Unsold pilot]
St. Elsewhere: 'Visiting Daze' (21.1.87)
Harry Anderson's Side Show (30.10.87)
Night Court: 'I'm Okay, You're A Catatonic Schizophrenic' (21.1.88)
Charles In Charge: 'Pickle Plot' (30.4.88)
The Saint: 'The Blue Dulac' (22.10.89)
They Came From Outer Space: 'UFO' (Part Two) (26.3.91)
Bonkers: 'Stressed To Kill' (1993) [voice only]
Burke's Law: 'Who Killed Alexander The Great?' (4.3.94)

Movies
West Side Story (1961)
That Touch Of Mink (1963)
The Wheeler Dealers (1963)
The Spirit Is Willing (1967)
Candy (1968)
Viva Max! (1969)
Bunny O'Hare (1971)
Two On A Bench (1971) TV
Every Little Crook And Nanny (1972)

Get To Know Your Rabbit (1972)
Evil Roy Slade (1972) TV
The Brothers O'Toole (1973)
Skyway To Death (1974) TV
Only With Married Men (1974) TV
The Dream Makers (1975) TV
Freaky Friday (1977)
Hallowe'en With The New Addams Family (1977) TV
National Lampoon's European Vacation (1985)

Director
McMillan & Wife: 'Murder By The Barrel' (29.9.71)
McMillan & Wife: 'Death Is A Seven Point Favorite'
(8.12.71)
CHiPs: 'Meet The New Guy' (10.10.82)
CHiPs: 'Rock Devil Rock' (31.10.82)
CHiPs: 'Brat Patrol' (27.2.83)

Carolyn Jones

Carolyn Jones was born in Amarillo, Texas, on 28 April 1929. She had always wanted to be an actress, and studied at the Pasadena Playhouse. She made her stage debut while still a teenager. She became a disc jockey at one point before finding success in minor TV shows and movies. She married writer/producer Aaron Spelling in 1953, but they divorced in 1964. She married conductor Herbert Greene in 1968, and this marriage also ended in divorce. Her final husband was actor Peter Bailey-Britton. She died of cancer on 3 August 1983.

The Addams Family (1964–66)
Roots (1977)
Capitol (1982–83)

Dragnet: 'The Big Sophomore' (1.10.53)
Pepsi Cola Playhouse: 'Account Closed' (15.1.54)
Pepsi Cola Playhouse: 'The Silence' (26.3.54)
Dragnet: 'The Big Frame' (22.4.54)
Schlitz Playhouse Of The Stars: 'Prisoner In The Town' (7.5.54)
Pepsi Cola Playhouse: 'Double In Danger' (18.6.54)
Dear Phoebe: 'Dear Phoebe' (10.9.54)
Treasury Men In Action: 'The Case Of The Careless Murder' (6.1.55)
Treasury Men In Action: 'The Case Of The Elder Brother' (10.2.55)
The Millionaire: 'The Story Of Emily Short' (16.2.55)
Treasury Men In Action: 'The Case Of The Black Sheep' (31.3.55)
Studio '57: 'The Black Sheep's Daughter' (26.4.55)
Dragnet: 'The Big Note' (5.5.55)
Your Play Time: 'Call From Robert Jest' (6.8.55)
Studio '57: 'Diagnosis Of A Selfish Lady' (23.10.55)
Fireside Theater: 'The Key' (15.11.55)
Alfred Hitchcock Presents: 'The Cheney Vase' (25.12.55)
Four Star Playhouse: 'The Answer' (29.12.55)
The 20th Century Fox Hour: 'The Hefferan Family' (13.6.56)
The Jane Wyman Theater: 'Little Black Lie' (1.1.57)
The Zane Grey Theater: 'Until The Man Dies' (25.1.57)
Wire Service: 'Dateline Las Vegas' (4.3.57)
Schlitz Playhouse Of The Stars: 'The Girl In The Grass' (15.3.57)
Panic: 'The Airline Hostess' (9.4.57)
GE Theater: 'The Man Who Inherited Everything' (19.5.57)
Climax: 'The Disappearance Of Amanda Hale' (30.5.57)
The Millionaire: 'The Story Of Matt Kirby' (18.9.57)
Wagon Train: 'The John Cameron Story' (2.10.57)

Schlitz Playhouse Of The Stars: 'High Barrier' (18.10.57)
Playhouse 90: 'The Last Man' (9.1.58)
The David Niven Show: 'Portrait' (16.6.59)
The Zane Grey Theater: 'Picture Of Sal' (28.1.60)
Playhouse Of The Stars: 'The Breaking Point' (1960)
The June Allyson Show: 'Love On Credit' (17.11.60)
The Zane Grey Theater: 'Blood Red' (26.1.61)
The Dick Powell Show: 'Who Killed Julie Greer?' (26.9.61)
Wagon Train: 'The Jenna Douglas Story' (1.11.61)
The Dick Powell Show: 'Goodbye, Hannah' (21.11.61)
Frontier Circus: 'Stopover In Paradise' (22.2.62)
The Lloyd Bridges Show: 'Just Married' (16.10.62)
Dr Kildare: 'The Mask Makers' (18.10.62)
The Dick Powell Show: 'The Sea Witch' (23.10.62)
Wagon Train: 'The Molly Kincaid Story' (16.9.63)
Burke's Law: 'Who Killed Sweet Betsy?' (1.11.63)
Burke's Law: 'Who Killed Madison Cooper?' (24.1.64)
DuPont Show Of The Month: 'Jeremy Rabbit, The Secret Avenger' (5.4.64)
Batman: 'Marsha, Queen Of Diamonds/Marsha's Scheme Of Diamonds' (23.11, 24.11.66)
Batman: 'Penguin Is A Girl's Best Friend/Penguin Sets A Trend/Penguin's Disastrous End' (26.1, 1.2, 2.2.67)
Rango: 'What's A Nice Girl Like You Doing Holding Up A Place Like This?' (17.2.67)
The Danny Thomas Hour: 'Fame Is A Four-letter Word' (30.10.67)
Bracken's World: 'King David' (3.10.69)
The Mod Squad: 'Lisa' (4.11.69)
Love, America Style: 'Love And The Geisha' (10.11.69)
The Name Of The Game: 'Why I Blew Up Dakota' (4.12.70)
Men From Shiloh: 'The Legacy Of Spencer Flats' (27.1.71)

Dan August: 'Assassin' (8.4.71)
Ghost Story: 'The Summer House' (13.10.72)
The New Perry Mason: 'The Case Of The Frenzied Feminist' (16.12.73)
Ironside: 'Raise The Devil' (12.9, 19.9.74)
Kolchak: The Night Stalker: 'Demon In Lace' (7.2.75)
Ellery Queen: 'The Adventure Of The Hardhearted Huckster' (21.3.76)
Wonder Woman: 'The Feminum Mystique' (6.11, 8.11.76)
Wonder Woman: 'Wonder Woman In Hollywood' (16.2.77)
Quincy, ME: 'Valley View' (13.5.77)
Quincy, ME: 'Last Of The Dinosaurs' (16.12.77)
The Love Boat (27.10.79)
Fantasy Island: 'Tatoo's Romance' (10.11.79)
Fantasy Island: 'Gigolo' (29.11.80)
Quincy, ME: 'Strain Of Guilt' (14.1.81)
Fantasy Island: 'Daddy's Little Girl/The Whistle' (30.1.82)

Movies
The Turning Point (1952)
The Road To Bali (1952)
The House Of Wax (1952)
Off Limits (1953)
The Big Heat (1953)
The Saracen Blade (1954)
Three Hours To Kill (1954)
Desiree (1954)
Shield For Murder (1954)
The Seven Year Itch (1955)
The Tender Trap (1955)
Invasion Of The Body Snatchers (1955)
The Opposite Sex (1956)

The Man Who Knew Too Much (1956)
The Batchelor Party (1957) [Oscar nomination, best supporting actress]
Baby Face Nelson (1957)
Marjorie Morningstar (1958)
King Creole (1958)
Last Train From Gun Hill (1958)
A Hole In The Head (1959)
The Man In The Net (1959)
Career (1959)
Ice Palace (1960)
Sail A Crooked Ship (1962)
How The West Was Won (1962)
A Ticklish Affair (1963)
Heaven With A Gun (1968)
Color Me Dead (1970)
Eaten Alive/Death Trap (1977)
Hallowe'en With The New Addams Family (1977) TV
Little Ladies Of The Night (1977) TV
Good Luck, Miss Wyckoff (1979)
The Dance Of Death (1979)
The French Atlantic Affair (1979) TV
The Dream Merchants (1980) TV
Midnight Lace (1981) TV

Jackie Coogan

Jack Leslie Coogan was born in Los Angeles, CA, on 24 October 1914. His parents, Jack and Illian Coogan, were vaudevillian actors, and he made his first film at the age of 18 months. He appeared on stage, where Charlie Chaplin was impressed by his acting. He cast Coogan in a two reeler, and gave him his first starring role – in *The Kid* – at the age of 6. This film made him the very first child star and brought him a small fortune, including a half-million dollar payment to switch from First National to Metro Films.

Troubles began when he started to grow up, and was no longer the mop-headed kid that the audiences loved. On 5 March 1935, he was involved in a car crash that killed his father and another child actor, Junior Durkin. They were returning from a trip to Mexico when another car forced them off the road and over a cliff. Coogan was the only survivor – with seven broken ribs and three bones broken in his back. He carried the bodies up the cliff and called his mother to tell her of the accident before collapsing.

His mother later remarried, to their financial advisor Arthur L. Bernstein, and Coogan was supposed to receive the monies owed him from his acting. When they didn't pay up, he successfully sued his parents for misuse of his earnings as a child actor. This led to the enactment of California's Coogan Law in an attempt to prevent the same happening to other child stars. By the time the case was settled, though, instead of the $4 million he was owed, he received just over $100,000.

He joined the Army shortly before the attack on Pearl Harbour brought the US into World War II. He moved to the glider corps, becoming a pilot. During the invasion of Burma, he flew the first glider that landed on 5 March 1944, and won the Air Medal for his actions.

He married actress Betty Grable in 1937, but stress over the money problems led them to divorce two years later. His second marriage was to movie extra Flower Parry, on 10 August 1941. They had a son, John Anthony, but were divorced a couple of months later. His third wife was Ann McCormack, by whom he had a daughter, Joan in 1948. They were divorced in 1950, and he married his final wife, Dodie, in 1952. They had a daughter, Leslie, in 1954. His younger brother, Robert, also became an actor, as did a son, Jackie Coogan, Jnr (who appeared on *The Munsters* the same time his father was in *The Addams Family*).

He remained active as an actor for over 60 years, making somewhere in the order of 1400 TV show appearances. He earned $35,000 a year for his role as Fester, but was unhappy with his initial treatment. The Network apparently had doubts about him (he'd been arrested twice for drinking and once for marijuana possession), but after he tested for the role, he was okayed by Harve Bennett (who later produced the *Star Trek* movies). For the first season, he was only credited at the end, but he managed to have his name added to the opening credits for the second season. He died of a heart attack in Santa Monica, CA, on 1 March 1984.

Pantomime Quiz (1950–55)
Cowboy G-Men (1952)
McKeever & The Colonel (1962–63)
The Addams Family (1964–66)
The Addams Family (1973–75) [Voice only]
The Red Skelton Show (14 appearances)
Racket Squad: 'The Christmas Caper' (25.12.52)
So This Is Hollywood: 'Reunion In Hollywood' (11.6.55)
Matinee Theater: 'The Old Payola' (8.8.56)
Playhouse 90: 'Forbidden Area' (4.10.56)
Damon Runyon Theater: 'Honorary Degree' (10.12.56)
Playhouse 90: 'The Star Wagon' (24.1.57)
Playhouse 90: 'The Troublemakers' (21.11.57)
Telephone Time: 'Death Of A Nobody' (31.12.57)
Studio One: 'Trial By Slander' (20.1.58)
Matinee Theater: 'The Iceman' (4.2.58)
The Loretta Young Show: '810 Franklin Street' (1.3.59)
Peter Gunn: 'Keep Smiling' (23.3.59)
GE Theater: 'The Indian Giver' (17.5.59)
Lineup: 'Wake Up To Terror' (30.9.59)
Alfred Hitchcock Presents: 'Anniversary Gift' (1.11.59)
Hawaiian Eye: 'Dangerous Eden' (4.11.59)

The Loretta Young Show: 'Ten Men And A Girl'
(15.11.59)
The Adventures Of Ozzie And Harriet (20.3.60)
The Ann Sothern Show: 'Surprise, Surprise' (18.4.60)
The Ann Sothern Show: 'Wedding March' (16.5.60)
Shirley Temple Theater: 'Tom And Huck' (9.10.60)
The Outlaws: 'The Rape Of Red Sky' (27.10.60)
The Tab Hunter Show: 'I Love A Marine' (30.10.60)
Guestward Ho: 'The Matchmakers' (15.12.60)
Klondike: 'Halliday's Cub' (19.12.60)
Shirley Temple Theater: 'Rebel Gun' (22.1.61)
Best Of The Post: 'Martha' (18.2.61)
The Americans: 'The Coward' (8.5.61)
Perry Mason: 'The Case Of The Crying Comedian'
(14.10.61)
The Andy Griffith Show: 'Barney On The Rebound'
(30.10.61)
The Outlaws: 'The Sisters' (15.2.62)
Follow The Sun: 'A Choice Of Weapons' (25.2.62)
Father Of The Bride: 'Stanley's Steamer' (24.8.62)
The Dick Powell Show: 'Thunder In A Forgotten Town'
(5.3.63)
Perry Mason: 'The Case Of The Witless Witness'
(16.5.63)
The Lucy Show: 'Lucy And The Military Academy'
(9.12.63)
Perry Mason: 'The Case Of The Fifty Millionth
Frenchman' (20.2.64)
The Bob Hope Chrysler Theater: 'Her School For
Batchelors' (20.3.64)
Burke's Law: 'Who Killed Annie Foran?' (10.4.64)
Perry Mason: 'The Case Of The Final Fade-Out'
(22.5.66)
The Hoffer (15.8.66) [Unsold pilot]
The Virginian: 'Trail To Ashley Mountain' (2.11.66)

Family Affair: 'Fat, Fat The Water Rat' (23.10.67)
The Wild, Wild West: 'The Night Of The Cut-Throats'
(17.11.67)
The Lucy Show: 'Lucy Gets Involved' (15.1.68)
The Outsider: 'Tell It Like It Is . . . And You're Dead'
(4.12.68)
My Friend Tony: 'Death Comes In Small Packages'
(12.1.69)
The Wild, Wild West: 'The Night Of The Winged Terror'
(17.1, 24.1.69)
Hawaii Five-O: 'Face Of The Dragon' (22.1.69)
I Dream Of Jeannie: 'Guess Who's Going To Be A
Bride?' (30.9, 7.10.69)
Hawaii Five-O: 'Which Way Did They Go?' (24.12.69)
Love, American Style: 'Love And The First Nighters'
(6.2.70)
The Name Of The Game: 'Man Of The People' (6.3.70)
Barefoot In The Park: 'Disorder In The Court' (12.11.70)
The Partridge Family: 'Did You Hear The One About
Danny Partridge?' (20.11.70)
Julia (8.12.70)
The Name Of The Game: 'The Glory Shouter' (18.12.70)
The New Andy Griffith Show (5.2.71)
The Interns: 'The Quality Of Mercy' (12.2.71)
The Jimmy Stewart Show: 'Guest Of Honor' (7.11.71)
Alias Smith And Jones: 'Dreadful Sorry, Clementine'
(18.11.71)
Longstreet: 'This Little Piggy went To The Marquette'
(2.12.71)
Ironside: 'License To Kill' (2.12.71)
McMillan & Wife: 'Death Is A Seven Point Favorite'
(8.12.71)
Adam-12: 'Adoption' (2.2.72)
Owen Marshall, Counselor At Law: 'Shine A Light On
Me' (3.2.72)

Alias Smith And Jones: 'Which Way To The O.K. Corral?' (10.2.72)

Love, American Style: 'Love And The Newscasters' (26.2.72)

The Brady Bunch: 'The Fender Benders' (10.3.72)

Emergency (11.11.72)

Love, American Style: 'Love And The Happy Days' (17.11.72)

Love, American Style: 'Love And The Tycoon' ????

Alias Smith And Jones: 'McGuffin' (9.12.72)

Marcus Welby, MD: 'The Problem With Charlie' (30.1.73)

Hawaii Five-O: 'Little Girl Blue' (13.2.73)

Barnaby Jones: 'Sing A Song Of Murder' (1.4.73)

McMillan & Wife: 'Two Dollars On Trouble To Win' (1.4.73)

The FBI: 'Break-In' (7.10.73)

Here's Lucy: 'Lucy's Tenant' (22.10.73)

The Partridge Family: 'Made In San Pueblo' (8.12.73)

Hec Ramsey: 'Dead Heat' (3.2.74)

Ironside: 'Class Of '40' (7.2.74)

McMillan And Wife: 'Cross And Double Cross' (17.2.74)

Dirty Sally: 'The Hanging Of Cyrus Pike' (5.4.74)

Gunsmoke: 'The Guns Of Cibola Blanca' (23.9, 30.9.74)

A Lucille Ball Special (1.3.75)

Police Story: 'The Witness' (11.3.75)

McCoy: 'Double Take' (30.11.75)

Movin' On: 'The Big Switch' (20.1.76)

Lannigan's Rabbi: 'Say It Ain't So, Chief' (17.4.77)

Sweepstakes (9.3.79)

Movies

Skinner's Baby (1917)

A Day's Pleasure (1919)

The Kid (1920)

Peck's Bad Boy (1921)
Oliver Twist (1921)
My Boy (1922)
Trouble (1922)
Daddy (1923)
Circus Days (1923)
Long Live The King (1924)
A Boy Of Flanders (1924)
The Rag Man (1924)
Little Robinson Crusoe (1925)
Johnny Get Your Gun (1925)
Old Clothes (1925)
Johnny Get Your Hair Cut (1926)
The Bugle Call (1927)
Buttons (1927)
Tom Sawyer (1930)
Huckleberry Finn (1931)
Home On The Range (1935)
College Swing (1938)
Kilroy Was Here (1947)
French Leave (1948)
Skipalong Rosenbloom (1951)
Outlaw Women (1952)
Lost Women (1956)
The Proud Ones (1956)
The Joker Is Wild (1957)
The Buster Keaton Story (1957)
High School Confidential (1958)
Lonelyhearts (1958)
The Beat Generation (1959)
Night Of The Quarter Moon (1959)
The Big Operator (1959)
Sex Kittens Go To College (1960)
John Goldfarb Please Come Home (1964)
A Fine Madness (1966)

The Shakiest Gun In The West (1968)
Million Dollar Legs (1972)
Marlowe (1969)
Cool Million/Mask Of Marcella (1972) TV
Cahill, US Marshal (1973)
The Phantom Of Hollywood (1974) TV
The Manchu Eagle Murder Caper Mystery (1975)
The Specialists (1975) TV
Sherlock Holmes In New York (1976) TV
Hallowe'en With The New Addams Family (1977) TV
Human Experiments (1979)
The Escape Artist (1982)
The Prey (1984)
Dr Heckyl And Mr Hype

Blossom Rock

Blossom MacDonald was born in Philadelphia on 21 August 1896, older sister of actress/singer Jeanette MacDonald. She married in the twenties, becoming Blossom Rock. She became an actress in the thirties, under the name 'Marie Blake', but reverted to her real name later. She started out in vaudeville and small acting troupes before breaking into films. She appeared as the switchboard operator in many of the *Dr Kildare* movies. She died on 14 January 1978.

The Addams Family (1964–66)

Goodyear Theatre: 'Wait Till Spring' (25.5.59)
Goodyear Theatre: 'The Incorrigibles' (12.10.59)

Movies
Mannequin (1937)
Everybody Sing! (1938)
Love Finds Andy Hardy (1938)

Dramatic School (1938)
The Women (1939)
Calling Dr Kildare (1939)
The Secret Of Dr Kildare (1939)
They Knew What They Wanted (1940)
A Child Is Born (1940)
Dr Kildare's Strange Case (1940)
Dr Kildare Goes Home (1940)
Dr Kildare's Crisis (1940)
Caught In The Draft (1941)
Remember The Day (1941)
The People vs. Dr Kildare (1941)
I Married A Witch (1942)
The Major And The Minor (1942)
Dr Kildare's Victory (1942)
Calling Dr Gillespie (1942)
Dr Gillespie's New Assistant (1942)
Dr Gillespie's Criminal Case (1943)
Pillow To Post (1945)
Between Two Women (1945)
Abbott And Costello In Hollywood (1945)
Dark Delusion (1947)
Mourning Becomes Electra (1947)
The Girl From Manhattan (1948)
Alimony (1949)
The Snake Pit (1949)
Love Nest (1951)
The FBI Girl (1951)
The Brigand (1952)
Hilda Crane (1956)
She Devil (1957)
From The Terrace (1960)
The Second Time Around (1961)
The Best Man (1964)

Ted Cassidy

Ted Cassidy was born in Pittsburgh, Pennsylvania, in 1932. He grew to six feet tall by the time he was 11, naturally being selected for athletics. He attended college on athletic scholarships, but majored in Drama. He wanted to become an actor, so he moved into radio, where his size couldn't be held against him. He was host, and sports and programme director for a station in Dallas, Texas, when he managed to get a break into TV. His size (6 feet 9 inches) and his deep voice made him a natural for villainous roles, though he is best known as Lurch. He provided voices for many animated shows. He and his wife, Jesse, had two children before they split up, a son, Sean, and a daughter, Lynn. He died following open heart surgery on 16 January 1979.

The Addams Family (1964–66)
The New Adventures Of Huck Finn (1968–69)
The Addams Family (1973–75) [v/o]

The Girl From UNCLE: 'The Montori Device Affair' (11.10.66)
Star Trek: 'What Are Little Girls Made Of?' (20.10.66)
Lost In Space: 'The Thief From Outer Space' (9.11.66)
Star Trek: 'The Corbomite Maneuver' (10.11.66)
Batman: 'The Penguin's Nest/The Bird's Last Jest' (7.12, 8.12.66)
Star Trek: 'Arena' (19.1.67)
The Man From UNCLE: 'The Napoleon's Tomb Affair' (27.1.67)
The Monroes: 'Wild Bull' (15.2.67)
Daniel Boone: 'The Scrimshaw Ivory Chart' (4.1.68)
I Dream Of Jeannie: 'Genie, Genie, Who's Got The Genie?' (Part Three) (30.1.68)
I Dream Of Jeannie: 'Please Don't Feed The Astronauts'

(13.2.68)
Banacek: 'Ten Thousand Dollars A Page' (10.1.73)
The Bionic Woman: 'The Return Of Bigfoot' (22.9.76)

Movies
Mackenna's Gold (1968)
Genesis II (1973) TV
Planet Earth (1974) TV
Harry And Walter Go To New York (1976)
The Last Remake Of Beau Geste (1977)
Hallowe'en With The New Addams Family (1977) TV
Benny & Barney: Las Vegas Undercover (1977) TV

Ken Weatherwax

Ken Weatherwax was born in Los Angeles in 1955, and is the nephew of Rudd Weatherwax, owner and trainer of the original Lassie. He worked for a while in commercials, but quit acting after *The Addams Family*, not really interested in pursuing it as a career.

The Addams Family (1964–66)

Movies
Hallowe'en With The New Addams Family (1977) TV

Lisa Loring

Lisa Loring was born in the South Pacific to parents serving in the US Navy on 16 February 1958. Her parents divorced shortly after her birth, and she grew up in Hawaii and then Los Angeles with her mother. Her role in *The Addams Family* brought her attention and money – which she wasted when it came to her as a teenager – but a lot of pressures. Her mother was an alcoholic and died while Lisa was in her teens. After *The Addams Family*, Lisa's career went nowhere, and she married at 15. She was divorced the following year, and developed a drug problem, which she overcame with difficulty. Her current husband is a former erotic movie actor, and the two of them have been making the rounds of the American talk shows in recent years.

The Addams Family (1964–66)
As The World Turns (1981–83)

The Girl From UNCLE: 'The Montori Device Affair' (11.10.66)
Fantasy Island: 'The Flight Of The Great Yellow Bird/The Island Of Lost Women' (25.11.78)
Barnaby Jones: 'Memory Of A Nightmare' (14.12.78)
Barnaby Jones: 'Indoctrination In Evil' (1.11.79)

Movies
Hallowe'en With The New Addams Family (1977) TV

Felix Silla

Felix Silla was raised just outside Rome. He trained as a circus performer, touring with the Ringling Brothers and Barnum & Bailey. His abilities brought him as a stunt man to Hollywood. He often doubles for children, and has his own group, The Original Harmonica Band.

The Addams Family (1964–66)
Buck Rogers In The 25th Century (1979–81)

Bonanza: 'Hoss And The Leprechauns' (22.12.63)
The Girl From UNCLE: 'The Romany Lie Affair' (6.12.66)

Movies

A Ticklish Affair (1963)
Don't Be Afraid Of The Dark (1973) TV
The Towering Inferno (1974)
The Black Bird (1975)
The Hindenberg (1975)
Hallowe'en With The New Addams Family (1977) TV
Battlestar Galactica (1978) TV
Buck Rogers In The 25th Century (1979)
E.T. (1982)

Fred Gwynne

Frederick Hubbard Gwynne was born in New York City on 10 July 1926, son of a stockbroker. He grew to 6 feet 5 inches tall. During World War II, he served in the Navy, then studied art on the GI bill. He graduated from Harvard in 1951 before turning to acting instead. He found it didn't pay well, and worked for a while as a copywriter at J. Walter Thompson. Then his career began to take off, starting with Broadway work in 1952, and he quit the agency. As well as acting, he was an artist in many media. He held his first show in 1989, consisting of artwork puns. A bell like a banana was 'Banana Peel', for example. He also wrote and illustrated a dozen children's books. He and his wife Deborah had four children. He died from pancreatic cancer on 2 July 1993.

Car 54, Where Are You? (1961–63)
The Munsters (1964–66)

You'll Never Get Rich: 'The Eating Contest' (15.11.55)
The Phil Silvers Show: 'For The Birds' (1956)
Studio One: 'The Landlady's Daughter' (26.11.56)
Kraft Theater: 'Sextuplets' (7.8.57)

Suspicion: 'Hand In Glove' (21.10.57)
Kraft Theater: 'The Big Heist' (13.11.57)
DuPont Show Of The Month: 'Harvey' (22.9.58)
DuPont Show Of The Month: 'The Hasty Heart' (18.12.58)
Play Of The Week: 'The Old Foolishness' (6.3.61)
DuPont Show Of The Month: 'Seven Keys To Baldpate' (24.1.62)
US Steel Hour: 'Don't Shake The Family Tree' (15.5.63)
NY Television Theater: 'The Lesson' (17.10.66)
NET Playhouse: 'Infancy' (15.12.67)
Guess What I Did Today? (10.9.68) [Unsold pilot]
Arsenic And Old Lace (2.4.69)
Anderson And Company (12.5.69) [Unsold pilot]
Hallmark Hall Of Fame: 'The Littlest Angel' (6.12.69)
NET Playhouse: 'Paradise Lost' (25.2, 4.3.71)
Hollywood Television Theater: 'The Police' (14.10.71)
Dames At Sea (15.11.71)
Hallmark Hall Of Fame: 'Harvey' (22.3.71)
Bound For Freedom (7.3.76)
Annyone For Tennyson?: 'A Tribute To Anonymous Poets' (4.5.77)
How, What And Witch (27.10.79)
American Short Story: 'The Man That Corrupted Hadleyburg' (17.3.80)
A Day With Conrad Greene (9.6.80)
American Playhouse: 'Any friend Of Nicholas Nickleby Is A Friend Of Mine' (9.2.82)
American Playhouse: 'The Killing Floor' (10.4.82)
Jake's M.O. (30.7.87) [Unsold Pilot]

Movies
On The Waterfront (1954)
Munster, Go Home! (1966)
Captains Courageous (1977) TV

La Luna (1978)
Sanctuary Of Fear (1979) TV
Simon (1980)
So Fine (1981)
The Munsters' Revenge (1981) TV
The Mysterious Stranger (1982) TV
The Cotton Club (1984)
Water (1985)
Kane And Abel (1985) TV
The Boy Who Could Fly (1986)
Vanishing Act (1986) TV
The Christmas Star (1986) TV
Ironweed (1987)
Murder By The Book (1987) TV
Disorganized Crime (1989)
Pet Semetary (1989)
Murder In Black And White (1990) TV
My Cousin Vinnie (1992)
Shadows And Fog (1992)

Books
Pigeon Toad
Chocolate Moose For Dinner
The King Who Rained
A Prince Of A Frog
The Story Of Ick

Al Lewis

Al Lewis was born upstate New York in 1910. At the age
of 12, he left home to join a travelling circus. After this, he
moved to New York, where he performed in vaudeville,
Broadway, radio and TV. His identification with the role of
Grandpa on *The Munsters* led to his hosting movie festivals
on cable TV, and a line of repackaged low-budget horror

276

film releases on video. In the eighties, he opened his own Greenwich village restaurant – 'Grandpa's Pasta and Pizza', which he later sold.

Car 54, Where Are You? (1961–63)
The Munsters (1964–66)
Super Scary Saturdays (1987–89)

Lost In Space: 'Rocket To Earth' (15.2.67)
Taxi: 'On The Job' (Part 2) (14.5.81)
The Magical World Of Disney: 'Save The Dog' (5.2.89)

Movies
Munster, Go Home! (1966)
Ring Of Passion (1978) TV
The Munsters' Revenge (1981) TV
Married To The Mob (1988)
Car 54, Where Are You? (1994)

Yvonne de Carlo

Yvonne de Carlo was born Peggy Middleton in Vancouver, Canada, on 1 September 1922. Her father was a New Zealander who deserted the family when she was 3. She was a dancer from childhood, and appeared as such in nightclubs before breaking into films. She was often cast in harem roles or as dancing girls in Westerns. She married stuntman/actor Robert Morgan, whom she met filming *The Ten Commandments*. She retired from work to raise their two sons, Bruce and Michael. Her husband was badly injured in a stunt, however, so she returned to work, accepting any part simply to support her family. After the success of *The Munsters*, she could afford to be a little more choosy. She still works in films occasionally.

The Munsters (1964–66)

Lights Out: 'Another Country' (24.3.52)
Ford Theater: 'Madame 44' (24.9.53)
Backbone Of America (29.12.53)
Screen Director's Playhouse: 'Hot Cargo' (4.1.56)
Star Stage: 'The Sainted General' (6.4.56)
Playhouse 90: 'Verdict Of Three' (24.4.58)
Bonanza: 'A Rose For Lotta' (12.9.59)
Adventures In Paradise: 'Isle Of Eden' (22.2.60)
Follow The Sun: 'The Longest Crap Game In History'
(5.11.61)
Follow The Sun: 'Annie Beeler's Place' (11.2.62)
Death Valley Days: 'The Lady Was An MD' (1962)
The Virginian: 'A Time Remembered' (11.12.63)
Burke's Law: 'Who Killed Beau Sparrow?' (27.12.63)
The Greatest Show On Earth: 'The Night The Monkey
Died' (10.3.64)
The Girl From UNCLE: 'The Moulin Ruse Affair'
(17.1.67)
Custer: 'The Raiders' (27.12.67)
The Virginian: 'Crime Wave At Buffalo Springs'
(29.1.69)
The Name Of The Game: 'Island Of Gold And Precious
Stones' (16.1.70)
Fantasy Island: 'The Mermaid/The Victim' (1.12.79)
Murder, She Wrote: 'Jessica Behind Bars' (1.12.85)

Movies
Harvard, Here I Come! (1942)
This Gun For Hire (1942)
Road To Morocco (1942)
Lucky Jordan (1942)
Youth On Parade (1942)
Rhythm Parade (1943)
The Crystal Ball (1943)
Salute For Three (1943)

For Whom The Bell Tolls (1943)
So Proudly We Hail! (1943)
Let's Face It (1943)
True To Life (1943)
The Deerslayer (1943)
Standing Room Only (1944)
The Story Of Dr Wassel (1944)
Rainbow Island (1944)
Kismet (1944)
Practically Yours (1944)
Here Come The Waves (1944)
Bring On The Girls (1945)
Salome, Where She Danced (1945)
Frontier Gal (1945)
Song Of Scheherazade (1947)
Brute Force (1947)
Slave Girl (1947)
Black Bart (1948)
Casbah (1948)
River Lady (1948)
Criss Cross (1949)
Calamity Jane And Sam Bass (1949)
The Gal Who Took The West (1949)
Buccaneer's Girl (1950)
The Desert Hawk (1950)
Tomahawk (1951)
Hotel Sahara (1951)
Silver City (1951)
The San Francisco Story (1952)
Scarlet Angel (1952)
Hurricane Smith (1952)
Sombrero (1953)
She Devils (1953)
Fort Algiers (1953)
The Captain's Paradise (1953)

La Castiglione (1954)
Border River (1954)
Happy Ever After/Tonight's The Night (1954)
Passion (1954)
Shotgun (1955)
Flame Of The Islands (1956)
Magic Fire (1956)
Raw Edge (1956)
Death Of A Scoundrel (1956)
The Ten Commandments (1956)
Band Of Angels (1957)
Mary Magdalene (1958)
Timbuktu (1959)
McClintock! (1963)
A Global Affair (1964)
Law Of The Lawless (1964)
Tentazioni Proibite (1965)
Munster, Go Home! (1966)
Hostile Guns (1967)
The Power (1968)
Arizona Bushwhackers (1968)
The Delta Factor (1970)
The Seven Minutes (1971)
The Girl On The Late, Late Show (1974) TV
The Mark Of Zorro (1974) TV
It Seemed Like A Good Idea At The Time (1975)
Satan's Cheerleaders (1977)
Nocturna (1979)
Silent Scream (1979)
Guyana Cult Of The Damned (1980)
The Man With Bogart's Face (1980)
The Munsters' Revenge (1981) TV
Liar's Moon (1982)
A Masterpiece Of Murder (1986) TV

Butch Patrick

Butch Patrick was born in Inglewood, California, on 2 June 1954. He made about $600 per show for *The Munsters*. He started taking drugs at 16, and was busted by the police and convicted in 1979. He spent the intervening years doing odd jobs, including waxing cars and selling Christmas trees.

The Real McCoys (1963)
The Munsters (1964–66)
Lidsville (1971)

Ben Casey: 'A Pleasant Thing For The Eyes' (16.4.62)
Death Valley Days: 'A Kingdom For A Horse' (1963)
Bonanza: 'The Prime Of Life' (29.12.63)
My Favorite Martian: 'How To Be A Hero Without Really Trying' (29.12.63)
Gunsmoke: 'Friend' (25.1.64)
I Dream Of Jeannie: 'My Master, The Author' (26.12.66)
Gunsmoke: 'Mad Dog' (14.1.67)
Daniel Boone: 'Copperhead Izzy' (30.1.69)
Marcus Welby, MD: 'All Flags Flying' (21.10.69)

Movies
Munster, Go Home! (1966)

Pat Priest

Pat Priest was born in Bountiful, Utah, in 1936. Her mother was treasurer of the United States while Eisenhower was president. She became a fashion model, then gained some work in commercials before starring in her own local TV show in Salt Lake City, Utah. When she was 19, she married Naval officer Pierce A. Jensen, Jnr. He was a Naval aide at the White House at the time. When he was posted to

California, she went with him. She auditioned there for a role on *Gilligan's Island*, and then became the second actress to play Marilyn on *The Munsters*. Her husband quit the Navy and went into real estate. Pat left acting to raise their two children.

The Munsters (1964–66)

Perry Mason: 'The Case Of The Tandem Target' (14.5.64)
Voyage To The Bottom Of The Sea: 'The Price Of Doom' (12.10.64)
My Favorite Martian: 'My Uncle The Folk Singer' (8.11.64)
Perry Mason: 'The Case Of The Crafty Kidnapper' (15.5.66)
Death Valley Days: 'The Left Hand Is Damned' (1969)
Death Valley Days: 'The Wild West's Biggest Train Holdup' (1969)

Beverly Owen

Beverly Owen was born in Iowa in 1939.

The Munsters (1964)

Wagon Train: 'The Myra Marshall Story' (21.10.63)

Al Lewis Interview

In a restaurant on a corner in Bleeker Street, in the heart of New York's famed Greenwich Village, Al Lewis is engaged in an unusual form of showbiz – a restaurant owner and host. He is perhaps best known as the crotchety old vampire from *The Munsters* that he played for two years – Grandpa – and 'Grandpa's' is the name of this Italian dining establishment. Stylized depictions of Al Lewis in the role adorn the doors, the menus, and boxes of special pasta.

The customers can hardly miss seeing him, because he sits at an empty table, dressed in a dark cowboy hat, wearing a number of rings, and smoking an Avanti cigar. By his side is the portable phone he seems almost attached to. When it rings, he answers the calls himself.

A group of youngsters, very obviously out-of-towners by their dress, stop by and ask if they can have a picture taken with him. 'Sure', he answers, and poses cheerfully. 'Only two', he cautions, and calls over a waiter. The kids group round him, and then he's back for the interview. It is interrupted from time to time as he greets customers or takes phone calls. 'No', he tells one caller, 'I don't have pictures of Schnauser. [His role in *Car 54, Where Are You?*] I have thousands of Grandpa.' In a New York infested with restaurants of all kinds of ethnic varieties and quality, you have to have a little something extra to make a new place work. Grandpa's has something extra-special – Grandpa himself, constantly on the premises.

And just how did he get to be here? It all began back in 1922, when a twelve-year old boy from upstate New York fulfilled a childhood fantasy that many youngsters have and joined the circus. 'At least', he cautioned, 'that's the way the myth goes. I don't know if children really dream of

283

running away and joining the circus. I think it's just that an author or two may have written that. I know you didn't dream of running away and joining a circus, and I've never run into anybody who did! In the true sense, I didn't run away from home. I left home; I didn't pack a lunch and disappear one day. I joined the circus, and I've been a performer ever since.'

'I worked my way up to being a clown, and I taught myself how to do a slack wire act, and I rode a trick unicycle. From there I went to carnival, vaudeville, burlesque . . . I've had my own medicine show. Then radio, Broadway, live television, off-Broadway, films . . . You name it. As a group, I find most interesting that which has a live audience. I very much enjoy the theatre. In vaudeville, I wasn't able to do a slack wire, because of the equipment set-up, but I did ride a trick unicycle. I taught myself how to play a musical saw, and, after a number of years, I taught myself to play a musical saw while riding a unicycle. Very, very difficult to do. You miss one stroke and you'll be singing in the boy's choir the rest of your life!'

'After that, I did eighteen years of radio. When live television came along, in the early days in New York City, I drifted into the Dumont Network. [An early network based in the city and now defunct.] I had established myself, as we used to say in the old days, as a talker – he who was able to talk. So it was very easy for me. I was a talker on radio, and I simply became a talker on television. I don't call myself an actor: I'm a performer. I don't want to split hairs on what the delineation is, but in the old days before television an actor was he who performed on the stage. Nowadays, of course, it's he who performs on stage or in front of a camera. I can perform – and have performed – in so many different mediums, doing things other than 'acting', that I always refer to myself as a performer. It's not really a bone of contention, but I'm a performer, and have been for 67 years. Acting isn't limited – when it calls for me to do acting, I do acting. I have done things other than acting, and still can. It doesn't really matter, though: if you want to call me an actor, fine. It's okay. It doesn't bother me.'

His initial fame came when he was cast for a small role in the Nat Hiken comedy series *Car 54, Where Are You?* He explained: 'I had worked with the man who created the show. We used to call him the King of Comedy, Nat Hiken. Nat had started out in college writing the humour column, then found himself on the west coast, working on a radio show. Then he was brought back to New York by the late Fred Allen, to do Fred's radio show for many years. Since he was a writer, he found it easy to transfer, and he went into the television field. He was with *The Colgate Comedy Hour*, *The Martha Raye Show*, *The Texaco Show* . . . He was one of the three geniuses that I ever worked with in the writing field. He created *Sergeant Bilko*, and I did a number of those. When he first cast *Car 54, Where Are You?* I was doing a Broadway musical with Phil Silvers and Nancy Walker, and when I came into New York in the Christmas week of 1960, Nat asked me if I would do a couple of guest shots on the show. The first thing I did on *Car 54* was the building construction superintendent trying to get a woman out of the building. About a week or so later I did another show where I had a car repair or paint shop. My brother-in-law talked me into painting cars, and I didn't know they were stolen.'

'In those years, most shows had a single sponsor, as differentiated from today. Our sponsor was Procter and Gamble, who buys the most time of anybody, with all the products they produce. Their response to the show was that they wanted Al Lewis added to the cast. I was doing a musical on Broadway at the time, *Do Re Mi*, and Nat asked me if I could do both. I said I'd give it a shot, and so he wrote in the part of officer Leo Schnauser. I did that for about three weeks, and again the response was such that, in order to broaden the part, they wrote in a wife for me, so as to take me out of the precinct. They brought in an extremely funny, talented lady called Charlotte Rae. That's pretty much it – I did the part for two years.'

Lewis and Fred Gwynne had an on-screen rapport that worked very well, and carried over to their next series. 'I get along with everybody', Lewis said. Judging from the greetings aimed in his direction, and the attention he was receiving from passers-by, this was not overstating the case. 'I have absolutely no problems. The only people I have problems with – and I can't even call it problems – are people who are not professionals. I'm a very, very trained mule. I go in, and I do my job. I pull my wagon and I get it home first. That's it.'

Joe Connelly and Bob Mosher had proposed a series to Universal (who owned all of the old movie monster rights) a comedy show based on this horror creatures, to be called *The Munsters*. Al Lewis and Fred Gwynne were the first of the regulars in. 'I was at home', Lewis recalled, 'and I got a telephone call from a gentleman named Jerry Henshaw: "We're doing the pilot for a new series, and wondered if you'd be interested." I said: "Well, I can't really tell you if I would or I wouldn't. I haven't seen any scripts." No problem – the following day I got a couple of scripts by air mail. I looked at the package; this must have been either a Tuesday or a Wednesday. We talked about it, and that Sunday I flew out. In the course of the conversations with Mr Henshaw, he told me: "By the way, a friend of yours will be coming out on the plane with you, Fred Gwynne." Whether we were the first ones for the show I don't know, and I don't really care!'

'Still, that may be right in a sense, because the pilot was

done without Yvonne de Carlo. It was another lady, Joan Marshall. The boy was different in the pilot; it was a boy named Happy Durman. I think he does a magic act now. Marilyn was the same, Beverly Owen. Whether she was the first or not, she was a contract player for Universal.' The pilot shot was actually a 15-minute clip from the episode 'My Fair Munster', where Grandpa concocts a love potion to help 'ugly' Marilyn catch a man. 'It was a presentation, not a full show', Lewis explained. The makeup for the Munsters was considerably different (though Fred Gwynne's Herman make-up lingered into the first few shows of the series before being toned down). 'I really don't know why they only shot the clip. People have to understand that even if you're the star, unless it's your own production, the actor or actress is low man on the totem pole. You're the last to find out anything – if you do find it out!'

'I remember what they shot. They filmed the opening scene of the house. They shot a family scene, a very short one, of the boy, Fred, Joan and the young lady, Beverly. Somebody said something about: "Where's Grandpa?" "He's down in the basement, whipping up something." And that was the longer part. I soloed and ad-libbed for five or six minutes down in the basement. That was it. That was the whole presentation.' On the subject of ad-libbing, he admitted, cheerfully, that: 'I always do. Except if I'm working for a genius. Those are so few and far between that you can say I always ad-lib. I have found that on my feet I can write better than most writers can sitting down in front of a typewriter for hours. I've been in the business for so long, I have a comic genius, I know exactly the rhythm of the thing . . . For various reasons – timing, that sort of thing. But I do that. If somebody doesn't like it, they tell me not to do it, and I don't. No big deal.'

What made him decide to accept the role? 'I never thought about it. It was a job. First of all, I had no indication that it would require us being what we had to be. Neither Fred nor I did – after all, all we'd seen was a piece of paper, the script! Neither one of us knew that it required that much makeup, and whatever! But I had a gloriously fun time doing it. It unquestionably comes through. It is very, very difficult to fool a camera. It's easier to fool a live audience than it is a camera.' As to why the show appeals so much that it's still being syndicated, and a new series has been filmed, he admits to being baffled. 'I'd be the last person in the world who could even guess at an answer', he confessed. 'One, I've never seen them. Two, you'd do better asking the viewers. I have no idea why a show which only ran two years and made only about 70 episodes is in its 24th year of syndication and has never been off the air in its entirety in the United States and is presently today running in 44 different countries of the world – in their respective languages. I've met all of these people here', he explains, gesturing about the restaurant. 'Unbelievable. Not just the major countries, like Europe, but . . . the island of Malta, Majorca, Zimbabwe, Malaysia, Czechoslovakia, every South American country, Finland – I didn't know it was playing in Finland! Switzerland! I mean, Germany, Italy, Scotland, yes, but the rest? I don't know what the appeal is, I really don't. I could guess at it, but if you've seen it, then your guess is a lot better than mine.'

Explaining this, he grinned. 'I've never seen anything I've ever done. I'm not interested. It's done. It's finished. I know what I did, and I know if I had to repeat something, I'd remember how I'd done it slightly differently so it might be better, or with better results, but I'm not interested. I have great difficulty watching myself shaving in the mornings. I'm not that enamoured of myself.'

Quite often, Grandpa would be seen hanging upside down in the closet. Lewis did this himself: 'on the trapeze bar. It's very easy. Not like if they turned the cameras around, and everyone else had to be upside down! Hanging from a trapeze? Easy! Very easy.'

Grandpa had his own car in several episodes of the show. 'They designed the Dragula for me', he explained. 'That was designed and built by the same customizers as the family hearse – the casket car was built by George Barris. He's still living in California and turning things out. He's built everything – the Batmobile and so forth. There was an episode of the show where Herman lost the family car in a bet ['Hot-Rod Herman'], so Grandpa had to build a car from a casket, the Dragula. I drove the car on the backlot for that episode. I think that was the only time I ever drove it. We didn't use it that often.'

'The history of the Munsters was: 70 shows, one Easter special – I don't know if it even still exists – that we did at the now-defunct theme park Marineland, in California. Then we did the movie, *Munster, Go Home*. Then we did *The Munsters' Revenge*, a TV movie. That's the last thing that Yvonne, Fred and myself did, in 1981. They recast Eddie and Marilyn, of course, since it was so many years later.' The show has recently been revived as *The Munsters Today*, with John Schuck as Herman, Lee Meredith as Lily and Howard Morton as the new Grandpa. The producers of the new series didn't seek the old actors out. 'I know they didn't approach Fred; Fred wouldn't do it. It's out of the question. I don't know if Yvonne would have done it, but I know she wasn't approached. The other two, Butch Patrick and Pat Priest, would have been difficult, because they've now aged. Butch is 35 years old, and obviously couldn't play the boy. Both girls (Beverly Own and Pat Priest) are grandmothers now! I think that the producers just made a decision to do a new show with new people.'

He watches very little television. 'For many years, I never even owned a television', he confessed. 'I'm not really that interested. I don't go to the theatre – I hate actors. Most of them are egomaniacs. I like automobile mechanics. At the studios, my friends were always the people behind the camera. I'd go out with them to a hockey game, or a basketball game. I don't like people, first of all, who talk shop, and who tell me how wonderful they were last week . . . I would appreciate that if Michaelangelo would tell me that, but the chances of my running into Michaelangelo on a film set are pretty low! I don't dislike actors, actually. I'm an omnivorous reader. I very rarely go to plays, and in the last ten years I've seen two films.'

He has one special souvenir of *The Munsters* that he treasures – and it is, curiously enough, from England. 'The number one political cartoonist in England at that time was David Lowe', he recounted. 'This was during the time when people were coming from the Colonies, and there was the whole furore and uproar about it. David did a cartoon, of which I have the original in California. What it shows is a typical street, with all the houses the same, a whole block of them, looking like they've been stamped out of cookie cutters. Right in the front are two English biddies, probably about sixty years old, and they're looking down the street. Down the street is a big moving van; someone is obviously moving into one of the houses. And that someone is Lily Munster, carrying a lamp and Grandpa and Herman carrying a couch. They're moving in. And one of the biddies says to the other: "Well . . . at least they're white . . . " Obviously the show was very popular, otherwise how would people have identified with the cartoon? I was not there then, I was in California filming, but a friend of mine knew David very well, and he arranged for me to get the original cartoon.'

After the show ended, Al Lewis continued acting. Fred Gwynne has complained that the show virtually wrecked his acting career for a number of years. He has re-established himself as a serious actor recently, and refuses utterly to talk about *The Munsters* at all. Lewis, on the other hand, didn't have the same troubles. 'Nobody said to me: "We're not casting comic Draculas this week." Nothing like that. It didn't bother me any, because before I did *The Munsters* I worked, and after it I worked. It was not a problem for me. *The Munsters* just made people say: "Gee, Al Lewis is funny." Well, Al Lewis had been funny for forty years before then. I did some guest shots, and I went out and did live theatre all over the country. I did an episode of *Lost In Space*, and I went back to playing gangsters. In the Joe Louis story I played the boxing promoter . . . That kind of thing. The show didn't typecast me in my mind. It may have in other people's minds, but I can't deal with that. That's their problem.'

He is still 'as active as ever' to this day. 'I did *Save The Dog, Married To The Mob*. I have three videos out. I just did two commercials for McDonalds . . . Pretty much the same things I've always been doing. I've been pretty busy in performing and other things, I've had to turn down parts. I turned down the new Mary Tyler Moore show, to play her father. I turned down a pilot to do with Harvey Korman. I operate this restaurant, and we're building more. I own a comedy club. I own my own pasta company . . . I have so many things outside of performing that I limit myself to how much time I can take away from them. I keep working. I have no regrets.' Asked if he aims to retire, he barked: 'No!! Never!'

Why a restaurant? 'Why not?' he returns, logically. 'To you, this is a restaurant. To me, this is showbiz. I deal with the people who come in here. It's true that the end product is food, they end up with dinner, but this is still showbiz to me. It's a nice place for me to hang my hat, and I'm building two more of them right now – one in Westchester, and one on Staten Island. There will be a fourth, and then I'll franchise.'

He's now branching out into pasta production. 'Within the next month, it'll be in every store in the United States. It's a natural offspring to an Italian restaurant.' He's not of Italian background, despite this interest in Italian food. 'I was in the merchant marine for about eight and a half years. During the Second World War, I was going from North Africa to Italy, bringing war supplies. I lived in Italy after World War II for four and a half years', he explained. 'It was extremely difficult making a living – unless you were extremely bilingual. What I did, along with Richard Basehart, Anthony Quinn and others, we scrambled to do dubbing. That was during the era of the great Italian films, and we used to do the voices before they were sent to America. It was a tough scramble for work.'

For cable channel TBS, he hosts *Super Scary Saturdays*, a collection of vintage monster and horror films aimed at the younger audiences. He films intros and end tags for each movie. 'I've been doing that for about a year and a half', he said, adding that it's fun. 'I don't do anything unless it's fun. If it ceases being fun, I quit. I go down to Atlanta to do those, about every seven to ten weeks, and film a batch of them, then return to New York.' He doesn't pick the films, and 'they don't even tell me what movies they're doing. I don't really care. Well, I would care if they asked me to help them make a choice. But since they don't, what am I going to say?'

For McDonalds, he was one of a number of old sitcom stars brought together for two spots. The others were from *The Beverly Hillbillies, Get Smart, Gilligan's Island* and *Leave It To Beaver*. They all drove in to a McDonalds, with Buddy Ebsen at the wheel, and Grandpa in Grandma's old chair on the back. 'I didn't do any more than that with Buddy Ebsen. I did my bits alone, and with Don Adams. I did my bits very quickly. I flew out there, did my part the following day and flew back that night because I had to do a concert at Avery Fisher Hall at Lincoln Center. I did four performances with the New York Philharmonic Symphony of "The Sorcerer's Apprentice".' He was not, however, playing the musical saw. 'I narrated! If they ask me, I do it.'

By now, you might be wondering if there is anything he hasn't done. 'There's thousands of things I haven't done!' he laughs. 'I've never gone off Niagara Falls in a barrel. And I'm not going to do it! I never had an ambition to do this, or be in that. I discovered a long time ago that the good Lord had given me a certain amount of talent, and I'm here, and I'm not going to leave until I use it all up. I'm grateful I've been able to do what I've done. I've always gotten great enjoyment out of performing in front of and entertaining people, making them laugh. I love that. I enjoy live performing because it's like ringing the register. I don't dislike television and I don't dislike film, but obviously if you're doing a show, there are a number of advantages. You get an immediate reaction. Also, you're challenged to repeat it, night after night. And if what you are doing isn't working, then you get an opportunity to change it to make it work. In film or television, you don't.'

This is clearly part of his origins in the vaudeville tradition. 'In vaudeville you work up an act. You might work out in the bushes for ten years before somebody invites you into a large city. You've got to hone it down, and it's got to be sharp. Otherwise, that's all you'll ever be. Television? Movies? That's easy. That's falling off a log.'

Note: This interview was conducted in March 1989, and first appeared in *Starburst* magazine.

Life After Deaths

Television being what it is, the concepts behind *The Munsters* and *The Addams Family* were not simply left to rot when the shows were cancelled. For example, there was *Struck By Lightning* (1979), in which a young Ted Stein (Jeffrey Kramer) inherited an inn, only to discover he's the descendant of Frankenstein and the caretaker of the inn, Frank (Jack Elam) was the monster – though a nice guy this time around. The show lasted for three episodes.

Even shorter lived – only pilots were ever filmed – were further attempts. ABC had *Mr & Mrs Dracula* (5 September 1980), starring Dick Shawn, who was far more notable as the singing Hitler in *The Producers* (1966). *13 Thirteenth Avenue* (15 August 1983) gave us Clive Revill (*Wizards And Warriors*) as a psychologist whose patients are such assorted monsters as a nervous werewolf and a witch with a temper. *A Little Bit Strange* (1989) tried mixing *The Munsters* with *Bewitched*. *Free Spirit* (1992) did make it as a short-lived series, with Corinne Bohrer as a wacky witch-cum-nanny.

None were ever very successful, so it's hardly surprising that the production companies keep returning to the graveyard of old shows and disinterring *The Munsters* and *The Addams Family* from time to time. As I write this, John Landis is reportedly working on a new TV movie of *The Munsters*. Paul Rudnick has completed a script for a third *Addams Family* film, which is almost certain to be made, given the box-office receipts of the first two films. Both shows, though they've been dead several times, keep rising once again.

But, all things considered, isn't that highly appropriate?

Other Books In This Series:

DOCTOR WHO – THE PROGRAMME GUIDE

Jean-Marc Lofficier

This indispensable handbook first appeared more than a decade ago, and immediately established itself as the single most important reference work about *Doctor Who*.

Since then it has been updated four times. This new edition contains all the important information about every *Doctor Who* story.

Each story entry includes the storyline, the full cast list, technical credits, and details of the novelisations, video cassettes and audio cassettes of the story.

An additional section gives details of the New Adventures that have been published since the TV series finished in 1989.

ISBN 0 426 20342 9

BLAKE'S 7 – THE PROGRAMME GUIDE

Tony Attwood

The perennial appeal of *Blake's 7* is reflected in this programme guide, which has been through three printings in hardback and paperback editions.

This latest edition has been revised, expanded and updated. In addition to a synopsis and cast list for each television story, and an alphabetical encyclopedia of the *Blake's 7* universe, the book contains the latest information about the actors and writers, the merchandise, the story continuations that have appeared since the programme ended, and about the fans' network.

ISBN 0 426 19449 7

RED DWARF – THE PROGRAMME GUIDE

Chris Howarth & Steve Lyons

Despite its new improved bang-up-to-dateness, this book still won't make you handsome or rich or popular at parties. But it will answer once and for all those embarrassing personal questions: When was Gazpacho Soup Day? Who had his appendix removed twice? How many rehydratable chickens are stored on *Red Dwarf*?

At last, the answer to all these questions, as well as thousands of other bite-sized chunks of non-essential information, can be found in this valuable yet temptingly smeg-free guide to the greatest cult SF comedy in this universe.

ISBN 0 86369 682 1

DOCTOR WHO – THE SIXTIES

David Howe, Mark Stammers & Stephen James Walker

The Sixties is the definitive record of *Doctor Who*'s early years, from the broadcast of its first episode on 23 November 1963, to its change into colour with the beginning of the Jon Pertwee era.

Illustrated throughout with colour and black and white photographs, most of which have never been published before, this is a meticulous record of the beginning of a cultural phenomenon. It is also a lovingly assembled history of the art of television in a decade perhaps less jaded than our own.

'. . . for the science fiction fan who's always wanted one book about the series, but who has been put off by the plethora of titles available, this is the one to get.'

Starburst

'This will probably rank as the ultimate book on the subject . . .'

Doctor Who Magazine

ISBN 0 86369 707 0

Also available:

DOCTOR WHO – THE SEVENTIES by Howe, Stammers & Walker

THE PRISONER

Alain Carrazé & Hélène Oswald

A spy story? A science fiction thriller? A critique of modern society? Or all of these things, and more?

Patrick McGoohan's startling television series broke new ground in the 1960s; and time has only emphasised the magnitude of McGoohan's achievement – and increased the programme's popularity.

This book, the most comprehensive study of the programme yet published, contains over 250 photographs as well as an episode-by-episode breakdown of the entire series, complete with script extracts.

ISBN 0 86369 557 4

THUNDERBIRDS, STINGRAY, CAPTAIN SCARLET – THE AUTHORISED PROGRAMME GUIDE

John Peel

In 1956, Gerry Anderson's small film company was commissioned to produce 52 episodes of a puppet series for children – *The Adventures of Twizzle*. There followed a decade of ageless, innovative and increasingly sophisticated science fiction programmes.

This book provides an overview of Gerry Anderson's works, and concentrates on his three most popular and enduring creations. Each series is described in detail, with a story synopsis, technical credits and background information, as well as photographs from the series' archives.

ISBN 0 86369 728 3

Other telefantasy books:

DOCTOR WHO: THE HANDBOOK – THE FOURTH
DOCTOR

David Howe, Mark Stammers & Stephen James Walker

Doctor Who is the world's longest-running science fiction
series, and Tom Baker was the longest-serving of the actors
who portrayed the title role.

This volume covers the reign of the fourth Doctor, from
1974 to 1981, when the programme achieved its highest
ratings in Britain, and became a sensation in the United
States.

As well as interviews with Tom Baker, the book includes
an in-depth study of the production processes and location
work used, and an episode-by-episode guide to the era.

ISBN 0 426 20369 0

Also available:

DOCTOR WHO: THE HANDBOOK –
THE SIXTH DOCTOR by Howe, Stammers & Walker
DOCTOR WHO: THE HANDBOOK –
THE FIRST DOCTOR by Howe, Stammers & Walker